International Screen Industries

Series Editors:
Michael Curtin, University of California, San ⟨...⟩ ⟨P⟩aul McDonald, King's College London, UK.

The International Screen Industries series offers original and probing analysis of media industries around the world, examining their working practices and the social contexts in which they operate. Each volume provides a concise guide to the key players and trends that are shaping today's film, television and digital media.

Published titles:
The American Television Industry *Michael Curtin and Jane Shattuc*
Arab Television Industries *Marwan M. Kraidy and Joe F. Khalil*
The Chinese Television Industry *Michael Keane*
East Asian Screen Industries *Darrell Davis and Emilie Yueh-yu Yeh*
European Film Industries *Anne Jäckel*
European Television Industries *Petros Iosifidis, Jeanette Steemers and Mark Wheeler*
Global Television Marketplace *Timothy Havens*
Hollywood in the New Millennium *Tino Balio*
Localising Hollywood Courtney *Brannon Donoghue*
Nollywood Central *Jade L. Miller*
Latin American Television Industries *John Sinclair and Joseph D. Straubhaar*
Video and DVD Industries *Paul McDonald*
The Video Game Business *Randy Nichols*

Latin American Film Industries

Tamara L. Falicov

THE BRITISH FILM INSTITUTE
Bloomsbury Publishing Plc
50 Bedford Square, London, WC1B 3DP, UK
1385 Broadway, New York, NY 10018, USA

BLOOMSBURY is a trademark of Bloomsbury Publishing Plc

First published in Great Britain 2019 by Bloomsbury on behalf of the British Film Institute
21 Stephen Street, London W1T 1LN
www.bfi.org.uk

The BFI is the lead organisation for film in the UK and the distributor of Lottery funds for film. Our mission is to ensure that film is central to our cultural life, in particular by supporting and nurturing the next generation of filmmakers and audiences. We serve a public role which covers the cultural, creative and economic aspects of film in the UK.

A catalogue record for this book is available from the British Library.

Library of Congress Cataloging-in-Publication Data
Names: Falicov, Tamara Leah, author. | British Film Institute, issuing body.
Title: Latin American film industries / Tamara L. Falicov.
Description: London ; New York, NY : Bloomsbury on behalf of the British Film Institute, 2019. | Includes bibliographical references and index.
Identifiers: LCCN 2018039451| ISBN 9781844573103 (pb) | ISBN 9781844573110 (hb)
Subjects: LCSH: Motion picture industry–Latin America.
Classification: LCC PN1993.5.L3 F33 2019 | DDC 791.43098–dc23 LC record available at https://lccn.loc.gov/2018039451

ISBN:	HB:	978-1-8445-7311-0
	PB:	978-1-8445-7310-3
	ePDF:	978-1-9112-3938-3
	eBook:	978-1-9112-3939-0

Typeset by Integra Software Services Pvt. Ltd.
Printed and bound in India

To find out more about our authors and books visit www.bloomsbury.com and sign up for our newsletters.

Contents

List of Figures

Acknowledgements

This book will always have a special place in my life. After completing tenure, I decided that this time around, I would firstly secure a book contract, and then complete the book, rather than the other way around. Little did I know that a new Chairship in a newly created Department of Film and Media Studies at the University of Kansas and three delightful *bambinos* were going to see the light of the world in the next five years! This book has been a long time in coming, and I must credit my ever-patient series co-editor Paul McDonald (with Michael Curtin cheering in the wings) for seeing this through. I owe Paul many great thanks for persevering with me, not letting me off the hook when I almost quit, and upholding the nearly annual tradition of having a drink at SCMS with Tamar, his lovely life companion and fellow film scholar.

I must extend my warmest thanks to the support team that was consistently there throughout this process. I am forever grateful to the administrators and teachers at the Berkley childcare centre on the University of Missouri-Kansas City campus for their efforts to educate, nourish and sustain my children while I was slogging through this process. I felt fortunate to entrust my 'precious cargo' with the fantastic people who fostered a welcoming and loving space for cultivating young minds. Special thanks go to Monica Houston and Beth Liss, who provided me with encouragement (and a great laugh every day when they asked, 'How's the book coming along?'). Thanks go out to my children's teachers over the years: Alyssa Morrow, Jessie Newman, Jessica Morris, Meghan Wanner, Monica Quiros, Karen Hutchinson, Kate Ghio (buddy!), Cecilia Harris and Darcy May. At Académie Lafayette, thanks go to Justin Jones, Amandine Brown, Caroline de Jonckheere, Marie Line Charles-Galley, Catherine Defosse, Yael Israel Nicole Fisher, Yamar Diack, Zacharie Méjean and to my favourite transportation caregiver extraordinaire and friend and life cheerleader, Sheila Baskin. Thank you ever so much! I would be remiss not to acknowledge Noa's fantastic caregiver for her first year, the inimitable Katherine (Kaki) Speicher. Helen Grantham, Eusebia (Essy) and Arturo Rodriguez, and Olga Gonzales helped me keep my home in order during these inordinately busy (and messy) years. I hope that you find this in a random vanity google search one day and smile.

Over the years I was fortunate to hire two graduate assistants at different stages of the process. To Bärbel Gobel-Stoltz, who is successfully pursuing the political economy tradition, and Courtney Aspen Sanchez, who is helping to move the field forward both in Latin American film studies and the medical field! Thanks to you both for being such diligent researchers and for being such great people with whom to work. And to my development editor, Anitra Grisales, who fortunately is not only an excellent editor and a patient one at that, but is also a fellow lover of foreign film, and we shared many lively exchanges together. A special thank you to Isis Sadek, who helped me copyedit and organise the book near the end of the project. Much appreciation to you both for your insights, helpful suggestions and being part of this team. I must thank my 'sweep' team members at the end of the process, Pam LeRow, who was gracious and a pleasure to work with, along with Linda Steigman, who has incredible editing acumen! (also acknowledged in the family section). Special thanks also go to the staff in the College of Liberal Arts and Sciences including Interim Provost Carl W. Lejuez, Interim Dean Clarence Lang, fellow 'conjoined' colleague Associate Dean Joy Ward, Tabatha Gabay, Margaret Brumberg, Linda Luckey, Kristi Henderson, Jim Mielke, Holly Storkel, Nicole Hodges Persley, Ben Eggelston and all those fabulous colleagues who make up the Dean's office.

To my fellow travellers in the writing process: To the KUKC faculty who met throughout the years to share their work and attempt to get writing done: Giselle Anatol, Kim Warren, Nicole Hodges Persley (again!), Mechele Leon, Ann Rowland and fellow summer writer Deepika Polineni. You are all so incredible, so dedicated, and I am so honoured to share ideas with you while sampling crêpes and coffee. Thanks to the staff and faculty in Film and Media Studies and the Center of Latin American and Caribbean Studies for being a great place to work. I am indebted to those who made my administrative job a little easier so that I could make time to complete this project (and not have all of my hair turn grey). Special thanks to Chair Michael Baskett for his extra support during this process, and members of FMS: Karla Conrad, Che Butterfield, John McCluskey, Germaine Halegoua, Meg Jamieson, Joshua Miner, Catherine Preston, John Tibbetts, Bob Hurst, Kevin Willmott, Matt Jacobson and Ron Wilson, and to Liz Kowalchuk and Henry Bial for their excellent leadership.

Thank you to all of my wonderful and supportive colleagues who make up the SCMS Latino/a Caucus and the Film Festivals SIG. You know who you all are: you have welcomed me into your communities of thought, and I am so grateful to have a home in my respective fields with people I truly love and admire. Much love and appreciation goes to Consuelo Tapia Morales and her wonderful husband Marcelo who hosted me in La Paz, Bolivia, and showed me the wonders of the city, including the market in El Alto. Thanks also to Atilio Roque González, who has always been a great resource and support, and for accompanying me to La Salada market.

And lastly, but not leastly, to my family: As all who go through this know, books cannot be written alone in a garret somewhere; research trips are involved, conference papers given, grumpy moods rear their heads occasionally. I cannot fathom how I could have completed this book without the help and encouragement of my life companion and dearest one, Stephen Steigman. He was so inspired by life in academe (haha) that he completed a graduate degree during this time, and I could not be more thrilled. He understood how important this manuscript was in my life, and has been a wonderful parent and support for the SATIN 5 (Stephen, Avital, Tamara, Ilan, Noa) beyond my wildest expectations. He also read a chapter draft and provided great observations. Thanks again to Linda Steigman, for all of her help, support, encouragement, and as mentioned, major help with copyediting skills at the final push. Thanks also to my children for their infinite patience and words of support. Each of them has been bestowed honorary names that I will document for posterity: Ilan Raul Stingray Paper Airplane Falicov Steigman; Avital Simone Art Baby Blue, Toilet Dreamer, Steigman Falicov; Noa Lilach Art Staple Tape Glitter Make Bed 'It Smells Like Cake' Steigman Falicov.

Concluding words go out to my sisters, Yael and Anna, and their wonderful respective partners and fantastic children, who make my life so incredibly enjoyable and enriching. They came to visit and help out near (what I thought was!) the tail end of the process and it was a breath of fresh air. Thanks too to my sister from another mother, Ellen Steigman, who shares my passion for writing. To my mother, Celia Haydée Jaes Falicov, who consistently inspires me every day with her wit, passion, hard work, clarity of vision and empathy towards others. She diligently took the time to read many chapter drafts (even while she was travelling!), and for this I am most grateful. A major shout out goes to Peter, my mom's supportive husband, who always has stimulating conversations and has encouraged me to strive for excellence. To the memory of my father, Raúl Esteban Falicov, whose lasting impact is seen daily. He worried, near the end of his illness, that we would forget about him, but rest assured (as we told him) *that* would be impossible. It is to him, and my family, that I dedicate this book.

Introduction

Latin American film industries are an industrial or mass form of culture that, at times, has been either commercially popular or critically acclaimed, and sometimes both. While films from this region have historically tried to reach domestic, and even international, audiences, their relation with other film industries constitutes a distinguishing feature: they have always already been in competition with the globally powerful and hegemonic neighbour to the north known as Hollywood.

This book both examines the countries that are the larger producers in Latin America (Mexico, Brazil and Argentina, known as 'the Trinity') and traces the development of emerging film industries in the Andean region, such as Bolivia and Peru, and in the Caribbean region (such as Cuba and the Dominican Republic). It also focuses on countries such as Colombia and Venezuela, and those in the Southern Cone such as Chile and Uruguay. Moreover, film production in Central America including Guatemala, Costa Rica and Panama will also be profiled. Attention will be paid to the varied and valiant attempts on the part of these emergent industries to gain access to production funding as well as participation in national exhibition and international film festivals and markets. While this book predominantly explores how feature-length films are produced, exhibited and distributed in Latin America, it also considers lower-budget films whose production process differs from an industrial framework. Indeed, some of the countries covered make films in a less standardised fashion than the larger, wealthier nations, in ways that invite discussion of differing budgets, formats and audiences.

The following chapters examine commonalities among Latin American film industries, such as the challenges of procuring financing, competition from Hollywood, battles over state funding and innovative 'DIY' (Do It Yourself) forms of independent filmmaking. The chapters also address exhibition and distribution problems that plague most independent filmmakers around the world, as well as the related piracy trade, while examining throughout the transnational nature of Latin American film industries.

Myriad reasons warrant the production of a book on Latin American film industries in the English language. For one, while Jorge Schnitman's *Film Industries in Latin America* (1984), the last book to have been published on the topic in English, is a valuable resource, it is in need of updating due to the many changes that have occurred (in mostly positive ways) in film production across the region. Moreover, film production has become easier and more finance models are available thanks to: (1) the changes in video technologies that make film production more accessible (as much of it is shot digitally), and (2) the ways in which a new generation is using the internet and social media to crowdfund and post videos on YouTube and other websites. A book that delves into this diversity of models for funding, exhibition and distribution may prove as useful for academics as for filmmakers in the region interested in a panorama of the various facets of production, exhibition and distribution of Latin American film in the contemporary era.

DEFINITIONS OF INDUSTRY IN A LATIN AMERICAN CONTEXT

Questions have been raised about whether 'film industry' is the most appropriate term to define film production in a region where industrial capabilities are limited and fluctuate over time. Octavio Getino (2007) argues that the term 'industry' was only accurate during the period from the 1930s to 1950s when studio production employed large groups of people full-time to produce multiple films per year, as part of a system of mass production that encompassed every step from writing the script to preparing prints for distribution. Despite these strict criteria for characterising what constitutes a film industry, Getino does acknowledge that some films produced in countries with a longer film tradition, such as Mexico, Argentina and Brazil, obtain financial support from national television chains and US film studios which have invested, co-produced and distributed some bigger-budget films with varying degrees of success (I will examine these relationships in Chapter 3).

There are vast differences between countries with a lengthy industrial history and smaller countries with a limited home market that produce only a few films per year. In 2006, Getino calculated that, during the decades between 1930 and 2000, 12,500 films were produced in Latin America. Of that total, 45 per cent were made in Mexico (5,500 films), 25 per cent in Brazil (3,000 films) and 20 per cent in Argentina (2,500 films). The remaining 10 per cent came from the other film producing countries in Latin America (Getino, 2006, 60).

Rather than speaking of film studios in Latin America, it is more fitting to describe them as production houses, as over 80 per cent of the films made are produced by small businesses which operate independently and work hard to compete against the large global oligopolies that dominate the film trade throughout Latin America (Getino, 2007).

Given these differences in the scale of production across the region, it is more accurate to say that some countries have 'film industries', while the others, which only produce one to two films per year, have a 'film tradition' (Middents, 2009). Many countries, including Paraguay, El Salvador and Honduras, generally make films in a more sporadic, piecemeal fashion. Hamid Naficy calls this type of intermittent production 'interstitial' or artisanal because there is no set formula for film production in the 'hand to mouth' methods employed in countries with limited resources (Naficy in Himpele, 2008, 18). While the main reason why films often fail to get produced in countries such as Honduras or Paraguay has much to do with these countries' economic situation, the lack of robust state or governmental policies that incentivise and protect national production puts these nations at a disadvantage (Getino, 2006, 60). Making films is an expensive endeavour. Film critic Pedro Susz opined that filming a movie in Bolivia is the equivalent of trying to build the Concorde airplane in a car garage (in Sousa Crespo, 2011).

Although films in Latin America can be categorised as part of the entertainment industry, as are television, video games and popular music, and other forms of culture (art, music and dance), they should also be regarded as a form of cultural expression that, in addition to providing entertainment, is capable of communicating identity, local or national social issues, and politics, all of which are specific to a geographic locality. One useful framework that examines film industries both as media industries and as a form of cultural expression is a cultural industries approach.

A CULTURAL INDUSTRIES APPROACH

Rodrigo Gómez García offers a useful way of conceptualising film industries as part of an overarching category of 'cultural industries' in his synthesis of the unique place that these industries occupy within society from the perspective of the marketplace:

> Cultural industries are based on an industrial capitalist logic (Garnham, 2000), highly pervasive in contemporary societies, oriented to manage, produce, operate, and distribute symbolic products (Hesmondhalgh, 2007) in accordance with ideologies, imaginaries, and identities characteristic of each context. Due to the link between symbolic symbols and the spread of ideology, scholars devote a considerable share of attention to analysing and understanding how media policy is shaped by social power. (Gomez García, 2012, 217)

Thus, the distinctive trait of cultural industries is that they have the simultaneous potential to function as industries – that is, producing commodities that circulate globally, and often as purveyors of local and national culture and identities. Lower-budget films that embody specific histories or local stories tend to be labelled as 'arthouse' cinema when they are exported globally, but they typically are not released in large theatres in major movie chains. However, Latin American countries do not only produce films that grapple with national or local identity. To be sure, examples abound of higher-budget genre films such as comedies, thrillers, action films, and in some cases horror and sci-fi films. One can also point to live-action, animation or 3D films that compete with Hollywood blockbusters with some modicum of success.

Film industries can be considered both 'cultural' and as 'industrial entities' which provide national employment opportunities and, ideally, are financially stable. Cultural and commercial objectives may not always overlap. Sometimes, they may even contradict each other, ultimately resulting in the failure of film productions. Unfortunately, the state's participation often perpetuates the bifurcation between issues of 'national culture' and the 'market'. In theory, from a Latin American point of view, national culture is conceived as an artefact or a form of expression that should be independent from the logic of the marketplace. In practice, however, as cultural theorist and anthropologist Néstor García Canclini has observed, with the increased commercialisation of all spheres of life, even artisanal crafts displayed in national museums cannot be separated from the marketplace (García Canclini, 1995, 155).

The state's role in sustaining all Latin American film industries cannot be underestimated (this is the case in almost all parts of the world) but legislation varies from one county to another (this topic will be explored in Chapter 6). Communications scholar Guillermo Mastrini argues that 'very few films amortise their high costs of production. If Latin American film industries were solely dependent on the laws of the marketplace, only the largest film industries such as Brazil, Mexico and Argentina would achieve a consistent level of production, which would still not reach the current levels today [without state support]' (Mastrini, 2014, 10).

The next section outlines some historical background regarding the pan-Latin American movement El Nuevo Cine Latinoamericano (New Latin American Cinema) (NLAC), which has had a profound effect on filmmaking, and also influenced how critics both inside and outside the region have labelled Latin American films: for example, in seeking to acknowledge traces of this movement in future generations' films, or in classifying films as 'commercial', 'non-political' (if such a definition exists), radical or something else.

THE IMPACT OF THE NEW LATIN AMERICAN CINEMA MOVEMENT ON LATIN AMERICAN FILM INDUSTRIES

Overview

As an anti-imperialist cinema movement, NLAC marked a historical juncture in which low-budget, gritty filmmaking stood in stark opposition to Hollywood's commercial output. As such, the films became important icons of oppositional work during the 1960s and 1970s. This political position was strengthened when, in the wake of successive military dictatorships throughout the Southern Cone in the 1970s (in Argentina, Chile, Brazil, Uruguay, Paraguay, Peru), a left-wing, radical film movement coalesced that mainly worked outside the state funding mechanisms (with the exception of Brazil) to create films that aimed to denounce the actions of the military, or to raise viewer consciousness about the domestic situation, to the limited extent within which they were allowed to express themselves freely. These rebel filmmakers were making documentaries, experimental and low-budget narrative fiction films that were often screened in union halls and spaces other than traditional movie theatres, which sometimes explicitly blocked the screening of such films. Whether focusing on marginalised sectors of society to tell their stories in aesthetically innovative ways or making an urgent anti-establishment cinema, these filmmakers moved away from both the Hollywood and national film studio models of filmmaking. In forging this new path, they were labelled part of a new cinema, the Nuevo Cine Latinoamericano, while their Brazilian counterpart, a movement of young college-educated filmmakers which took shape in the late 1950s, was dubbed 'Cinema Novo' (New Cinema).

While the majority of filmmakers were preoccupied with making films under clandestine conditions as part of an attempt to survive the terror of right-wing military dictatorships, one group of filmmakers in Cuba were working under more favourable conditions. The state-sponsored Instituto Cubano de Arte e Industria Cinematográficos (Cuban Film Institute) (ICAIC) both created the stable conditions for the growth of a Cuban national film industry and soon, given its radical pan-Latin American thrust, also became the social nexus for the NLAC movement. The ICAIC's sponsorship often allowed exiled filmmakers to complete their films, as was the case for Brazilian Glauber Rocha and Chilean Patricio Guzmán. Film culture in Cuba during that time was part of a broader political atmosphere of Third World solidarity, culminating in the annual Festival del Nuevo Cine Latinoamericano (The International Festival of New Latin American Cinema), founded in 1979, which became a hub where Latin American filmmakers could meet, share work and discuss issues of common interest. This group also included US Latinx filmmakers such as Jesús Treviño, Sylvia Morales and other radical Chicano directors making films in the 1970s.

The Havana film festival continues to be held today, even if it has ceased to fulfil its original political function, in the 1970s and 1980s, as a meeting place for radical dialogue and exchange.

THE NLAC MOVEMENT'S INFLUENCE ON CONTEMPORARY FILMMAKING

The emergence of a new generation of filmmakers in countries such as Chile, Bolivia, Guatemala, Costa Rica, Panama and Peru, to name only a few, has generated a bounty of new and exciting films dealing with a diversity of topics. Throughout the book, a number of case studies illustrate productions from a range of countries within the broad and variegated landscape that is the contemporary Latin American film industry.

That these productions are often made in countries facing economic hardship begs the question: what new spaces make it possible for these stories to be told and heard? What confluence of events occurred so that a first-time feature filmmaker from Guatemala, Ana V. Bojórquez, trained at a film school in Cuba, could meet a Mexican producer at a workshop in Panama five years prior to the completion of a small, intimate film about a young indigenous girl living in the Guatemalan highlands? The film, *La casa más grande del mundo* (*The Greatest House in the World*, dirs. Ana V. Bojórquez and Lucía Carreras, 2014), a minimalist drama that focuses on a young Maya Mam

[Figure 0.1 Gloria López in *La casa más grande del mundo* (*The Greatest House in the World*, 2014). Directed by Ana V. Bojórquez, © Prisma Cine y TV S.A. & Filmadora Producciones S.A. de C.V.]

shepherd girl who loses a sheep from her flock one day, explores innocence and the necessity of confronting one's fears. This film can be compared to the allegorical style of Iranian cinema and it played well to audiences including the Berlin and Panama film festivals, stimulating curiosity about the movie's possible political significance.

Audience members in Panama wanted to know whether the film's indigenous cast was in any way a commentary on the massacre of indigenous peoples during the past military dictatorship/civil war (1982–96). They also asked if it was a religious allegory. The directors replied with a resounding 'No'. The film was simple and lyrical; it did not conform, contrary to some audience members' expectations, to the NLAC tradition or have a religious slant. If the film's focus on childhood is familiar, its decision to feature an indigenous girl in a central role is bold. The film was funded thanks to the efforts of its two directors, who came from different countries (Guatemala, Mexico) and spent many years obtaining no fewer than eleven development training opportunities, co-production funds and grants before working extensively with the cast and crew. (This process through which first-time feature filmmakers cobble funds together is discussed in Chapter 2.)

Since the 1990s, Latin American film industries have produced an abundance of aesthetically appealing and commercially successful films both at home and abroad. Examples include *Amores perros* (*Love's a Bitch*, dir. Alejandro G. Iñárritu, 2000), *Nueve reinas* (*Nine Queens*, dir. Fabián Bielinsky, 2000), *Cidade de Deus* (*City of God*, dirs. Fernando Meirelles and Kátia Lund, 2002), *Diarios de motocicleta* (*The Motorcycle Diaries*, dir. Walter Salles, 2004) and *Y tu mamá también* (dir. Alfonso Cuarón, 2001). Some of these productions have benefited from private sector investment in addition to co-production and distribution deals with Hollywood majors (e.g. Disney's distribution wing Buena Vista International, Sony's Columbia Pictures and Warner Bros.). Another important source of pan-Latin American funding is the Ibero-American film finance pool Programa Ibermedia, housed in Spain, which has successfully funded hundreds of award-winning Latin American co-productions, many of them box-office successes.

Latin American films have budgets of all scales. They range from low- or no-budget films that receive limited circulation, such as the Guatemalan/Mexican film mentioned above, to commercial hits that take a country by storm, as did the Argentine box-office explosion *Relatos salvajes* (*Wild Tales*, dir. Damián Szifron, 2014). This film comprised six vignettes starring well-known stars, including Argentina's most famous actor, Ricardo Darín. These tales of repression gone wild, and fantasies unleashed by frustrated characters, touched a raw nerve among Argentine audiences. Selling 3.3 million tickets at the box office, the film reached an all-time record in the history of Argentine cinema. With this astounding success, Argentine cinema took 17.5 per cent of the box-office share against primarily Hollywood films (Batlle, 2015) when Argentine films typically obtain between 10 and 12 per cent of market share each year (which tends to be the average for the larger film industries).

Relatos salvajes was a US$4 million Argentine/Spanish co-production. Seventy per cent of the film's budget was raised in Argentina and the remainder financed by Spanish director Pedro Almodóvar and his producer brother Agustín Almodóvar's company, El Deseo productions. Warner Bros. distributed it nationally; Sony Pictures bought the rights for the United States, Canada and Australia, and Warner Bros. purchased them for Argentina, Spain, and France (Appelo, 2015). After winning awards at the Cannes Film Festival, in San Sebastián, Spain, and other European festival prizes, the film garnered box-office success in Italy, Spain and Germany, generating over US$40 million worldwide. In Spain, it drew one million spectators and, in France, 500,000 moviegoers attended (Anon., 2015b). The film also won the top award for best Ibero-American fiction film, and seven others at one of the most important awards shows for Ibero-American cinema, the Premios Platino (Platino Awards) sponsored by the Spanish EGEDA, the Entidad de Gestión de Derechos de los Productores Audiovisuales (Audiovisual Producers' Rights Management Association).

Chapter Overview

Chapter 1 provides an overview of the sound era in motion pictures in the three most developed film industries, those of Argentina, Brazil and Mexico. This chapter discusses the rise of these studio systems, including profiles of the top studios in each context, and examines how they were able to remain financially solvent prior to the rise of television. The impact of runaway productions or Hollywood foreign location shooting is discussed as a phenomenon spanning various historical periods in a section on Mexico and Argentina. Newer industrial models developed by socialist countries Cuba and Venezuela are also profiled.

Chapter 2 examines the role of the state in funding Latin American film production. Space is devoted to outlining the histories of the three oldest and most established film institutes in 'the Trinity'. Moreover, attention is paid to co-productions between state institutions facilitated by the Ibero-American film finance pool Programa Ibermedia, as well as the smaller but equally important fund (now temporarily suspended), Cinergia, set up expressly for Central American film production. Co-productions are spotlighted as a successful method of financing, exhibiting and distributing films.

Chapter 3 looks at the role of the private sector, tracing how the private model of funding resurfaced in Latin America in the 1990s, after state funding was slashed in the wake of governments' neoliberal economic policies during that era. Examinations of privately funded studios in Argentina, Brazil, Mexico and Colombia serve as case studies of how these studios created films and television programmes with investment not only from national and multinational companies and business people but also with assistance from MPA-backed US studios, such as Buena Vista (Disney) and Warner Bros. In addition to examining the role of private television channels both as producers and exhibitors, newer, more grassroots forms of funding from the private or non-governmental sector, notably crowdfunding, are explored.

Chapter 4 explains how film distribution functions in Latin America, highlighting the ways in which national distribution companies operate and manage to survive in the face of competition from foreign, primarily Hollywood distributors. Case studies examine small independent distributors, such as the Colombian company Multiplex, and the myriad ways they encourage the circulation of national cinema.

Another important platform for independent film distribution is the film festival circuit. These festivals have become a crucial vehicle for small, low-budget, independent and/or arthouse films to secure distribution in the global marketplace. Newer technologies, such as digital production and the role of new distribution platforms (video on demand [VOD], Latin American sites such as Cuevana and others, Netflix), will be framed as new possibilities for furthering the reach of a cinema that is always in search of a larger audience.

Chapter 5 outlines the rise of multiplex movie theatres in Latin America, discussing the ownership of these chains – mainly multinational firms from the United States and Australia – and the impact this has on the kinds of films screened. The politics of exhibition slots for national films and the demographics of moviegoers in various Latin American countries constitute another significant topic. The success of Mexico-based chain Cinépolis and the space it has afforded to national productions merits discussion. Another successful Brazil-based chain, the now-defunct Rain Network, built 100 digital theatres – the largest in the world in the mid-2000s – and beamed films via satellite, thus eliminating costs related to celluloid and transportation. The chapter concludes with an exploration of rural exhibition initiatives in Cuba in the 1970s and in present-day Mexico and Brazil, respectively, through the examples of the Ambulante project, along with urban movie theatres funded by the municipality in urban neighbourhoods of Rio de Janeiro.

Chapter 6 examines the impact of film legislation to understand how national governments supporting national films are always in competition with Hollywood. Newer trends such as the revival of protectionist measures like the screen quota will be framed in contrast to the United States' push for trade policy liberalisation. Case studies include the screen quota policy enacted in Argentina in 2004. The chapter then moves into a discussion of film piracy in Latin America and the mixed results yielded by the efforts of MPA-sponsored anti-piracy organisations to pressure Latin American governments to impose tougher anti-piracy measures.

The scope of this project means that it will necessarily have lacunae in its coverage of a vast region where production practices are ever-shifting. Since this book focuses predominantly on the creation and sustenance of industries, the production of feature-length films is central, with some mention of documentary, but little discussion of films made outside of the mainstream circles of production and distribution. Therefore, experimental, and non-theatrically distributed independent films (underground, Super 8, mobile phone films, neighbourhood cinema, home movies), along with independently distributed political films (which are proliferating in numbers across the region) are not examined, even though they are a part of the increasingly complex fabric of filmic production in the region. Moreover, this book has sought to balance coverage of the major film producing countries and their emerging counterparts. To be sure, more countries deserve inclusion than was possible here. Conversely, there are larger industries that might have needed additional coverage given the sheer volume of their production. The hope is that the featured range of this incredibly diverse work by talented Latin Americans might mobilise scholars to pursue future research on this subject. Furthering the lines of enquiry in a cinematic field that is already gaining prominence will only help disseminate what Latin Americans themselves already know: that film sector creatives throughout Latin America belong both to a rich tradition and to a newly emerging creative field. This unstoppable drive, constant innovation and wilful energy could certainly be edifying for creative producers in the United States (especially those with hefty Hollywood budgets), Europe and other parts of the 'advanced industrialised' world.

1

A Brief History of the Film Studios

Film industries in Latin America were collectively launched as part of a worldwide process in which representatives of the Lumière brothers distributed moving pictures by dispatching teams on planned itineraries designed to shore up the fascination which the new invention generated everywhere. Tasked with showing short films – either cheap amusements or filmed *actualités* – two teams went to Latin America: one was dispatched to Rio de Janeiro, Montevideo and Buenos Aires, while the other one went to Mexico and Havana (Chanan, 1996, 427). During the silent era, entrepreneurs (many of them immigrants from France, Germany and Italy) living in Argentina, Brazil, Mexico and elsewhere tried their hand at creating their own films, typically filmed on the street and exhibited in itinerant roadshows. This chapter initially examines the development of modern movie studio facilities in the three largest film producing countries (Argentina, Brazil, Mexico). This is followed by a discussion of how the push to build studios in the contemporary era in some ways helped strengthen national film industries while incentivising foreign film shoots from abroad to film 'runaway productions' in Latin America. An exploration of socialist film studios in Venezuela and Cuba caps off the chapter.

The studio system came into existence in the 1920s during the silent era and transitioned to sound in the 1930s. This demarcation is significant because sound films based on national musical styles played a role in the success of the Argentine *¡Tango!* (dir. José Moglia Barth, 1933) and *Allá en el rancho grande* (*Out on the Big Ranch*, dir. Fernando de Fuentes, 1936), a *comedia ranchera* (ranch comedy) featuring singing cowboys performing distinctly Mexican folk music. While Argentine and Mexican studios were privately funded, this was not always the case in Brazil. Well-known privately owned film studios Vera Cruz and Atlântida also relied on the state to help them in difficult financial times from the 1950s onwards (Dos Santos, 2009).

During this period, Latin American governments with the strongest economies (Argentina, Brazil, Mexico) passed various forms of legislation in support of the construction and maintenance of national film studios. To that end, screen quotas (mandatory time given to national films on screens) were enacted in Brazil as early as 1932. These measures were taken in response to the Hollywood studios' growing dominance in Latin America and elsewhere, despite the temporary effects of the Great Depression on the US film industry.

PIONEERING STUDIO SYSTEMS

Brazil

In the case of Brazil, two film studios established thanks to private capital in the early 1930s formed the nucleus of an industrial method of filmmaking that flourished up until the early 1960s. Entrepreneur Adhemar Gonzaga founded Cinédia Studios in Rio in 1930, and Carmen Santos followed suit by opening her Brasil Vita Filme in the same city three years later (King, 2000, 55). Cinédia was furnished with four sets of sound equipment, a studio large enough to accommodate several simultaneous productions, and two laboratories (de Usabel, 1982, 146). Cinédia would be known from this decade onwards as a producer of musical genre films called *chanchadas*, as well as carnival films, a subgenre that *Carmen Miranda* popularised worldwide beginning in the 1940s (de Usabel, 1982, 146). These films' incorporation of the day's popular musical stars from radio and theatre made them highly successful at the box office. Similar to the success of tango films, launched during the same period in Argentina, these films were an extension of the popular amusements to which working people had grown accustomed with the nickelodeon and vaudeville theatre (or, in the Latin American context, the theatre sketches known as *sainetes*). Cinédia Studios constitutes the first attempt at concentrated industrialisation in the history of Brazilian cinema (Johnson, 1987, 44). In 1933, Carmen Santos, the actor and producer who became a film studio owner, founded Brasil Fox Film Studios, a name which Twentieth Century Fox studio obliged her to change in 1935. It was renamed Brasil Vita Filme and became the second-largest studio in Brazil (Shaw and Dennison, 2007) and the first to be owned by a woman.

[Figure 1.1 Carmen Santos: actor, producer, film studio owner and pioneer.]

The two most important industrialised film studios during the 1940s were based in the two largest centres of commerce: Atlântida was constructed in Rio in 1941 and the Vera Cruz studio in 1949 in São Paulo. The latter was built during a period of rapid industrialisation in São Paulo; the city saw the creation of approximately twenty-nine companies between 1949 and 1953 (Schnitman, 1984, 57). The powerful industrial group Matarazzo invested massive amounts of money to create a studio they hoped would be capable of making quality films that were commercially successful, both domestically and abroad. They made use of imported European equipment, as well as personnel. Despite Vera Cruz's short-lived boom, which produced such studio hit films as Oscar-winner *O Cangaceiro* (dir. Lima Barreto, 1953), its history serves as a cautionary tale about how a large studio can fail. The government support obtained by Brasil Vita Filme was insufficient to save it from bankruptcy, which it declared in 1954, due to the studio's excessive investments in infrastructure and its inability to reach foreign markets (Johnson, 1987, 63). Atlântida, however, continued to make studio-style *chanchadas* until it closed in 1962. Its demise has been attributed mainly to changes in viewing habits due to the rise of television. Filmmaking in Brazil was revived from the late 1950s through the 1970s, but this revival yielded progressively political films, made independently outside the model defined by the studio system. As mentioned in the Introduction, Cinema Novo strove to expose socio-economic class disparities, racial inequalities and other ills that plagued society; it was part of the continent-wide, anti-imperialist movement known as New Latin American Cinema (see Introduction, Pick, 1993; Martin [ed.], 1997).

While commercial production waned with the rise of television, it ultimately resumed thanks to investment funding from powerful television conglomerates, with Rede Globo leading such initiatives. However, the Brazilian film industry was almost completely gutted in the mid-1990s when President Collor de Mello slashed all remaining funding with the closure of EMBRAFILME (the Brazilian Film Enterprise, founded in 1969) and CONACINE (the National Cinema Advisory Board, founded in 1982). As a result of these measures, production reached its lowest level yet, at three films in 1993 and four in 1994 (Johnson, 2007, 87). In response, two laws were passed, one in 1991 and the other in 1993, under a new administration that took over when Collor was impeached. The Rouanet Law and the Lei do Audiovisual (Audiovisual Law) offered tax incentives to large corporations that invested funds in national productions (mainly commercial films that might provide some return on investment). The Lei do Audiovisual also gave foreign film distributors in the country a chance to invest up to 70 per cent of their revenue in national film production (Johnson, 2007, 89). This law proved to be extremely successful at reviving film production, with the release of twenty-three films by 1998. Around the same time, the multi-media conglomerate Globo, which had created its film wing Globo Filmes in 1997, began to produce in earnest more commercial films in the new economic climate (Johnson, 2007, 95). Globo's involvement stimulated interest among Hollywood majors to co-produce films; they eventually distributed seven Globo-produced films that reached over one million spectators (Johnson, 2007, 92). This relationship between the US movie studio cartel, the Motion Picture Association of America (MPAA) and Globo is discussed in Chapter 3.

Mexico

The rise of the Mexican studio system was undoubtedly influenced by the Hollywood model of film industrialisation, but, as John King (2000, 42) points out, 'North American styles and technical expertise would be alternately revered and reviled within Mexican cinema.' This dominant influence mainly resulted from the fact that the personnel working on first studio films was comprised of production heads, actors and technicians who had all been trained in Hollywood before or while they worked in Mexico. While films had a similar look and form to their Hollywood counterparts, they were funded with national capital and the themes were typically home-grown.

Though films with sound had been introduced in the late 1920s in Mexico, the 1931 film *Santa*, directed by Spanish actor Antonio Moreno, was the first Mexican 'talkie' which synchronised image and sound on the same celluloid strip (García Riera in Gurza, 2001). The film was shot in a Hollywood style of continuity editing and was an exemplar of the familiar 'fallen woman' genre, but the narrative was based on a melodramatic Mexican novel written by Federico Gamboa. The lead actors, Lupita Tovar and Ernesto Guillen (who also went by the US stage name Donald Reed), had experience working in both silent and sound films in the United States. The film was set in a brothel and the narrative revolves around Santa, a young, innocent girl who falls into prostitution and lives a life of underworld dealings and vice – a life not of her own making. While the film was a popular box-office success, critics gave it mixed reviews. The crux of the debate was whether it was too closely tied to a Hollywood format or if it had its own merits as a Mexican film. Two critics at the magazine *El Ilustrado* lauded the effort that *Santa* represented but felt there was too much US imitation at play. While one reviewer acknowledged the advantage of gaining technical expertise and 'commercial experience' from abroad, he noted it should 'avoid hewing too closely to the "standardised" products of Hollywood and instead make films ... which interest all of Spanish America and Spain ... films with American technique but Mexican substance' (Jarvinen, 2012, 99). *Santa* marked a watershed year for production; six more films were produced, many of which used the same professionals who had worked on *Santa* or who had come from Spanish-language filmmaking in the United States (Jarvinen, 2012, 99).

These melodramatic films often employed popular music and folklore that were familiar in everyday life and became more popular with the advent of famous stars who sang their own renditions. Thus, productions such as *Santa* began a successful run of 'cabaret' films that lasted through the 1930s. The film *Allá en el rancho grande* later helped launch a wave of popularity for *ranchera* music in 1936. Indeed, the film landed Gabriel Figueroa (Emilio 'El Indio' Fernández's famed cinematographer) a prize at the Venice Film Festival, and succeeded financially at home and abroad. In 1938, film was the second-largest industry in the country after oil (King, 2000, 47). This emphasis on the popular music of Mexico led to the formation a very successful film genre known as the *comedia ranchera*, which helped propel the Mexican film industry into a position of stability and provided an opportunity for growth. This, in part, paved the way for Mexico's entrance into its famed 'Golden Age' of cinema, which began in the 1940s and ended around 1953.

Seth Fein notes that unlike the Hollywood studio system, Mexican studios were not controlled by single producers; instead, production companies rented services from studio operators (1994, 102). Some studios were privately owned and some were supported by the state. In 1935, for example, CLASA (Cinematográfico Latino Americana, SA) was furnished with the most up-to-date equipment and received subsidies from the Mexican government to foster a domestic cinema that could demonstrate national (or perhaps nationalistic) values (Noble, 2004, 14). Mexican Estudios Churubusco Azteca was founded in 1945 in an agreement between the Manuel Ávila Camacho government, RKO and Televisa.

Mexico's movie studio system flourished during the 1940s and 1950s, when it was the largest film industry in Latin America. Seth Fein notes that, by the time Emilio Fernández's critical success *Río Escondido* (*Hidden River*, 1948) was released, 'movies represented Mexico's third largest industry by 1947, employing 32,000 workers. Mexico had 72 producers of films, who invested 66 million pesos (approximately US $13 million) in filming motion pictures in 1946 and 1947, four active studios with 40 million pesos of invested capital, and national and international distributors' (1994, 103).

Many scholars have focused on Mexico's 'Golden Age' cinema due to the success and popularity of various auteurs, such as Emilio 'El Indio' Fernández, Spaniard Luis Buñuel, who made films in Mexico during this time, and other more commercial filmmakers such as Julio Bracho, Roberto Gavaldón and Ismael Rodríguez. Famous actors of the time included Cantinflas (Mario

Moreno), María Félix, Dolores del Río, Lupe Vélez, Ramón Novarro, Jorge Negrete, Pedro Armendáriz, Pedro Infante and many others. Work by film historians Jorge Ayala Blanco (1968) and (1974), Emilio García Riera (1992), Carl M. Mora (2005), Charles Ramírez Berg (1992, 2015) and Andrea Noble (2004), as well auteur studies (Dolores Tierney, 2007, and Ernesto Acevedo-Muñoz, 2003), detail the effervescent period when Mexico's cinemagoing culture flourished due to an industrially robust studio system that relied on support through private funding. Funds came from both national investments and the United States, which supported national film production as a bulwark against what they perceived to be communist infiltration in other Latin American film industries. While some critics might debate the term 'Golden Age', Noble notes that figures confirm that characterisation: production went from thirty-eight features in 1941 to eighty-two in 1945, reaching a record high of 123 in 1950 (2004, 15). This was also an age of transnational collaboration between the United States and its trusted ally, Mexico, in the ideological fight against communism. The Mexican 'B' film *Dicen que soy comunista* (*They Say I'm a Communist*, dir. Alejandro Galindo, 1951), among others, perpetuated Cold War propaganda (Fein, 2000, 93).

The special treatment that the Mexican film industry received from the United States in part explains why it flourished. According to *Variety* (written in its customarily choppy style), the desire to position Mexico as the most prolific and popular film producer in Latin America was no secret:

> A terrific US pressure is being exerted to eliminate Argentina as the world's greatest producer of Spanish-language films, and elevate Mexico into the spot. Action is part of the squeeze being exerted by this country to blast Argentina from its friendly attitude toward the Axis. Francis Alstock, film chief of the Office of the Coordinator of Inter-American Affairs (OCIAA), is constantly in and out of Mexico helping the industry. WPB [War Production Board] has cracked down hard on the volume of raw stock being shipped to Argentina, and is lavish with Mexico. (Anon., 1943a)

In 1942, the Mexican film industry produced forty-nine films, and by 1944, its production had increased to seventy-eight. That same year, Argentina's production slid down to twenty-four films, a more than 50 per cent decrease from its 1942 level of fifty-six (Schnitman, 1984, 88). In 1944, a film critic for *Variety* commented: 'the WPB is still awaiting word from the State Department on what the 1944 quotas to the various countries should be. You will recall that about a year ago, the allotment for Argentina was cut back because of her flirting with the Axis and Mexico received a "super-colossal footage"' (Lowe, 1944).

Reports stated that, rather than receive forty million feet of film from the United States, Argentina would receive 50 per cent less in 1943. This represented the deepest cut in Latin America. In contrast, Mexico would be 'well taken care of' (Anon., 1943b). An interdepartmental memo from the Motion Picture Division of the OCIAA explains the Hollywood film industry's motivations for providing technical, material and financial aid to the Mexican film industry:

> The fact is that Mexico will never be a competitor of the American companies
> no matter how much help is given to the Mexican industry. But if better Spanish
> speaking pictures were made through the help extended to the Mexican industry, it
> should result in larger audiences, new theatres, and a strong and better motion picture
> situation in Latin America. It should strongly stimulate and develop the market
> for American pictures. It should help them become more profitable. The American
> company which helps the most may reap the greatest benefit. (Bohan, 1942)

Other justifications were connected to tax incentives for Hollywood that neu-tralised the risk in investing in their Mexican counterparts. Finally, the author of this internal memo felt that the plan could potentially result 'in developing Mexican talent, the best of which might be utilised in America' (Bohan, 1942). Other OCIAA efforts to assist the Mexican film industry included donating film equipment to help build film studios. John Hay Whitney and Francis Alstock (both representatives of the OCIAA) stated in a memo that, in order to avoid a monopoly of film studios, the OCIAA would help 'consolidate the interests of the Azteca and Stahl studios, and the other unit [was] to be the Clasa studios'. In addition, they committed to help set up a finance fund for Mexican motion pictures and promised to send Hollywood film experts to participate in train-ing Mexican technicians. Finally, the OCIAA offered to 'negotiate with the American Moving Picture industry for the commercial distribution of Mexican pictures in those countries and territories requested by the producers of the Mexican Committee' that met with representatives of the OCIAA (Whitney and Alstock, 1942).

Film scholar Román Gubern (1971, 95) has also provided an explanation for why the United States aided the Mexican film industry – a measure that debilitated Argentina:

> The OCIAA policy to favour the Mexican film industry has a double advantage
> from the point of view of United States interests. From an ideological perspective,
> an Allied country was a better guarantee of suitable motion picture content; from
> an economic point of view, reducing the importance of the Argentine film industry
> in Latin America spared North American film companies a competitor from

some sectors of the Latin American film market, and it gave North American entrepreneurs the opportunity to participate in the development of the film industry in Mexico. For instance, in 1945, 49 per cent of the stock of Churubusco studios (the most important in Mexico in the 1940s) was owned by RKO.

Ultimately, it was a confluence of ideological and economic factors which caused the United States to take sides in supporting one Latin American country's film industry over another.

The 1950s marked a decline in the number of quality films made in Mexico, when shooting was reduced from five to three weeks at a time to cut production costs and save money on the high wages that Mexican film stars were earning (Noble, 2004, 16). Along with other factors, this financial constraint contributed to the rise of rapidly made, inexpensive films that lacked artistic merit. These movies were known as '*churros*', as Anne Rubenstein (2000, 665) notes: 'like [the dessert fritter], [they] were not nourishing, rapidly made, soon forgotten, identical to one another and cheap'. Apart from a few exceptional films made during that period – *Macario* (dir. Roberto Gavaldón, 1960) and *El ángel exterminador* (*The Exterminating Angel*, dir. Luis Buñuel, 1962) – Mexican films failed to attract large numbers at the box office or to get exported abroad.

In the 1970s, under the left-leaning Echeverría administration, the film industry underwent a radical change. Once in office, Luis Echeverría set out to establish himself as a progressive president and self-appointed spokesperson for the Third World (Treviño, 1979). 'He gave a new direction on all cinematographic fronts,' remembers Jorge Fons, a quietly spoken and bearded new-wave director who made more than five features during the Echeverría years. 'He opened up the traditionally strict censorship of themes, promoted new directors, encouraged co-productions with the state, he created a new promotion department in the film industry, and began to concentrate on improving the distribution and exhibition of Mexican films' (quoted in Treviño, 1979, 28). During this period, the state contributed to the formation of new independent film production companies through the nationalised Banco Nacional Cinematográfico (National Film Bank), run by the president's brother, Rodolfo. They helped produce the majority of the independent films during the period through companies such as Marco Polo Productions, Alpha Centauri and Scorpion Productions. The Banco Nacional Cinematográfico was a unique institution, as no other national cinema had created a bank dedicated to financing film production. As such, it placed the film industry on a firmer footing (Noble, 2004, 16).

The 1970s were also marked by an important increase in state institutions that helped foster film production and culture in general. These include the Centro de Producción del Cortometraje (Centre for Short Film Production, 1971), the Cineteca Nacional (National Cinematheque, 1973), the Centro de Capacitación Cinematográfica (The National Film School (CCC), 1975), the Corporación Nacional Cinematográfica (National Film Corporation, 1974) and the Corporación Nacional Cinematográfica de Trabajadores y Estado (National Film Corporation of Workers and the State, 1975) (Piva et al., 2011, 24). The Cineteca Nacional remains one of the main exhibitors for foreign and artistic films in Mexico City; it also functions as the repository for all national commercially released films. By law, every producer who exhibits a commercial film in Mexico must donate one print to the Cineteca (Maciel, 1999, 197). The National Film School, the CCC, was well conceived as an important teaching institution and remains so to this day. The other organisations, however, did not fare so well. The state-run National Film Corporation and the National Film Corporation of Workers and the State were intended to act as producers and co-producers of films (Rossbach and Canel in Maciel, 1999, 201). Unfortunately, these institutions were all dismantled during the following presidential administration led by López Portillo. Filmmaking was then thrown into crisis, as most filmmakers from the 1968 generation, comprised of left-leaning directors who created low-budget independent cinema, had relied on state funding to produce quality films. Many filmmakers shifted over to television or had to rely on making low-budget, commercial genre films such as action movies, risqué comedies and US–Mexico border films with violent themes (Maciel, 1999, 210). Later chapters will offer further discussion of the history of Mexican cinema.

Argentina

Film studios in Argentina were established in the 1930s when two major production companies, Argentina Sono Film (1933) and Lumiton Studios (1932), opened. Sono Film was founded by the Mentasti family, Italian immigrants who started out in the wine-selling business in the province of Buenos Aires and expanded their activities to cinema in 1932 when the patriarch, Angel, met a fellow immigrant who had ties to a film distribution company and teamed up with him to import German films (España, 1992, 50). According to film historian Claudio España, screenwriter and silent filmmaker Luis J. Moglia Barth approached Angel 'El Viejo' Mentasti about producing a talkie called *Tango*, which would feature tango singers and stage actors performing alongside those who had popularised the songs on the radio (actors Azucena Maizani, Luis Sandrini, Libertad Lamarque, Pepe Arias and Tita Merello with well-known musicians of the time, including 'El Viejo', who was also a musician). Mentasti agreed to hire the ensemble cast, and the film propelled Argentina Sono Film to fame, creating a lasting brand that continues to be relevant today. Though it is still run by scions of Mentasti, the studio has merged with Telefe, a private television channel owned partially by the Spanish telecoms company Telefónica.

Lumiton Studios was founded by a group of doctors in the suburb of Munro where they produced their first film (and box-office hit), *Los tres berretines* (*The Three Amateurs*, dir. César José Guerrico, 1933). The company continued to make studio dramas such as *Los martes, orquídeas* (*On Tuesdays, Orchids*, dir. Francisco Múgica, 1941), which was famed actress Mirtha Legrand's debut. Throughout its history, Lumiton produced ninety-eight films; the studio is currently maintained and rented out to independent film companies. These pioneering studio experiments were followed by the studio Artistas Argentinos Asociados (AAA), founded in 1941 by a group of unemployed actors who contracted Lucas Demare to make the nationalist epic *La guerra gaucha* (*The Gaucho War*) in 1942. Their next big hit was *Pampa bárbara* (*Savage Pampa*, dirs. Lucas Demare and Hugo Fregonese) in 1945. The studio disbanded in 1958, and the company distributed films until 2000.

In 1935, Argentina produced twenty-two sound films, and fifty films had been released by 1939. Argentina was the most popular and prolific producer of films in Latin America, and was a considerable competitor to Hollywood in the Spanish-speaking world (Falicov, 2007a, 16). Each major studio could produce approximately twelve features a year, making Argentina the world's largest producer of Spanish-language films (Anon., 1942a). According to Getino (2005, 28), this film industry was the most technologically advanced in all of Latin America. As Argentine cinema grew in popularity at home, it began to be exported throughout Latin American countries, competing on some level with Hollywood films for box-office share. In 1941, Sono Film and Lumiton opened film distribution offices in Mexico. These Argentine studios began to distribute films throughout the country, making up 34 per cent of the total production exhibited in the regional capitals (Getino, 2000, 300). Film studios such as Lumiton, Sono Film, AAA and others were at the peak of their popularity in 1942, when there were six majors and fifteen to twenty smaller units (Anon., 1942b).

Ana M. López describes how legislation was enacted, both before and during President Juan Perón's first administration (1946–52), mandating state support for film industries with the aim of strengthening Argentina's industrial development and its position in international markets. This legislation included a variety of measures such as screen quotas, state bank loans for financing film productions, a film production subsidy programme funded through a tax on film admissions, and restrictions on the withdrawal of earnings from Argentina by foreign-controlled companies (López, 1987, 50). In response to the gradual decline of the studio system, the Instituto Nacional del Cine (National Film

Institute) (INC) was founded in 1957. The creation of this institution and its continued function is discussed further in Chapter 2, on the importance of the public sector in funding Latin American cinema.

In the contemporary era, the studio system in its traditional form has become a rarity, with the exception of Argentina Sono Film. Instead, it has been replaced by smaller, modern production companies which are fully or partially owned by megamedia conglomerates such as Argentina's Grupo Clarín, or Disney's Buena Vista International. In other cases, films are commissioned by a studio, such as the Mexican Televisa Cine, but are then produced through a system of subcontracting to be co-produced or distributed by large multimedia conglomerates (Brazil's Globo) or US majors (Fox, Warner Bros. and Columbia, for example).

In the case of contemporary Argentina, Barnes, Borello and Llahí (2014, 33–5) have identified four distinct typologies to describe the current industrial models: (1) Small production companies that solely make films and are not involved in making television shows or advertising. Although this model is not the most common, examples include Matanza Cine (owned by Pablo Trapero), BD Cine (run by Daniel Burman and Diego Dubcovsky until 2013) and 4L films (owned by Lisandro Alonso). (2) Film, advertising and television production for broadcast and cable are all functions that production companies take on in order to make films. Many film directors work in the advertising world and the connections they make in this sector prove particularly beneficial in the process of making their films. Examples of this model include Adrián Caetano's production house, Lucrecia Martel's company, the late Fabián Bielinsky's company and many others. (3) A company that provides services related to the production chain. These include post-production houses, colour correction labs, visual effects houses and equipment rental houses. And (4), an entrepreneurial model of production that works exclusively within the realm of co-production with other countries, private companies and the state. This might mean a financial group rather than one dealing with the production process (Barnes, Borello and Llahí, 2014, 34). This categorisation may prove problematic in some respects – for example, how might one differentiate a production house from one that provides support for ancillary services – but it nonetheless accounts for the shift away from the traditional studio model in which every facet of pre-production, production and post-production was handled in house.

While Hollywood studios are increasingly opting to diversify their portfolios and invest in lower-budget Latin American films, they are also continuing to participate in the reigning studio practice of 'runaway productions' encouraged by tax-incentive policies in various Latin American countries, as well as skilled workers who command lower wages, and lower infrastructural costs.

RUNAWAY PRODUCTIONS

The decades-old practice of luring 'runaway productions' from advanced indus-trialised countries is an increasingly global phenomenon, and one which has prompted countries from all over the world to consider constructing movie stu-dios in locations which offer incentives to do so. In this model, capital investment is put forward by a studio, typically one of the large Hollywood studios, which then locates the cheapest studio labour and infrastructure, either out-of-state or abroad, with which to make films. For highly skilled film crews trained in coun-tries such as Mexico, Chile, Argentina, this model also affords the possibility of persuading international film companies to shoot their films abroad in order that these skilled crews are potentially hired on the set.

Runaway productions are not new in Hollywood's history. Historians cite the origins of this practice when US film studios opened satellite branches abroad (such as Paramount's Joinville Studios in France in 1930), where low-budget, multiple-language versions of the same film were produced for foreign audiences at 33 per cent below the cost of the original Hollywood film (Shurlock, 1931, 22). A decade later, Hollywood studios teamed up with the US government to pro-mote what was known as the 'Good Neighbour Policy'. Orchestrated through the OCIAA, the policy's cultural wing was a concerted effort to create Holly-wood films with positive images of Latin America in order to persuade Latin American nations to join forces with the Allies in World War II. These early forms of 'runaway productions' include cartoons blended with live-action films, such as Walt Disney's *Saludos Amigos* (1943) and *The Three Caballeros* (1945). The actual phrase 'runaway production' appears in the 1950s (Davis and Kaye, 2010), following the famous Paramount Case of 1948 (known as the Hollywood Anti-Trust Case) in which a US Supreme Court ruling challenged the studios' monopoly by mandating that they divest themselves of their exhibition houses. This, in turn, reshaped the studios, which started to produce films abroad through subcontractors. The Paramount Case significantly shifted the production of US films from a lower-budget model focused on regional content produced for studio-owned movie theatres, to a system premised on the production of fewer, higher-budget films for movie theatres both domestically and internationally. Ironically, this model generated more profit than its older, vertically integrated predecessor: when 'blockbuster' films such as Universal Pictures' *Jaws* (dir. Steven Spielberg, 1975) was released on 1,200 screens throughout the US, it brought in sixty-seven million viewers nationwide. From then on, a small number of films would generate extraordinary profits, whereas the bulk of productions would make little or no money at all (Humphreys, 2013). One way to maintain budget-ary restraint in this new model based on subcontracting involved a continuous search for lower labour and location costs abroad.

Hollywood in Mexico

The contemporary history of Hollywood production in Mexico purportedly began with the filming of *Night of the Iguana* (dir. John Huston, 1964) in the once-sleepy town of Puerto Vallarta. The film's fame purportedly transformed the town into a showy commercial and tourist destination. Restaurants and bars bearing the film's name cashed in on the tourist market, and in 1999, the movie set was resurrected into two theme restaurants based on the film (Koehne, 1999). During an earlier period, Hollywood Westerns such as John Ford's *Treasure of the Sierra Madre* (1948) were partially filmed in Mexico, given the landscape (which was faithful to the Western genre) and the geographic proximity to Hollywood. From 1954 onwards, following the establishment of a film commission in the northern city of Durango, over 100 Hollywood films were shot in the city, including *White Feather* (dir. Robert D. Webb, 1954), *The Magnificent Seven* (dir. John Sturges, 1960), *The Wild Bunch* (dir. Sam Peckinpah, 1969) and *True Grit* (dir. Henry Hathaway, 1969).

Big-budget productions of summer blockbusters did not return to Mexico until the mid-1990s when *Titanic* (dir. James Cameron, 1997) – the most expensive film at that point in history (US$200 million) – was filmed at a huge custom-built studio in Rosarito, Baja California Norte (Hawley, 2004). According to the Mexican government, the film injected US$85 million into the local economy. Built in 1996 by Fox Studios Baja, this same facility has since produced *Master and Commander* (dir. Peter Weir, 2003), *Pearl Harbor* (dir. Michael Bay, 2001) and the comedy *Beverly Hills Chihuahua* (dir. Raja Gosnell, 2008), a hit in both the US and Mexico.

What advantages does this practice hold for Hollywood studios? Wages for Mexican film crews are roughly 75 per cent lower than their US counterparts, according to Hugo Alonso Reyes Mejilla, the secretary for technicians at the Union of Cinema Production Workers (Hawley, 2004). This therefore cuts labour costs for the Hollywood studios by at least one-third (Tegel, 2002). The Mexican government additionally benefits from a potential influx of money, including the tourism dollars generated by having images of the Mexican landscape projected globally. Tourism has been further promoted, as the presence of Fox Studios Baja developed a theme-park element to the studio following the production of *Titanic*. When Fox sold the studio to private investors Baja Acquisitions in 2007, it was renamed Baja Studios, and functioned as a film studio and tourist destination, similar to its earlier incarnation. The facility has been recently used to film US television series, such as AMC's *Fear the Walking Dead* (2015–) (de la Fuente, 2017a).

Contemporary debates on US runaway productions focus predominantly on the Canadian case, as Canada offers one of the most enticing tax incentives to Hollywood producers. Moreover, compared to Latin American countries and to other non-English-speaking nations, Canada has closer cultural and linguistic ties with the US (indeed, this is why New Zealand and Australia are key filming locations for Hollywood crews, despite the enormous geographic distance). Nevertheless, in the quest for ever-cheaper labour and exotic locales, Latin America has continued to be on US film producers' radars, with the region ensuring continued attention by marketing its low-cost and touristic locations. The visibility of Latin American locations has increased thanks to initiatives involving: (1) tax incentives and legislation, as has recently occurred in Mexico; (2) the creation of national and regional film commissions championed by both Mexican and Argentine regional governments as well as other Latin American countries; (3) presence in location conferences (such as the annual Locations Trade Show in Santa Monica, CA); and (4) ad placement in trade publications. For example, for the 2015 Locations Trade Show, the following film commissions were represented: Dominican Republic Film Commission, Durango, Mexico Film Commission, Film Commission Chile, Panama Film Commission and the Colombian Proimágenes Film Commission. The presence of these film commissions has dramatically increased compared to a decade earlier when only Buenos Aires and Durango attended. This shift is a sign that the playing field has broadened throughout the region, and that the once-dominant industries are being challenged by the emerging ones, in both service offerings and in obtaining valuable production funds from the public and private realms (Villegas, 2015).

Despite the fact that government subsidies and incentives for film industry investment have not materialised in Mexico (to the same extent as they have for the private sector in Brazil, for example), legislators have made an attempt to encourage multinational investment. In 2004, Mexico introduced a 15 per cent Value Added Tax (VAT) rebate on local film production services, on the condition that they contract with a Mexican production service or a local producer (de la Fuente, 2004, 18). In recent years, however, a handful of Hollywood films have been shot in Mexico, due to the lower cost of services, which can be advantageous for the bottom line, especially of higher-budget blockbuster movies. After a rash of drug-gang-related violence in 2008–9, and in an attempt to lure Hollywood producers back to the country, in March 2010 President Calderón's administration announced a new cash rebate policy. The initial funding pool of US$20 million offered 17.5 per cent rebates on Mexican shoots, combining cash rebates and sales tax refunds administered through the ProAudiovisual Fund, a part of ProMexico, a government body set up to encourage the export of Mexican products (de la Fuente, 2014b). It is unclear whether this fund convinced the producers of the James Bond film *Spectre* (dir. Sam Mendes, 2015) to film in Mexico, but documents leaked online via the

December 2015 Sony hack prompted speculation that Mexican authorities had given the MGM and Sony producers upwards of US$20 million to guarantee specific changes in the script: for example, that a Mexican mayor would not be assassinated in the plot, that no villains would be Mexican and that the next 'Bond girl' would be Mexican (Young, 2015). James Wilson, the film's producer, has refuted these allegations (Olivares, 2015). In 2017, the ProAudiovisual Fund (ProAV) was shuttered due in part to a lack of foreign companies taking part in the programme (Gutiérrez, 2017).

Foreign Production Services: Pros and Cons

Mexico's tax rebate was designed as a means to make the country as competitive as other Latin American countries such as Colombia, Costa Rica and Puerto Rico. These countries attract foreign producers by offering substantial cash rebates, along with highly competitive pay scales (Young, 2010). According to the Wharton School of Business's web magazine, the reigning king of filming locales in Latin America and the Caribbean has been Puerto Rico, a US territory that offers a 40 per cent tax credit on payments to local film crews. Since its currency is the US dollar, the island has an innate advantage of simplifying transactions for production companies. The industry has become a major contributor to the island's economy, as the country's film commissioner Demitrio Fernández notes. In '2009 alone, $22 million in credits generated $118 million in total economic activity in the film and television industries' (Wharton School, Anon., 2013d). Moreover, Puerto Rico has become a stand-in for Mexico in films such as *22 Jump Street* (dir. Phil Lord, 2014), a sequel starring Jonah Hill and Channing Tatum (Anon., 2013a).

In an age defined by mobility, the ability to offer this level of specialisation in production services might tip the scale in favour of a specific country looking to attract a production. Indeed, it might prove to be a competitive advantage, paving the way for more specialised local technicians to work on future projects. Goldsmith and O'Regan discuss this fierce competition among countries that build state-of-the-art facilities with the aim of giving competitive bids to foreign countries. Studios and locations are now competing against each other on the basis of their ability to provide a range of generic skills, services and expertise to individual films, augmented by what are claimed to be unique or compelling local advantages, including the availability of state-of-the-art studio infrastructure, particular creative individuals or firms, and the proximity to specific locations (2005, xii).

The Dominican Republic is a newer player that is attempting to compete with Puerto Rico by offering its own tax incentive package and facilitating the construction of purpose-built Pinewood Dominican Republic Studios, built in collaboration with Pinewood Studios, the studio that has hosted such hits as the

Harry Potter and James Bond series. This US$70 million investment by Lantica Media includes a water tank for filming scenes set 'at sea' or underwater. The 60,500 sq. ft Horizon Water Tank contains a full diving and marine unit (Wharton School, 2013). In 2013, the Dominican government added more provisions to its 25 per cent tax credit law, including measures to incentivise Dominican companies to also invest in local productions (Mango, 2013). Panama also offers a 15 per cent cash rebate on all local expenditures, and Puerto Rico extends a 40 per cent tax credit on payments to Puerto Rico residents, and a 20 per cent tax credit on non-resident talent.

The need to obtain financial investment is one factor that accounts for the motivation of these nations to create 'incentive' policy initiatives and to work with regional and municipal governments to provide such competitive bids for what Canada calls 'foreign service production' (Elmer and Gasher, 2005, 5). It is projected that nearly 20 per cent of all out-of-state production budgets are spent within local economies. More specifically, when a foreign shoot comes into town, the following are hired and used: labour, transportation, lodging, car and truck rental, motor fuel and service stations, food and beverage companies, to name only a few (Harrison and Gnuschke, 2005).

[Figure 1.2 Horizon Water Tank, Dominican Republic. The Pinewood Studios website advertises its foreign location shooting in the Dominican Republic with images of water tanks: 'Shooting in and around water is a specialty of Pinewood Dominican Republic. The eight acre water effects facility includes a 60,500 sq ft horizon water tank with 4,300 sq ft inner tank and blue screen capabilities' (https://www.pinewoodgroup.com/studios/pinewood-dominican-republic-studios/stages-and-facilities/water), © Lantica Media. All rights reserved.]

On the downside, Davis and Kaye (2010, 58) succinctly state that host coun-tries need to be concerned about the following three risks if runaway productions are the main avenue for the development of autochthonous production: oppor-tunity costs, integration with Hollywood and the race to the bottom. In their view, the competition by each country for the best cash rebates and the like will ultimately prove damaging (that is, at a certain point, they will no longer be the most competitive country). Moreover, the process can generate power dynamics between the foreign and the local crew that reflect hierarchies in the global world system. This is what happened when Roger Corman's production company worked in Argentina during the 1980s on nine low-budget films of varying genres. Argentina was chosen at a time when the economy was faltering and costs were extremely low. According to production designer María Julia Bertotto, during the filming of a sword and sorcery film, *Wizards of the Lost King-dom* (dir. Héctor Olivera, 1985), Corman's above-the-line crew acted offensively towards the Argentine crew. She recalled that some members of the US crew felt uncomfortable working with the locals, despite the fact that many of the latter spoke English. She remembered that Corman's people 'essentially gave orders and refused to hear our suggestions. It was as though they had preconceived notions of Argentina and thought we were "Indians with feathers on our heads"' (Falicov, 2004, 33). Another problem stemmed from the plan to market the film for the Anglophone market. To this end, the credits were modified, with Argen-tine names replaced by anglicised pseudonyms – for example, Américo Ortiz de Zarate was changed to Andrew Sargent – with the aim of increasing the film's chances of selling in the English-language market (Falicov, 2004, 34).

This power dynamic raises the question of whether countries participating in runaway productions, such as Mexico and Argentina, thrive or are exploited under these conditions. While, on some shoots, unskilled crew members tend to be overworked and underpaid, as has been documented in the case of the *Titanic* (Falicov, 2008), in other situations, having an international crew composed of specialised technicians may provide an opportunity for locals to learn new skill sets, thus promoting knowledge transfer. As a counterexample to the case of *Wiz-ards of the Lost Kingdom*, Corman's runaway productions also had some positive outcomes. Film critic Diego Curubeto describes how Argentine visual effects technician Alex Mathius and makeup artist Jorge Bruno had never had the opportunity to work in the fantasy genre until Roger Corman came to Argen-tina in the 1980s to make films such as *Deathstalker* (dir. John Watson, 1983). They gained valuable expertise by learning the craft from veteran special-effects makeup artist John Carl Buecheler, whose credits include numerous 'B' movies and horror films such as the 1995 release *Halloween: The Curse of Michael Myers* (dir. Joe Chappelle) (Curubeto, 1993, 155).

The presence of foreign film crews in particular countries therefore involves aspects that go beyond costs and benefits: while some local industries will benefit, workers will be exploited in other instances. Some may gain valuable technology transfer skills. Taking a cue from the Canadian case, which has a longer track record, Charles Davis and Janice Kaye conclude that one must distinguish between two different facets of home-grown productions: one consists of production capabilities, such as below-the-line crew positions, while the other involves the higher-order film and television-related 'business and creative capabilities'. The authors argue that both are necessary for a local film industry to thrive, but, while runaway productions strengthen crews' training and the economic stability of local film industries, they are not advantageous for local production houses or firms (Davis and Kaye, 2010, 58). The two afore-mentioned examples from Corman's runaway productions exemplify how this model generates both winners and losers. In a nutshell, runaway productions can benefit a host country if sufficient resources are involved (cash that stays in the country and is spent on salaries and services) and if skill sets are honed to allow for improved technical training of the local crew. Over time, this might help invigorate the local film infrastructure, as new studios, post-production facilities and so on can function as a form of investment that may lead potentially to local films being produced *in situ*.

SOCIALIST STUDIO MODELS

While the dominant mode of industrial filmmaking throughout Latin America and the world is a capitalist one, the importance of socialist models for film production in Latin America should not be neglected. Initially launched in the 1920s with the Soviet school of filmmaking, these models were shaped distinct-ively by Latin American socialist governments after the Cuban revolution of 1959, and in Venezuela after Hugo Chávez came to power in 1999.

Cuba

Although Cuba has never been a prolific producer of films, the impact of this industry is important to the region because of the way the country has incor-porated socialism to foment its national film industry. The Cuban film model has subsequently had a profound influence on the cinema of Latin America, especially on smaller, emerging and, in some cases, politically left-leaning coun-tries – one such example can be found in filmmaking in Chile during the Allende government (1970–3).

The Instituto Cubano del Arte e Industria Cinematográficos (Cuban Film Institute) (ICAIC) is an example par excellence of a state-run and funded institution. Founded in 1959 as an inherent part of Fidel Castro's revolutionary government, the ICAIC was charged with making films in line with the aims of revolutionary socialist ideology. Accordingly, filmmaking was to be transformed into a democratic art, becoming an 'imperfect cinema', an expression coined by filmmaker and theorist Julio García Espinosa to characterise it as distinct from a glossy, commercial, 'First World' type of movie. It encouraged a model of film practice that related more to Cuban reality and sought to change it in a 'committed' socialist fashion.

The socialist model of filmmaking involved a dramatic removal of any and all traces of the Hollywood studios that had peppered the film industry landscape, working against the image of Havana as a foreign shooting location used by studios such as Warner Bros. throughout World War II. During the period marked by the arrival of sound cinema in Cuba, filmmaking was mainly influenced by France (as the first films to arrive were from the distributors Gaumont and Pathé), but by the 1930s, Hollywood had erected studios and had begun to use Havana as a backdrop for musicals and other genre films. By the 1940s and 1950s, Cuban films would be either heavily influenced by Mexican cinema or stem from co-productions with Mexico.

Following the triumph of the revolution in 1959, Cuba, and particularly the ICAIC, became beacons of support for left-leaning filmmakers oppressed by military dictatorships and other repressive regimes. In this era, within the orbit of social movements, we see the first instances of alliances between Latin American filmmakers, giving rise to numerous meetings, reunions and film festivals held at Viña del Mar (Chile) in 1967 and 1969, Mérida (Mexico) in 1968, Caracas (Venezuela) in 1967, Havana on numerous occasions and under the auspices of the ICAIC, and in Montreal in 1974 (Rodríguez, 2007, 16).

As mentioned in the Introduction, in 1979 the ICAIC organised the Festival del Nuevo Cine Latinoamericano, or 'The Havana Film Festival', which not only acted as a high-profile showcase for Cuban cinema but also served as a space where filmmakers from across Latin America (including Chicano filmmakers from the US) could attend and discuss matters that affected all of these nations equally. For example, one issue was how to create distribution linkages among themselves, thus gaining freedom from Hollywood's stranglehold on film distribution. The festival became a space to view each other's work, to exchange ideas and to work collaboratively. From the outset, the ICAIC operated as a film studio in a specific sense: screenwriters, technicians and directors were employed full-time and people moved up the ranks via an apprenticeship system. One could begin at an entry-level position and ideally then work up to directing a film. Many famous filmmakers got their start this way. This included Sara Gómez, an Afro-Cuban woman filmmaker who directed a feature in 1974 after working in documentary.

The founders of the ICAIC began setting up the institute a mere three months after the triumph of the Cuban revolution on 1 January 1959. The filmmakers chosen to assume the helm – Alfredo Guevara, Julio García Espinosa and Tomás Gutiérrez Alea, among others – had been committed members in the struggle against the Batista regime, working hand in hand with Fidel Castro to construct a radio communications network called Radio Rebelde (Rebel Radio). Therefore, when Castro successfully overthrew the Batista regime, these same filmmakers went about dismantling the traditional studio system of film production that had very much modelled itself upon Hollywood.

The Cuban film industry became the first nationalised film industry in the Caribbean. Utilising the former Biltmore studios that had been constructed in the 1950s, the ICAIC renovated three movie studios and furnished them with new, imported film equipment, two film labs, projection rooms and editing suites. This was to be the largest cinema production centre in Latin America (Villaça, 2006). The ICAIC became synonymous with all aspects of Cuban cinema: from production to exhibition and distribution. It was the place where screenwriters were trained, newsreels assembled and directors 'greenlighted' after proving their mettle by apprenticing on various films. According to Julianne Burton (1978, 17), 'beginning in 1975, large numbers of university graduates (the majority of them women) began to enter the ICAIC to do everything from film criticism to script research and assistant directing. Many of the ICAIC's future directors were drawn from these ranks.'

The post-1959 film industry in Cuba was different from others in Latin America because it had been established and shaped by the revolutionary gov-ernment; as such, it was unabashedly part of the revolutionary project which was anti-imperialist in nature. Alfredo Guevara, the founding head of the ICAIC and its director until 1982, stated that

> in making or analysing a work of art, we cannot ignore its historical, economic, social or ideological context; our work is closely tied to the defence of the Revolution. We cannot be neutral. But if we reject neutralism, neither do we advocate an official culture ... The Revolution as a theme in films is not propagandistic nor superficial; it is life itself. (qtd. in Sutherland, 1961, 47)

In sum, the ICAIC's function was to act as an arm of the government to foster its revolutionary ideals, one of which was to make art and culture democratic rather than elite-oriented. Accordingly, films were screened across the country in both rural and urban settings, featuring topics which working people could relate to rather than privileging the triumphs and travails of wealthy people or the display of gratuitous sex and violence.

During the first twenty-five years of the ICAIC's existence, the institute produced 112 feature-length films (including documentaries), some 900 short documentaries (animation, fictional and educational) and more than 1,300 weekly newsreels. In comparison, it is estimated that, during the sixty years of filmmaking on the island before the revolution, no more than 150 features were produced, while non-commercial documentaries were practically non-existent (Burton, 1985, 126).

In the mid-1980s, the ICAIC's annual budget was roughly US$7 million, which covered not only the filmmaking but also the salaries of 1,100 employees (Fanshal qtd. in Burton, 1997, 137). Approximately six to eight films were produced per year during the 1980s (Chanan, 2004, 89). During this period, an attempt was made to give creative producers more agency, with the implementation of the Grupos de Creación (Creation Groups) model under the supervision of filmmaker and theorist Julio García Espinosa. This model organised filmmakers into three teams with the hope that these groups, headed by a filmmaker, would give producers more creative control and authority than the ICAIC had (Fernandes, 2006, 45). After the 1991 disintegration of the Soviet Union, a superpower on which Cuba and its film industry depended, these groups were disbanded and the industry struggled to survive. During what is known as the 'Special Period', production diminished to two or three films per year, depending on whether directors could obtain co-production financing. In other words, the collapse of Cuba's largest trading partner affected the ICAIC's ability to make films without being heavily subsidised. An increased use of international co-productions helped Cuban cinema persevere, since the funding model was radically reorganised around the search for hard currency abroad. Cuba's main collaborators were Mexico, Spain, Venezuela, Peru and Nicaragua (Fernandes, 2006, 46). Other sources of hard currency generated by the ICAIC at the time included service fees for international camera crews that came into the country to shoot, along with the distribution and sale of Cuban films abroad (Soles qtd. in Fernandes, 2006, 46).

Some Cuban films achieved international recognition. *Fresa y chocolate* (*Strawberry and Chocolate*, 1994), co-directed by Tomás Gutiérrez Alea, one of Cuba's finest directors, confronted Cuba's legacy of discrimination against homosexuality. Fernando Pérez directed *Madagascar* (1994), *La vida es silbar* (*Life Is to Whistle*, 1998) and *Suite Habana* (*Havana Suite*, 2003), all lyrical films that showed the everyday lives of Cubans. Other Cuban filmmakers have managed to cut costs by using digital video. Humberto Solás's *Miel para Oshún* (*Honey for Oshún*, 2001) was the first Cuban feature film made digitally. Lower-budget films such as Alejandro Moya Iskánder's *Mañana* (*Tomorrow*, 2007) were shot digitally but featured veteran actors Mario Balmaceda and Enrique Colina. Some films have been made independently of the ICAIC. Directors Gloria Rolando, Esteban García Insausti and Arturo Infante are among those who have raised funds on their own, typically working on video. A hybrid 'inside-outside' model has recently emerged when young entrepreneurial filmmakers such as Alejandro Brugués, trained at the Cuban Film School in San Antonio de los Baños, was forced to seek film financing to produce films outside the ICAIC's normal channels of production. Brugués's first film, a Cuban-Spanish comedy/horror film *Juan de los muertos* (*Juan of the Dead*, 2011), instantly became a popular and critical success both at home and abroad. The dominant 'insider', the ICAIC, then offered to distribute it both domestically and internationally, giving the film access to a distribution circuit and legitimising it domestically. In this way, some Cuban films are produced both from the outside, but also the inside the system.

In the current scenario, Cuba has allied with Venezuela, its oil-rich friend to the south. Although the countries do not engage much in filmic exchange (compared to the past when Cuban filmmakers would travel to the USSR and Czechoslovakia to study film), they share a similar history, as Venezuela created a film industry along with a national film and television culture under the late socialist President Hugo Chávez. The following sections explore how, under current president Nicolás Maduro, Venezuela has established a modern state-run film studio, Villa del Cine, that represents the government's involvement in film and media production.

Venezuela's Villa del Cine

Under the direction of the late President Hugo Chávez, Venezuela launched a massive effort to promote the visual arts and culture, seeking to challenge the global hegemony of US Hollywood studios. When Chávez rose to power in 1999, he implemented stronger protectionist measures to strengthen Venezuela's film industry. For example, a screen quota was introduced whereby national films were mandated to be screened in movie theatres, and exhibitors were required to keep them on the marquee for a minimum of two weeks. In addition, the screening of a Venezuelan short film (*cortometraje*) was required before each feature film.

Perhaps most grandiosely, on 3 June 2006, the largest film studio in Venezuela was inaugurated: the Villa del Cine (Cinema City), located 30 km west of Caracas in the working-class city of Guarenas. This 2,400 square-metre, state-owned complex cost US$42 million to construct, and is fully equipped with lighting, audio and video equipment, and soundproof facilities for casting, wardrobe and post-production (Márquez, 2007). As of 2010, Villa del Cine had produced twenty-three features, including both fiction films and documentaries, and participated in thirty co-productions (Gómez and Romero, 2010, cited in Zweig,

2011, 134), some of which were directed by Venezuelan auteurs Román Chal-
baud and Fina Torres. In 2015, a record thirty films were produced, though there
were not enough exhibition slots to screen them all, and so some productions
stayed on the marquee for weeks. For example, two years earlier, Venezuela's first
thriller, *La casa del fin de los tiempos* (*The House at the End of Time*, dir. Alejandro
Hidalgo) was the biggest box-office hit of 2013, attracting 575,000 spectators
and drawing in the highest box-office revenue at US$4 million.

The Ministry of Culture's express goal was to surpass the record of eighteen
national films produced per year to reach twenty-four (Cobo cited in Villazana,
2008, 165). According to media scholar Carlos Delgado Flores, Villa del Cine
was modelled on other government-sponsored cinema projects such as the
Italian Cineccitá (founded in 1937 under Mussolini) and the Mexican Estudios
Churubusco Azteca (Flores qtd. in Zweig, 2011, 133). As part of this larger
objective to promote home-grown media products, Chávez's government helped
create the counterhegemonic television network Telesur, labelled the 'Anti-CNN
network', with additional funds from Uruguay, Cuba and Argentina. Villa del
Cine and Telesur, alongside the Centro Nacional Autónomo de Cinematografía
(Venezuelan Film Institute) (CNAC) and the state-run film distribution company Amazonia films (which distributes films produced out of Villa del Cine),
have been hailed as an institutional form of cultural nationalism aimed at dis-
rupting the hegemonic position that Hollywood film and television continue to
occupy in Venezuela and beyond. In the words of Chávez, the Villa del Cine was
intended to break through the 'dictatorship of Hollywood' (van der Zalm, 2007).

News of this astounding movie studio complex attracted US left-leaning actors
to take a tour of Villa del Cine's facilities when it opened. In a gesture that was
seen as a form of resistance to the Bush administration, American actors Sean
Penn, Kevin Spacey and Tim Robbins were among those interested in finding
out more about the direction in which Venezuelan cinema was headed; Robbins
even contemplated shooting a project there (Kozloff, 2008). One of the causes
célèbres linked to Villa del Cine is US actor Danny Glover's quest to make a
US$27 million epic film about Haitian independence leader Toussaint L'Ouver-
ture. Slated to be released in 2013, it was supposed to star Don Cheadle, Angela
Bassett and Wesley Snipes. However, many critics, ranging from the political
Right (e.g. Republican Senator Connie Mack, who had criticised Glover for
cutting a 'sweetheart deal' with Chávez) to filmmakers in Venezuela, felt Glover
had not gone through the same vetting processes as others, and denounced the
anti-democratic implications of this lack of procedure. Claudia Nazoa, president
of the Venezuelan Chamber of Feature Film Producers, said: 'what worries us
is this trend for neo-colonisation by international figures who come to talk of
their support for Chávez's government – and leave with money for their projects'

(Kozloff, 2008). Nikolas Kozloff also points out that Venezuelan directors complained that the budget for Glover's film equalled the entire state budget for domestic films from 2003 to 2008 – a sum they said could 'finance 36 Venezuelan films' (Kozloff, 2008). Those defending the project felt that it could compete against Hollywood and join the 'major leagues of cinema' (Kozloff, 2008). They argued that this film could make Venezuelans proud, as it would recount histories that had not been told accurately on the big screen. Still, at this time of writing, the film has yet to be made.

CONCLUSION

This chapter has summarised how, beginning in the 1930s, film industries in Argentina, Brazil and Mexico utilised a studio system model of filmmaking. This factory model was created by entrepreneurs who employed actors from the radionovela and *sainete* (one-act theatrical sketches) tradition of popular culture to create films which launched national and international movie stars, directors and popular songs. Hollywood invested in movie studios, such as those in Mexico, partly as as a political move during World War II, but also to compete against the strongest Spanish-language film industry at the time, Argentina. The periods of systematic filmmaking are referred to as the 'Golden Age' of Mexican and Argentine cinemas. Beginning in the late 1950s, however, television was overtaking film and the state was forced to intervene to help sustain film production throughout the region.

Hollywood film studios also concentrated on Latin America following the collapse of European markets during World War II. This competition proved to be fierce for Latin American studio filmmaking, which eventually gave way, with only a few surviving into the contemporary era. Hollywood studio heads have also sent film crews and actors to various Latin American countries, principally Mexico and Argentina, for 'runaway productions' or 'foreign location shooting'. While undoubtedly helping to create jobs and teach production skills to sections of the workforce, at the same time, many low-skilled workers have been exploited and this model has been criticised as a 'race to the bottom' given the tax rebates and incentives offered to US and European companies. Finally, a socialist model of film studio filmmaking was profiled, examining Cuba's ICAIC and Venezuela's Villa del Cine. The history of filmmaking using a studio model has laid a foundation for the oldest and most established film industries, namely Argentina, Brazil and Mexico, but other countries have begun building their own modern studio facilities as well as smaller, more flexible patterns of production, not unlike advertising and other audiovisual companies. The next chapter will describe how national cinemas rely on state funding (loans, subsidies, training opportunities and the like) in order to continue producing films on a consistent basis.

2

State Film Funding

State funding is arguably the most essential component in fostering a regional film industry in Latin America. In an age characterised by a shift from the study of national cinemas to that of transnational and global formations, we might recall British film scholar John Hill's words when he argues that the concept of national cinema is of vital importance when analysing state policy, particularly as a means of promoting cultural diversity and attending to national specificity (Hill 1992, 1996, in Higson, 2006, 23). Ultimately, the present-day justification for funding state film institutes, state film legislation and other forms of government support (e.g. annual contributions to Ibero-American finance pools such as Programa Ibermedia) is to promote and sustain film industries in the face of the specific challenge posed by the prevailing hegemony of US Hollywood studios within the global film market. This chapter examines various institutions and initiatives, operating both regionally – the aforementioned Programa Ibermedia, and the Central American fund Cinergia, among others – and on a national scale, including film institutes and government agencies created to assist in the branding, marketing and circulation of national cinema abroad.

Filmmakers in Latin America often depend on state institutions and initiatives to help fund, exhibit and distribute films. Since commercial interests dominate the marketplace for film, most investors in the private sector shy away from funding some of these films, possibly perceiving them as not 'commercially' profitable enough. Clearly, the state's role as a bulwark for the maintenance and support of small- and medium-sized film industries is crucial when compared to its dominant Hollywood film industry counterpart that generates US$60 billion worldwide annually (Quartesan, Romis and Lanzafame, 2007, 15). According to researchers from the Inter-American Development Bank (IADB), all of the Latin American film industries put together generate a mere 3 per cent of global film production, roughly 400 million Spanish speakers and 260 million Portuguese speakers worldwide (Quartesan, Romis and Lanzafame, 2007, 15).

Despite the current tendency to examine film industries in transnational terms, this framing can fail to account for the specificity of the Latin American context in which region-wide sources of funding function alongside state-run organisations. It is therefore vital to avoid any generalisations about the impact of neoliberalism by assuming that the state's participation has weakened across the board. Indeed, in the case of most Latin American film industries (perhaps with the exception of Mexico), the state remains the main purveyor of essential funding and support for filmmakers in their respective countries to produce cinema and circulate it nationally and globally. While some countries are increasingly finding ways to involve the private sector in funding initiatives (primarily in Brazil and Mexico), the majority of countries offer limited resources for granting funding and other kinds of support to filmmakers. The state thus becomes de facto the most important mechanism by which a film industry can thrive and remain financially healthy in the realms of pre-production, production and post-production.

The countries with the political will to support legislation that carves out a space for films to be funded, or provides other forms of support, are the ones that have historically had the strongest and most stable film industries (Argentina, Chile, Colombia, and socialist countries such as Venezuela and Cuba, to name a few). On the contrary, those countries lacking a film law or legislation to assist filmmakers in obtaining low-cost loans or other forms of financial support (Paraguay, most countries in Central America including Honduras and Guatemala) have historically had the most difficulty in creating any significant annual film production output. Recall Getino's observation from Chapter 1 that countries that typically do not have state or governmental policies that incentivise and protect national production are at a major disadvantage (Getino, 2006, 60). Instead, these nations must rely on a few prodigious filmmakers who have been successful in obtaining international or private-sector funding.

The development of Latin American film industries can be traced, as is shown below, by examining the role of film institutes in providing support and fostering a sense of stewardship over the industry. In addition to profiling the oldest and largest film institutes – those of Argentina, Brazil and Mexico – this chapter will explore how each institute offers benefits to filmmakers even if these fluctuate over time, and are subject to changes in government and budgetary constraints (see Appendix A).

Other initiatives discussed later in the chapter include: a case study of CinemaChile, taken here as an example of the marketing and branding of national cinema as a symbol of quality; and an examination of the film finance pools Programa Ibermedia, funded by Spain, Portugal, Italy and Latin American countries, and Cinergia, a fund for Central American and Cuban filmmakers, supported through European foundation grants (currently on hiatus).

Other important infrastructure that often receives state support includes training programmes such as film schools, film training seminars and development labs that are typically sponsored in part by the state and funded by other non-profit entities, frequently from European media funds or film festival funds.

Our focus on the state's role in supporting national industries should not prevent us from acknowledging – and potentially problematising – the Ibero-American infrastructure linking Latin American states. Specifically, the Spanish state plays a substantial role (and in the case of Brazil, the Portuguese state, though to a much lesser degree) in fostering Ibero-American cinematic production, circulation and distribution at home and abroad. For example, the Instituto de la Cinematografía y de las Artes Audiovisuales (Spanish Film Institute) (ICAA) facilitates co-production agreements between Spain and Latin American countries; it is the host and founding member of La Conferencia de Autoridades Cinematográficas de Iberoamérica (Conference of Ibero-American Cinematographic Authorities) (CACI), which governs the most important film finance pool in Ibero-America, the Madrid-based Programa Ibermedia. Moreover, Spain's public television channel (Televisión Española) is mandated by law to allot 6 per cent of their revenue from public television towards the support and broadcast distribution of Latin American films and Spanish/Latin American co-productions.

This Ibero-American partnership has made a substantial contribution to film production in the region. A 2006 study demonstrated that, between 1986 and 1992, Spanish television had contributed on its own more than US\$20 million for Latin American co-productions. This exceeded the contribution of governments from the region who provided state funds during the same period (Getino, 2006, 77). Finally, despite constituting an indirect form of state funding, it is notable that Spanish film festivals are heavily involved in running specifically Latin American sidebars and competitions such as the festivals held at Huelva and Lerida, among others. These sidebars and competitions are also features at festivals such as San Sebastián (Díaz López, 2014, 17). Though Spain's involvement in Latin American film industries is seen as a windfall by many, some regard the country as a historic, fraught symbol of colonial relationships, and speculate that Spain is trying to compensate for the legacy of five centuries of colonisation, which remains a constant reminder of historical oppression and subjugation. It is therefore not surprising that, outside of national film institutes, the biggest supporter of state funding is the Agencia Española de Cooperación Internacional para el Desarrollo (Spanish Agency for International Development Cooperation) (AECID) (Díaz López, 2014, 17), which supports Latin American productions through Spanish embassies, consulates and other cultural spaces. The funds from this agency provide support for organisations such as Programa Ibermedia, as well as for the exhibition of co-productions between Spain and Latin America in the form of screenings at the Instituto Cervantes cultural centres located worldwide, with the aim of increasing the influence of the Spanish language internationally (Díaz López, 2014, 17). Before the economic crises that befell Spain in 2008 and again in 2010, funding for Programa Ibermedia surpassed the combined contributions of all the Latin American states.

In Portugal, the Instituto do Cinema e do Audiovisual (Film and Audiovisual Institute) (ICA) is primarily responsible for supporting the production, distribution, exhibition and promotion of Portuguese cinema and audiovisual products, within the country and abroad. The institute annually sets aside funding to support co-productions with other Lusophone countries including Brazil.

THE ROLE OF FILM INSTITUTES

In the 1930s and 1940s, existing film industries such as those of Argentina, Brazil and Mexico relied primarily on the private sector to produce films within the framework of an industrialised studio system modelled in many ways on the classical Hollywood system. By the 1950s, however, many film industries were facing competition from television and the increased concentration of Hollywood products in the region, resulting in part from the collapse of European film markets during World War II. In response to this, state officials began considering the creation of national film institutes to help support, fund and promote national cinema. While all film institutes fulfil a central function in each country, some are fairly new and have limited resources to support national filmmaking, while others leave little room for films made independently of the state (though this is changing slowly). For example, the Cuban ICAIC was the central institution for film production in the country. It is only in recent years, as mentioned in Chapter 1, that a new generation of directors have begun to produce films outside of the system, even though the ICAIC still distributes their work.

Some countries currently do not have a film institute. This is the case in Nicaragua, which has not had a film institute since the closure of INCINE (Instituto Nicaragüense de Cine) (Nicaraguan Film Institute), which operated during the Sandinista government in the 1980s. At present, the Nicaraguan Film Association (Asociación Nicaragüense de Cinematografía) (ANCI) has constituted the support system for directors, who have been responsible for organising a Central American Film and Video Showcase since 2004 (Durón, 2014, 56). Costa Rica's film institute, the Centro de Cine (Film Centre), sponsors a newly revamped film festival, the Costa Rica Festival Internacional de Cine (Costa Rica International Film Festival) (CRFIC), and assists with archival restoration, as well as providing service support for international production companies who film in the country. A new law enacted in 2015 stipulated the creation of a fund that was to offer grants later that year, but this was postponed until 2016 when the 'Fawn Fund' (Fondo para el Fomento Audiovisual y Cinematográfico el

Fauno), a general competition for production funding, was given the following year (Anon., 2015e). The Centro's funding model is based on Spain's, whereby the Costa Rican public television channel, 13, supports the film institute financially and broadcasts a number of national films.

Since the history of film institutes constitutes a long, varied and often discontinuous trajectory, a brief overview of three film institutes – Brazil, Argentina and Mexico – will illustrate their central role in the development, protection and promotion of Latin American film industries.

Brazil

Legislation was enacted as early as 1932 to protect the Brazilian film industry. Measures included a required screening of a Brazilian short film (*cortometragem*) before every feature, and a screen quota (*quota de tela*) mandating that a varying percentage of national films had to be screened monthly in national movie theatres (Almeida in Harvey, 2005, 45). Getúlio Vargas's populist Estado Novo government made a more formal push to institutionalise the Instituto Nacional do Cinema Educativo (National Institute for Educational Cinema) (INCE), which characterised cinema as a form of educational mass communication and oversaw the production of documentaries. The screen quota was revived in 1939 when laws mandated that each movie theatre in the country was obligated to screen one national film for seven days over the course of the year (or 2 per cent of film programming per year per cinema) (Harvey, 2005, 46). An interesting trend throughout the various types of film institutes in Brazil is that there were always measures legislating varying degrees of the screen quota, despite the fact that it was not an easily enforceable law. Between 1980 and 1990, the number of obligatory days during which theatres were required to exhibit national films increased to 140 per year (Harvey, 2005, 47). In 1966, the Instituto Nacional do Cinema (National Film Institute) (INC) was established to perform essential functions such as film production financing and the implementation of regulatory measures to ensure that exhibitors reported accurate box office revenues, as underreporting was hurting producers. Most significantly, the INC administered a subsidy in which the funding Brazilian films received was based on their relative success at the box office (Schnitman, 1984, 68).

In the midst of a military dictatorship, during 1969, EMBRAFILME (Brazilian Film Enterprise), the institute's promotion and distribution arm, was created. In 1972, notable Cinema Novo director and new head of the organisation Roberto Farias created a more open environment, despite military government rule. This prompted Brazilian Cinema Novo directors to return from exile (most of whom had left after 1964) and to begin working within a more open atmosphere. Financial support for production was now authorised to directors prior to approval by a censorship board, who normally pre-approved a script. By funding films that could subsequently be censored by a different branch of the state apparatus, the Brazilian military government installed a paradoxical system in which government-funded cinema could potentially be censored (Schnitman, 1984, 70). Brazilian critic Jean-Claude Bernardet argues that one of the Brazilian government's strategies to weaken the opposition consisted of co-opting intellectuals (Dennison and Shaw, 2004, 171). This was also a period during which many light, sexual comedies, or *chanchadas*, were produced as a way of promoting the commercial side of the industry without posing an ideological threat to the government. Even exhibitors invested money and produced films in this genre to make up any revenue lost on screening foreign arthouse cinema. It also served as insurance against the inroads television was making in Brazilian households (Dennison and Shaw, 2004, 74). In his exhaustive study of the Brazilian cinema industry, Randal Johnson outlines the debates that took place during the creation of EMBRAFILME and focuses on whether the state should be supporting a cinema that had 'cultural importance' regardless of its capacity to attract a large audience, or whether it should back a more commercial model. This debate exemplifies EMBRAFILME's attempts to be 'all things to all people', in ways that ultimately ensured the failure of its aim to consolidate Brazilian cinema as a self-sustaining industry (1995, 373). Nevertheless, the 1970s were a watershed for Brazilian cinema: hits such as *Dona Flor e Seus Dois Maridos* (*Dona Flor and Her Two Husbands*, dir. Bruno Barreto, 1976), *Xica da Silva* (*Xica*, dir. Carlos Diegues, 1976) and *A dama do lotação* (*A Lady on the Bus*, dir. Neville de Almeida, 1978) amassed millions of spectators at the domestic box office, doubling audience numbers between 1975 and 1980 (Dennison and Shaw, 2004, 171). Dennison and Shaw accordingly argue that EMBRAFILME was a more successful experiment than previous scholarship has asserted.

EMBRAFILME was disbanded in 1990 under President Collor de Mello, who practically dismantled the film industry. It was not until 2001 that the new institute, ANCINE (National Film Agency), was created under the auspices of President Henrique Cardoso. Working under the tenets established by the 1993 Audiovisual Law and building on the provisions of the 1991 Rouanet Law (discussed in Chapter 3), ANCINE created the conditions for the process called '*retomada*' or the 'relaunching' of Brazilian cinema to levels reminiscent of its most prolific periods in the 1930s and 1970s. Scholar Natália Pinazza argues that ANCINE has played a key role in the development of a contemporary film industry in Brazil, by incorporating private investors into funding schemes and sponsoring competitions for screenwriters and debut filmmakers (2013, 33). (ANCINE's current programmes and resources are listed in Appendix A.) In 2015, for example, the agency earmarked 500 million reals (US$145.5 million)

[Figure 2.1 ANCINE logo.]

for production and distribution aid. As *Variety* journalist John Hopewell points out, that figure dwarfs many Western European nations' incentive systems. Spain's main film subsidy budget in 2016, for instance, was just €30 million (US$33.7 million) (2016).

Mexico

In Mexico, the first instance of state intervention in the cinema begins in 1913 when then-President Huerta ordered the regulation of how movie theatre owners conduct their business (Salcedo qtd. in Bordat, 2010, 7). The second decree was passed under the Carranza administration (1917–20) and established rules for government censorship of films in reaction to US oil companies using films to wage a defamatory campaign against the Mexican government. Although this law was not adhered to, it served as a catalyst for the Mexican government to begin producing their own films (Bordat, 2010).

Under the López Portillo administration (1976–82), the Departamento de Radio, Television y Cine (Radio, Television and Film Department) was created to replace the Banco Nacional Cinematográfico (National Film Bank). During this period, film production was high, at seventy films per year, but the type of cinema produced was more commercial in scope than 'high quality'. As a result, the film institute IMCINE (Instituto Mexicano de la Cinematografía) was created in 1983, existing to this day to assist the Mexican film industry in achieving a balance between industrial, commercial films and 'quality' cinema that can circulate at film festivals and abroad. IMCINE's home page includes the following mission statement: 'To promote and incentivise the development of national film activity, with the end result being the guaranteed continuity and artistic and cultural achievement of Mexican cinema via incentive programmes for filmmakers, support for feature length production and audiovisual production. The mission is also to promote and distribute national cinema in Mexico and abroad' (https://www.imcine.gob.mx/).

In the early 1980s, the private sector and the state forged a partnership: the private sector funded 80 per cent of the more commercial films, while 20 per cent of the budget was dedicated to the production of 'quality films' that IMCINE funded with the hope of exporting them to international film festivals (Bordat, 2010, 12).

Mexican film industry scholar Misha MacLaird notes that, in 1997, a new fund, the Fondo de Inversión y Estímulos al Cine (The Investment and Incentive Fund for Cinema) (FIDICINE) was created to 'focus on primarily commercial and potentially profitable films', while the existing fund, the Fondo para la Producción Cinematográfica de Calidad (Fund for Quality Film Production) (FOPROCINE) – housed within IMCINE – supported films with greater artistic, cultural and educational value but which possibly posed a more significant investment risk (2013, 29). The existence of these two funds is indicative of the tensions with which many film institutes contend. Such tensions stem from how film industries are conceptualised in a given country: are they commercial industries with a capacity to be self-sustaining and even profitable? Are they products which comprise the national patrimony and thus need to be protected on cultural rather than economic grounds? These are internal debates that the majority of film industries worldwide (save the most commercial) have to contend with.

In 2013, a new law was put in place – the Ley de Impuesto Sobre la Renta, known as EFICINE. This law gives companies a 10 per cent return on taxes if they invest up to 650 million pesos annually in film production or post-production. This incentive led to a large surge in production, whereby annual film output averaged well over 100 films a year (Hinojosa Córdova, 2014). In 2014, however, only 68 films were released out of the 130 made due to distributor and exhibitor

[Figure 2.2 IMCINE logo.]

reluctance to risk screening them. In that period (and continuing to the present), finding funds to make films was less of an issue and challenge. Indeed 20 per cent of the films produced were funded solely with private funds (IMCINE, 2014).

Argentina

In 1957, two years after Argentine President Juan Perón was ousted by a military junta, concerned film lobbyists convened with Congress and demanded that a national film institute be created to administer and regulate cinematic activity in a systematic fashion. The INC was subsequently established in the same year on the basis of the new cinema law (62/57). The INC was founded to oversee:

1. The development of Argentine cinema as an industry, business, art, and medium of communication and education.
2. The guarantee of freedom of expression for the cinema, similar to that of the press.
3. The creation of an organisation dependent on the Minister of Education and Justice, which would be transferred to the Director General of Entertainment.
4. The categorising of films for exhibition in terms of quality, according to two categories: 'A' designated the films that received mandatory exhibition, and 'B', the films whose showing was not mandatory.
5. An approval system of rating movie theatres and a determination of exhibition cycles and the percentage of payment that exhibitors would receive per national film.
6. A system for rating films designed to protect minors.
7. A film development fund which received revenues from a 10 per cent tax on box-office admissions as well as a tax on film imports.
8. The authorisation of economic benefits for the industry (bank credits, tax credits, special loans for film projects, film equipment, etc.).
9. The distribution of 'A' category films abroad. (Calistro, 1992, 109).

The creation of other laws helped strengthen the national film industry, but it was unable to overcome the political instabilities that plagued the INC's management between 1957 and 1967. In this volatile ten-year period, no fewer than ten INC directors were hired and fired. Because the directors were constantly subject to the scrutiny of the film community and mass media, they were routinely accused of mismanagement and dishonesty in financial transactions. This scepticism on the part of the leadership within the film production sector, as well as a general societal mistrust of state institutions, continued throughout the history of the INC, which was renamed the Instituto Nacional de Cine y Artes

Audiovisuales (National Institute for Cinema and Audiovisual Arts) (INCAA) after a new law was passed in 1994.

> As part of the Ministry of Culture, but still an autonomous entity, the INCAA is a public agency responsible for fostering and regulating Argentine film activity at home and abroad. The agency's functions are outlined as required by the Cinema Law and its new functions as part of Law No. 26.522 Service Law of Audiovisual Communication. Dubbed 'The New Cinema Law' (*La nueva ley del cine*), this legislation built on an existing 1969 law which stipulated that 10 per cent of every movie ticket purchased at theatres would be earmarked for national film production. However, due to the rise of television, cable, and home video, directors also demanded compensation for films aired on television. Famed film director Luis Puenzo stated: 'television has become the new space for viewing films, rather than movie theatres. So, this ten percent law is no longer viable. We want to rectify this situation and compensate for this displacement of exhibition revenue.' (qtd. in Anon., 1993, 20)

Responding to the need to create a brand for Argentine cinema, the film logo 'CA' (Cine Argentino) was adopted in 2008, roughly a decade after the start of the movement known as the New Argentine Cinema (see Falicov, 2007a). It replaced the brand logo created in 2006 as the result of a visual identity contest. This exercise in nation branding was part of a broader initiative to shine an international spotlight on the country. The campaign also gained municipal support in 1999 with the establishment of the Buenos Aires International Independent Film Festival (BAFICI), a new, edgy, youthful, independent festival. The next section profiles Brazil, Argentina and Chile in their quest to shore up name (and nation) recognition for their brand of filmmaking abroad.

[Figure 2.3 INCAA logo.]

[Figure 2.4 Cine Argentino brand.]

THE ABCS OF BRANDING AND MARKETING FILMS ABROAD: ARGENTINA, BRAZIL, CHILE

Given that marketing and distribution poses one of the most notable impediments to circulating Latin American film, some national film industries have jumped on the 'branding' bandwagon to help boost their visibility and circulation. In Argentina, Brazil and Chile, their respective film industries have taken cues from private companies in order to brand their national cinema by using discernible logos screened before each national film.

Their actions are a subset of the practice of nation branding, a process whereby governments hire experts to create greater brand awareness and exposure for their nations. As globalisation and neoliberal economic trends have become more prevalent, many countries, especially emerging economies in Eastern Europe, Africa and some parts of Latin America (Chile, Colombia, Argentina, Brazil and Ecuador), have worked to gain visibility within the global marketplace. By creating nation branding campaigns, they have sought to improve their image abroad, using survey research to launch national logo campaigns to capture the attention of a global audience.

Branding experts typically engage in a national survey known as the 'Nation Brand Index' (NBI) to help gauge how countries can improve their image abroad (Aronczyk, 2013). Cinema, of course, plays an important role in this process – for example, through the global film festival circuit with stands at marketplaces such as Berlin and Cannes. In some cases, nations have invested in a specific film logo which calls attention to their 'cinema brand'; there is currently a discernible push by film institutes to shape their film repertoire into an identifiable and distinctive brand of quality which would translate into widespread recognition.

In Argentina, the INCAA declared the main objectives of their branding campaign as follows: first, to 'instil the idea that *cine argentino* includes a variety of genres'; second, to 'communicate that *cine argentino* is seen all over the world and awarded internationally'; and third, to 'transmit that *cine argentino* moves, entertains, and is catchy. That it has excellent scripts, actors, music, photography and directors. That it is really "cool," and is worth watching' ('En busca del público merecido', *Raíces: Cine Argentino*, qtd. in Zullo-Ruiz, 2009, 17). The INCAA's campaign invests in reworking the previous *brand association* by countering it with three talking points regarding the qualities or characteristics of Cine Argentino, in order to distinguish it from the other 'brands' of cinema in the marketplace (Zullo-Ruiz, 2009). One might speculate that the INCAA's initiative aims to make their products more 'recognisable' by specifically ensuring the acknowledgement of a certain seal of quality which helps them export more product abroad.

Brazil is similarly committed to making its film brand more visible at international film festivals and other venues. The Ministry of Culture, the government trade agency APEX Brazil and the film union of the state of São Paulo (SICESP) banded together to form Cinema do Brasil, a 'program designed to globalise the Brazilian film industry and to increase its visibility in the international film community' (Woo, 2006). This initiative took shape in the production and circulation of glossy magazines and brochures detailing the latest Brazilian films at European film festivals, with the aim of selling more films abroad, branding national films, bolstering international co-productions and creating jobs within the industry. In 2009, Cinema do Brasil assisted ten independent film producers to the tune of US$15,000 each to help cover the costs of releasing national films in foreign territories, including the high costs of P&A (prints and advertising) (Hopewell, 2009).

In Chile, both the cultural and business sectors have provided film industry support. In 2005, the Consejo Nacional de la Cultura y las Artes (National Council for Culture and Arts) (CNCA) was subdivided to include the Consejo del Arte y la Industria Audiovisual (Council of Art and Audiovisual Industry) (CALA), which continues to serve as an umbrella organisation for all of the various government-sponsored bodies that support the film sector. The Corporación de Fomento (the National Small Business Development Corporation) (CORFO), an agency founded in 1939 to support national small business development, expanded its offerings in 1999 to include a filmmaker grant programme.

Paralleling to some extent the return of democracy to Chile in 1990, a wave of films contributed to the birth of the *novísimo cine chileno* (the 'newest' Chilean cinema; Cavallo and Maza, 2010), which made its first appearance at the Valdivia International Film Festival in 2005. The critical success reaped by this new group of filmmakers spurred the creation of various government initiatives in Chile to better orient national cinema towards an international audience, towards fashioning film to a certain extent as a high-quality export commodity similar to the country's successful wine and fruit exports. It is not coincidental, then, that Chile began to engage in talks with members of the OECD (Organisation for Economic Cooperation and Development) in 2007, becoming the first South American country to be admitted as a member in 2010. Supporting filmmakers and film sector representatives accordingly became a government priority, to ensure Chilean cinema's presence at international film festivals. This function was entrusted to the government agency CinemaChile, a subagency set up within ProChile in 2009, in partnership with the La Asociación de Productores de Cine y Televisión (Association of Television and Film Producers) (APCT). CinemaChile 'looks to position the national audiovisual sector abroad as a novel emerging industry with much capacity for work and the ability to create original and fresh scripts' (ProChile, 2017). CinemaChile is also responsible for 'represent[ing] Chilean documentary, dramatic feature, short film, animation and television productions in the world's major film markets and festivals' (CinemaChile, 2017). CinemaChile has succeeded in improving Chilean cinema's visibility at international film festivals and markets through diverse initiatives, including a stand at the Berlinale's marketplace (which the author viewed in 2012), and participation in Buenos Aires' Ventana Sur and international film markets.

Chilean films have consistently garnered prestigious awards internationally in recent years. Sebastian Leilo's film, *Una mujer fantastica* (A Fantastic Woman) won many international awards including a 2018 Academy award in the US for best foreign film. Sebastián Silva's *La nana* (*The Maid*) earned the top international prize at Sundance in 2009, and three of Andrés Wood's films have won international prizes: *La buena vida* (*The Good Life*, 2008) collected a Goya award (Spanish Academy awards) for Best Foreign Film in 2009, and *Machuca* (2004) picked up ten major film festival awards, including top prizes at Valdivia (Chile), Vancouver and Havana (for Best Cinematography). *Violeta se fue a los cielos*

[Figure 2.5 CinemaChile logo.]

(*Violeta Went to Heaven*, 2011) garnered ten prizes, including another Sundance win. Finally, a number of films have premiered at Cannes, including *Tony Manero* (dir. Pablo Larraín, 2008), *Huacho* (dir. Alejandro Almendras, 2009) and *Bonsai* (dir. Cristián Jiménez, 2011), among others.

Through film festival awards and international film sales, contemporary Chilean cinema is increasingly gaining recognition on the international arthouse circuit as part of a 'new wave' or boom, both in terms of the record number of films released, with an average of forty-five per year (Laborde, 2014). Still, this success has prompted a national debate about how Chilean cinema has attracted more critical acclaim abroad than at home. Constanza Arena, head of CinemaChile, was asked on television why so many of Chile's well-made films were so poorly attended, with the exception of the higher-budget smash hit *Stefan v/s Kramer* (dirs. Sebastián Freund, Stefan Kramer and Leonardo Prieto, 2012), which beat the all-time record for any film at the Chilean box office with two million moviegoers (Anon., 2012a). In her response, Arena attributed this to the following policy shortcomings: the absence of a national movie theatre chain (such as Espacios INCAA in Argentina); a lack of funds to market Chilean films; and an absence of legislative measures which would help sustain a national film culture such as a screen quota (2015).

CO-PRODUCTIONS IN LATIN AMERICA

From the 1960s onwards, Latin American countries have had increasing difficulty in providing state funding to filmmakers. While director-producers may receive some form of domestic funding (as they did, for example, in Cuba, up until the beginning of the economic hardships of the 'Special Period' in the early 1990s), reduced budgets, devalued currencies and soaring production costs have made co-production and other forms of collaborative financing the only ways of ensuring that films get made (Stock, 2006, 154). Even if most filmmakers in the region have adopted the less costly technology of digital production, some segments of the production chain, such as post-production, continue to be very expensive. Moreover, the process of making films 'festival-ready' for the international circuit implies additional costs. This is why co-production agreements forged as early as the 1960s have paved the way for trade ties, typically between Latin American countries and wealthier nations such as Spain, Canada and the United States. An Ibero-Latin American co-production treaty was signed in 1989, in addition to separate treaties articulated around regional trade blocs such as Mercosur.

The balance of power between old and new industries has more recently shifted, as the newer Latin American film producers such as Chile, Colombia and Venezuela have been actively supporting co-productions from the once-dominant industries, including Argentina, Brazil and Mexico. This shift is due to these countries' newer state funding systems, which spawn additional sources of financing, encouraging the growth of directors and producers. According to Argentine producer Ignacio Rey, European funding is becoming more difficult to access and, when it is granted, favours social realist projects that can be harder to sell for commercial release (Newbery, 2011). Co-production agreements signed between film institutes have provided important linkages between producers from several countries, which grant access to additional markets and state institute funds. The benefits that co-productions offer producers include: pooling financial resources; accessing foreign government incentives and subsidies; entering a partner's or third-party market; and learning from that partner.

Launched in 2012, the Europe/Latin America co-production forum at the San Sebastián Film Festival exemplified a recent way of using the space of a film festival to enable co-productions. Its aim was to bring together producers from both regions to facilitate a space for pitch sessions, which usually led to a line-up of meetings between interested potential co-producers. Many venues at European and Latin American film festivals have created such spaces to facilitate networking and production deals, including the Festival Internacional de Cine en Guadalajara (The Guadalajara International Film Festival) (FICG) and the Producers Network at Ventana Sur in Buenos Aires.

PROGRAMA IBERMEDIA, AN IBERO-AMERICAN CO-PRODUCTION FUND

We now turn to the oldest and most established Ibero-American film finance pool: Programa Ibermedia. Ibermedia is a co-production film fund sponsored by Spain, Portugal and nineteen Latin American member countries. While it is arguably the most effective and longest-lasting fund of its kind, critical scholarship has debated its ideological aims (Falicov, 2013a; Moreno Domínguez, 2008; Villazana, 2009). Housed in Spain and funded primarily by Spanish public funds, Ibermedia receives funds from each member country. Currently, the twenty-one member countries are Argentina, Bolivia, Brazil, Chile, Colombia, Costa Rica, Cuba, Dominican Republic, Ecuador, Guatemala, Italy, Mexico, Nicaragua, Panama, Paraguay, Peru, Portugal, Puerto Rico, Spain, Uruguay and Venezuela. Each country makes an annual commitment (minimum US$100,000) to the fund. Members then compete via production companies for backing from Ibermedia's various programmes, such as the script development fund, co-production fund, training grants, exhibition and distribution funds, and an international sales loan known as 'delivery', which was introduced in 2006 but later discontinued.

Ibermedia is supervised by the Ibero-American organisation La Conferencia de Autoridades Audiovisuales y Cinematográficas de Iberoamérica (Conference of Ibero-American Audiovisual and Film Institutes) (CAACI). Established in 1996 by the heads of the national film institutes during a meeting on Venezuela's Margarita Island, Ibermedia's goal is to promote the interchange of audiovisual professionals of member countries (see www.programaibermedia.com).

In a document produced during the Summit of the Americas in 1996, Ibermedia's function was described as 'contribut[ing] to the development of an Ibero-American film and television industry that is competitive in the world market, that is oriented towards the technological future, that is capable of projecting its own culture' (Ibermedia, 1996). The industrial growth facilitated by Ibermedia would have the additional benefit of 'creating employment and reducing the commercial deficit' (Ibermedia, 1996).

Ibermedia is modelled after the success of the European Union's Eurimages programme (1988–) in which Western, Central and Eastern European countries contribute to a fund according to what each nation can afford. The EU's production initiative, MEDIA Plus Programme, has also served as a model for Ibermedia. As with Eurimages, there are economic disparities among member countries in Latin America and Europe, but regardless, member countries are eligible to compete for the large sums of money awarded to film projects at various stages of completion. Ibermedia prides itself on the fact that all member countries have an equal chance at reaping large benefits (Fermin, 2003). Ecuador, for example, gives an annual instalment of US$150,000, but through the success of its co-production competition outcomes has gained between US$300,000 and US$400,000 per annum on average. Before 2007, Ecuador did not work in co-production, with the exception of high-profile directors such as Sebastián Cordero (Anon., 2012c).

Ibermedia development grants are awarded most typically to first-time filmmakers, as they provide workshop training funds which directors can use to improve and polish the script. The co-production fund is less likely to be awarded to first-time projects, as only a maximum of 50 per cent of a project's funding may be conferred. The eligibility requirements for the co-production fund specify that films must be in Spanish or Portuguese; the competition is a loan, not a grant; and the director, actors and technical crew must originate from an Ibero-American country. Competitions are held annually, except between 2006 and 2012 when they were held biannually.

Since Ibermedia's inception, 636 co-production grants have been awarded, as well as 698 development grants, and 270 films promoted and distributed with its support. US$85 million were invested between 1998 and 2015, and over 500 films screened (Ibermedia, 2015). In 2016, Italy joined as the first non-Ibero-American member of Ibermedia, and the following year, Nicaragua became the newest member.

Films that have benefited from Ibermedia funding include the aforementioned *Machuca* (a co-production between Chile, Spain, the UK and France); *La jaula de oro* (*The Golden Dream*, dir. Diego Quemada-Diez, Mexico/Spain, 2013); *Relatos salvajes* (*Wild Tales*, dir. Damián Szifrón, Argentina/Spain, 2014); *Pelo malo* (*Bad Hair*, dir. Mariana Rondón, Venezuela/Peru/Argentina/Germany, 2013); *Princesas rojas* (*Red Princesses*, dir. Laura Astorga, Costa Rica, 2013); *El elefante desaparecido* (*The Vanishing Elephant*, dir. Javier Fuentes-León, Peru, 2014) and the documentary *Invasión* (*Invasion*, dir. Abner Benaim, Panama, 2014). Since 2003, funding has targeted the perennially weak distribution link that has routinely beset Latin American film producers, as a consequence of the virtual monopoly held by the US majors in the region. Ibermedia sought to counter this by subsidising distribution. Unfortunately, however, the fund was eliminated in 2011, a measure which drew heavy criticism on the part of film producers and critics (Bettati, 2012b). In 2018, funds were doubled for animation development support, from US$15,000 to US$30,000.

As co-productions allow for the sharing of costs and markets, they constitute an essential mode of ensuring that films get made in Latin America. Still, this approach can pose challenges when the diverse participant countries try to build a narrative that aspires to transcend borders and offer audiences 'something for everyone' across national specificities. As with the European concept of 'Europudding', attempts have been made at understanding the narrative constraints that co-productions can impose on a film's script (see Falicov, 2007b). Another criticism, made by a producer who has successfully obtained Ibermedia co-production grants and who prefers to remain anonymous, is that the organisation should create two tracks of funding: one would be intended for low-budget projects, adhering to the current schema stipulating that grants must be paid back, while the second track would be reserved for more veteran producers with higher-budget projects. This system offers the advantage of involving less bureaucratic paperwork. It was the interviewee's observation that the paperwork currently associated with this fund is so extensive that it inhibits higher-budget producers from applying for funds, which are modest anyway (Anon., 2015c).

Finally, criticisms have been lodged against Spain, the home of Ibermedia and who until only recently was the largest contributor, as theoretically having the greatest say over the operation of the fund. Some critics allege paternalism and a way to maintain good relations with ex-colonists (Falicov, 2013b). More recently, in 2015, however, Brazil contributed the most funding towards the initiative, with US$1 million, Venezuela provided US$600,000 and Argentina US$500,000, compared to Spain's US$411,000 (Cine&Tele, 2016). It remains to be seen if Spain is losing some of its power over the fund, witnessed perhaps by

Programa
IBERMEDIA

[Figure 2.6 Ibermedia logo.]

the entrance of Italy. Furthermore, Brazil's influence over the fund is something
to observe in the coming years.

One of Ibermedia's most successful initiatives was the creation in 2010 of
Ibermedia TV, broadcasting Ibero-American films that had received Ibermedia
support on public television channels in member countries. Entitled 'Nuestra
Cinema/Nossa Cinema', this weekly programme format was promoted on
Ibermedia TV as having a potential audience reach of 500 million viewers.
Although this declaration is somewhat overstated, it responds to the criticism
that to truly be recognised and seen as a cultural form in Ibero-America, Iber-
media must reach a wider audience through free public television broadcast
rather than cable, which remains economically prohibitive for many (García
Canclini, 2007, 9).

Cinergia

Based in Costa Rica, Cinergia is a film finance pool for Central American and
Cuban filmmakers with member countries that include Belize, Costa Rica, El
Salvador, Guatemala, Honduras, Nicaragua, Panama and Cuba. Cinergia was
founded in 2004 by María Lourdes Cortés, the then-head of Veritas, a private
film school in Costa Rica. She felt that countries with emerging film industries
that could not afford the US$100,000 minimum required for contributing to
Ibermedia needed to have alternative access to funding for co-productions.
Cortés pooled funds from Veritas, the Hivos Fund from the Netherlands and
the Foundation for New Latin American Cinema (founded by the late Gabriel
García Márquez). Subsequently, the Ford Foundation was willing to partner with
Cinergia as long as Cuba could participate in the fund. Cortés agreed but was
concerned that the Cubans had a longer-standing tradition of filmmaking and
would most certainly dominate the funding competition. For this reason, Cinergia decided to exclusively fund first- and second-time directors, thus ensuring a
more equitable playing field (Cortés, 2015).

After some Central American countries later became members of Ibermedia,
Cortés observed that smaller member countries had a harder time competing

against the more developed filmmaking nations. For instance, Puerto Rico became a member in 2002 but was not awarded a co-production credit until 2004 due to logistical and monetary problems (González, 2006). Central American countries therefore needed a smaller regional fund to help producers increase their professionalisation before competing against larger industries such as those of Argentina and Brazil (Cortés, 2005). In addition to providing competitive production grants, Cinergia invited directors to participate in screenwriting workshops, convening with well-known distributors and producers from other parts of Latin America and Europe. This support to filmmakers is part of Cinergia's aim of creating a regional pan-American source of collaboration.

Since its inception, Cinergia has been the pre-eminent model for funding Central American countries. This is especially important in the case of countries that have a history of instability in which various governments have reneged on their commitments due to funding shortages. For example, when Guatemala joined Ibermedia in 2009, it was unable to send the promised amount to the pool for two years, rendering the country's filmmakers ineligible to apply for funding.

At the time of writing, Cinergia faces an uncertain future. In the past, reliance on non-governmental organisations has made the creation of this fund possible, but in 2015, Hivos, the main benefactor, had to discontinue its US$100,000 annual commitment due to a change in the Dutch government. Thus, Cinergia has had to suspend its funding to Central American filmmakers after a twelve-year run of subsidies that has seen it support 544 filmmakers throughout the region. Cortés hopes to raise smaller amounts from various companies in the private sector (Mata, 2015).

Guatemalan Ana V. Bojórquez is an example of how Ibermedia and Cinergia have helped a director from a Central American country without any state support for filmmakers. Bojórquez moved to Mexico to be eligible to apply for Ibermedia funding (her co-director and producer are Mexican). Her specific story, which involved physically relocating to another country in search of funding, sheds light on the very tenuous process of financing films from Central America.

Case Study: *La Casa Más Grande del Mundo* (2014)

In 2010, Bojórquez attended a co-production workshop in Panama as a co-director. There, she met a producer from Mexico, Sandra Paredes, who stayed on the project through to its completion. Bojórquez and Paredes attended no fewer than eleven training seminars, including workshops, co-production meetings, script labs and other opportunities for Bojórquez to hone her script, network with professionals and better learn best practices of making a feature that could circulate abroad.[1] Bojórquez stated that the major benefits of attending workshops at film festivals are the education, training and networking these opportunities afford, but additionally, the exposure to multiple films that would never reach theatres in Guatemala, both because of their limited circulation and the dearth of movie theatres. In addition to Cinergia's support, the film received financial assistance from Mexican initiatives: the EFICINE tax incentive programme via the IMCINE fund. Bojórquez's film, *La casa más grande del mundo* (*The Greatest House in the World*, 2014), was completed in five years but premiered in the 'Generations' section of the Berlinale, where it garnered praise and was subsequently invited to film festivals around the world.

As with the great majority of films from Guatemala, the production required international financing. This was also the case with *Ixcanul* (dir. Jayro Bustamante, 2015), which won the Silver Bear at Berlin, and the many films of Julio Hernández Cordón, including *Gasolina* (*Gasoline*, 2007), *Marimbas del infierno* (*Marimbas from Hell*, 2010) and *Te prometo anarquia* (*I Promise You Anarchy*, 2015). For better or worse, this model has become the standard for Guatemalan independent, low- and medium-budget films. In addition to the lack of governmental support, filmmaking in Guatemala is not seen as a profit-making enterprise, which is similarly the case in countries with smaller populations lacking an existing tradition of filmmaking (Díaz, 2014). In 2018, film festival seminars in Central America such as the Festival Ícaro were keen to persuade private sector companies that investing in the film sector can be potentially lucrative. This hopeful or aspirational shift in discourse towards the private sector will be discussed in Chapter 3.

THE POLITICS OF TRAINING INITIATIVES

As part of industry events at film festivals, recent decades have witnessed a proliferation of workshops, training residencies, development grants, pitching fora, film schools and temporary educational spaces which bring together newer filmmakers and seasoned professionals to impart the craft of film production. These events begin by inviting successful industry professionals, mainly from abroad (specifically from Europe and the United States), to help train local filmmakers in aspects such as screenwriting, the pitching of film projects, the search for film funds, meeting international producers, receiving critique in sessions, the legal aspects of filmmaking, etc. These opportunities are extremely valuable for those filmmakers who are unable to travel abroad to study, and they provide additional resources for the next generation of students who wish to pursue the craft of filmmaking.

These training courses include both well-established programmes such as the Berlinale Talents initiative, the Cannes residence programme, Produire au Sud in Nantes, France, but more recently, newer schemes in Latin America proper, such as the Primera Residencia Andina de Guión Documental (first Andean Documentary Script Residency), a programme co-sponsored by the Ecuadorian film institute CNCINE (El Consejo Nacional de Cinematografía de Ecuador) (National Film Council of Ecuador), along with the French Docmonde, whereby six Ecuadoran filmmakers and one from each of four other Andean countries (Bolivia, Perú, Colombia and Venezuela) spend roughly two weeks in the city of Cahuasquí (Ecuador) and work with two specialists, Chantal Steinberg from France, and Alain Paul Mallard from Mexico (LatAm Cinema, 2015). The two-week screenwriting residency Cine Qua Non Lab is a non-profit programme run by Mexican filmmaker Jesús Pimentel Melo. Founded in 2008, it is held in the small town of Tzintzuntzan, Michoacán, Mexico, and its funding formula is a combination of public and private monies, in addition to the funds paid by the ten selected filmmakers, who pay fees to defray costs.

Screenwriting workshops are an example of a prevalent practice that most participants in the field value as helpful in their development as filmmakers, as they afford opportunities for networking and professionalisation (de Valck, 2013). Some critics, such as the Nicaraguan-based French filmmaker Florence Jaugey and the Nicaraguan director Rossana Lacayo, nevertheless feel that training programmes and workshops are a poor substitute for establishing more permanent film schools in underserved countries. They argue that these short-term courses fail to address discontinuities and tend to be helpful only to students currently attending film school (Abascal, 2015).

Still, when countries without film schools (such as Panama) attempt to institute film school degrees, bureaucratic difficulties can often turn their implementation into a decades-long process (Benaim and Allen, 2015). In contrast, private schools can be costly for students and are not ideal for starting film degrees as they can often solely depend on the will of dedicated film professionals to get film programmes up and running. Panamanian director Abner Benaim and Argentine producer Gema Juárez Allen have opined that no easy solution has emerged to solve the issue of establishing a national film school, as progress in this matter has stalled, despite the fact that these challenges have been debated in film circles. They believe that the most that can be achieved is to organise workshops and encourage students interested in film to attend the annual film festival in Panama where training opportunities abound (Benaim and Allen, 2015). As in the aforementioned case of Ana V. Bojórquez, who attended multiple workshops, these meetings no doubt helped her launch her first film, which premiered at Berlin.

Film schools in the region are critical for the proliferation and education of film students throughout Latin America. Students of middle- and upper-socioeconomic status who did not have film schools in their own country typically travelled abroad to Cuba, Spain, France, Mexico and other countries to learn the craft of filmmaking. This began most famously in the 1950s when Cuban and Argentine directors travelled to Rome to study at the Centro Sperimentale di Cinematografia, whose participants included the late Nobel Prize-winning Gabriel García Márquez, who was a novelist but also an erstwhile screenwriter. The oldest film school in Latin America is the Centro Universitario de Estudios Cinematográficos (University Center for Film Study) (CUEC), founded in 1963 and located at the Universidad Nacional Autónoma de México (National Autonomous University, in Mexico City) (UNAM), a highly ranked public university and the largest in Latin America. The CUEC trained such notable directors as Alfonso Cuarón, Jaime Humberto Hermosillo, Fernando Eimbeke, Jorge Fons and cinematographer Emmanuel Lubezki. Ecuador, too, benefited significantly from having a prestigious film school in the region, the result of the participation of a group of film students at the school in the late 1980s (Avilés Molina, 2013, 43).

In 1986, the creation of the Escuela Internacional de Cine y Televisión, or the School of the Three Worlds (EICTV), in San Antonio de los Baños, Cuba, was another watershed moment in the formation of a whole generation of home-grown filmmakers. Initially, attendance at this signature school in Cuba was free of charge for young, aspiring filmmakers throughout the Third World. (The 'Three Worlds' in the name of the school signified Asia, Africa and Latin America.) This made an important difference for Latin American filmmakers, especially in Central American countries where for many years it remained the only film school in the region. The EICTV was co-founded by Cuban director and film theorist Julio García Espinosa in collaboration with Argentine director Fernando Birri, who served as the school's first director in 1986. It was initially funded by the Cuban government and benefited from a large sum contributed by Gabriel García Márquez's Foundation for New Latin American Cinema. While the EICTV continues to subsidise enrolment for Cuban students, foreign students must currently pay tuition fees.

The EICTV's School of the Three Worlds' philosophy emphasised the idea of Third World solidarity and internationalism, promoting collaboration among Latin American filmmakers in ways that became highly evident in Central America (Durón, 2014, 46). For example, many of the films screened in the Central American sidebar section at the 2015 Panama International Film Festival (IFF Panama) featured the work of directors from various countries who had trained in Cuba. It was at the EICTV that Dominican Laura Amelia Guzmán met her co-director and life partner Mexican Israel Cárdenas. Moreover, the honourable mention prize (US$5,000) of the post-production fund competition Primera Mirada (First Look) at the Panama film festival was given to Costa Rican Ariel Escalante – who had received formal training from the Cuban school – for his work-in-progress *El sonido de las cosas* (*The Sound of Things*, 2016). Additionally, one of the films in competition for the First Look post-production fund (*Kenke*, 2015) was directed by Panamanian director Enrique Pérez Him, who is part of the filmmaking collective Best Picture System comprised of ten filmmakers from all over Central America (Guatemala, Costa Rica, Panama and other countries). These filmmakers were all trained at the EICTV; and, as part of the collective, they pooled together scripts and resources for each project and rotated locations with each film. *Puro Mula* (dir. Enrique Pérez Him, Panama, 2010) was the first endeavour produced using this model. They continue to produce work collectively and have geared their scripts to a youth audience within the region rather than to arthouse audiences on the film festival circuit.

Training in Cuba was particularly crucial to the Central American context, creating a space and opportunity for films to be professionally made and for students to return to their respective countries where they would create their own production companies. In time, these graduates also founded their own film schools, such as the Casa Comal in Guatemala, started by alumnus Rafael Rosal. After graduating from the EICTV, Rosal was hired as the school's director for two years (2011–13) and then returned to Guatemala, founding Casa Comal and launching the Ícaro Festival Internacional de Cine en Centroamérica (Ícaro Central American Film Festival) in 1998, which would become an important platform for new Central American cinema. Along with a competition section, Ícaro organises supplementary activities such as workshops, conferences and international film sidebar programmes (Durón, 2014, 55). Casa Comal also organises throughout Central America a touring showcase of the previous year's winning films. By 2017, Ícaro had become a moving film festival, visiting various countries throughout the year: Nicaragua in August, Guatemala, El Salvador, Panama and Honduras in September, and Cuba in October. Moreover, it has expanded its reach to include six sidebar sections of Central American cinema at film festivals in Havana, Cuba, San Juan, Puerto Rico, New York and Miami in the US, Buenos Aires and Vienna. These festivals provide incredible platforms for premiering and screening national cinema, such as the case of the Ícaro film festival in Honduras, which features the newest short fiction, documentary and feature-length fictional films at its annual festival. The Ícaro festival in Guatemala is co-sponsored by the Guatemalan government and European agencies in the UK, Spain and Norway (Durón, 2014, 55).

Film institutes have sponsored ancillary programmes and funded filmmakers or producers to attend the ever-increasing number of workshops and labs offered throughout the world. Argentine documentary producer Gema Juárez Allen credits these labs and workshops as excellent networking events whereby people can meet future co-producers, receive invitations to similar events in other locations and engage in productive exchanges with more seasoned participants (Juárez Allen, 2015).

CONCLUSION

Filmmakers in Latin America often depend on state funding bodies such as film institutes and various initiatives to help fund, exhibit and distribute films. This reliance is in response to the extensive commercial interests that dominate the region's marketplace for film. Most of the time, investors in the private sector are not interested in funding films they perceive as uncommercial, a definition which is, of course, debatable. Therefore, in addition to state film institutes such as Bolivia's CONACINE or Mexico's IMCINE, funding comes from state co-production funds, such as Ibermedia.

Historically, the state has either fully supported or fallen short in its funding of various Latin American film industries in contrasting periods of economic feast or famine. This chapter demonstrates that the state matters more than ever before in creating and enforcing laws to help sustain national film industries, via film institute programmes, support to the private sector via legislation (the subject of the next chapter), and in forming linkages with other Ibero-American countries though co-productions and initiatives such as Ibermedia and Cinergia.

3

The Role of the Private Sector

How do filmmakers navigate the often harsh terrain of film financing in a region where the state alternately undergoes periods of economic stability and chaos? This chapter delves into seemingly disparate forms of private funding for all stages of the filmmaking process across Latin America. Although some governments use federal film legislation to set up provisions so that corporate entities can receive incentives for investing in films (as in the cases of Brazil, Colombia and Mexico, for example), in other contexts, the lack of funding opportunities or state infrastructure, particularly in emerging economies, frequently forces filmmakers to seek out non-traditional channels of funding. These are discussed at the end of this chapter in the case studies section. While transnational corporations (telecommunications companies such as the Spain-based Telefónica or Hollywood studios such as Warner Bros. Entertainment Studios, Disney and Sony) have invested in film industries, they have mostly opted to minimise their risk by focusing on countries with a stronger industrial base (Brazil, Mexico, Argentina).

This chapter examines the myriad ways in which the private sector intersects in varying degrees with film production in Latin America, including industry-friendly legislation, as illustrated by Brazil; the newly redefined role of the Motion Picture Association of America (MPAA) in the region's film investment; the emergence of new business-friendly legislation in Colombia; the role of private television channels, particularly Spanish ones; and the recent participation of private equity firms from various countries including the US. The bulk of these modes of private funding are a consequence of the neoliberal shifts of the 1990s, specifically of free trade agreements and the downsizing of state participation in cultural industries.

Finally, the chapter examines how limited state funding during this period created the push for alternative sources, including grassroots fundraising and crowdfunding campaigns, along with various new revenue opportunities. Particular attention will be paid to filmmakers in Guatemala, Costa Rica and Mexico.

STATE–PRIVATE PARTNERSHIPS WITH HOLLYWOOD STUDIOS

In the 1990s, a steady stream of private funding resurfaced in Argentina, Brazil and Mexico for the first time since the industrial studio era of the 1940s–50s. Within the framework of the neoliberal economic policies adopted by several governments (Brazil, Peru, Argentina and others), during the decade many state-funded entities were cut. The following study of Brazil offers an example of how the state may work in conjunction with the private sector to increase film investment.

Industry-Friendly Film Legislation: Brazil

As mentioned in Chapter 1, President Collor de Mello's 1990 decree to dismantle Brazil's film production sector exemplified the near-complete slashing of state funding for the maintenance of a film industry. Without support from the state, few filmmakers could finance their projects and, perhaps more importantly, the idea that the private sector would fill the void when state funding was practically eliminated did not materialise. This was, to some degree, because there was no attempt to institute tax incentive policies enticing the private sector to invest in the practically moribund industry. This drastic change had disastrous consequences for Brazil's industry: only nine films were produced in 1992, down from fifty-eight films in 1990 and seventy-four films in 1989 (Silva Neto, 2002, 936–7). Soon after, Brazil began to adopt other recently created neoliberal models to establish a public–private partnership that would enable industrial film production to survive.

As a response to the annihilation of state funding under Collor de Mello, film legislation was instituted in the early 1990s to encourage national and transnational corporations to invest in a medium in which private sector television had rarely participated. For the first time in Brazil's history, the 1991 Rouanet Law offered a tax credit to those who invested in the cultural field. More importantly, the 1993 Lei do Audiovisual (Audiovisual Law) allowed public and private businesses and corporations to invest a portion of their income tax in audiovisual projects, thus generating the (often remote) possibility of making a profit at no risk, since the invested funds would otherwise be paid to the federal government (Johnson, 2005, 20). Moreover, the law, which continues to be in effect today, permits foreign film distributors in the country to invest up to 70 per cent of their income taxes in national film production (Johnson, 2005, 20).

The emergence of Globo Filmes (tied to TV Globo, the largest television network in Brazil) in 1997 was one consequence of the Lei do Audiovisual; it created a commercial boost for Brazilian cinema, employing Globo actors and producing spin-offs of Globo telenovelas and films. This success prompted Hollywood majors to invest in co-productions to distribute these popular-themed films domestically and sometimes internationally. From 1999 through to the following decade, megastar Xuxa's feature-length films became box-office successes, due in part to her fame as the host of a popular children's television show. They garnered two million spectators per film on average. Although the films were deemed as not 'exportable' given their formulaic nature, three of them were directed or co-directed by Brazilian auteur Tizuka Yamasaki.

HOLLYWOOD INVESTMENT IN HIGHER-BUDGET LATIN AMERICAN CINEMA

Since the 1960s, the parable of David and Goliath has been commonly used to denounce the dominance exerted by the Hollywood 'Goliath' over small, defence-less but noble national film industries. This characterisation seemed particularly appropriate as the Motion Picture Association (MPA) represents the major six Hollywood studios: Walt Disney Studios Motion Pictures; Paramount Pictures Corporation; Sony Pictures Entertainment Inc.; Twentieth Century Fox Film Corporation; Universal City Studios LLC; and Warner Bros. Entertainment Studios Inc. Described as a cartel, the MPA has historically done everything in its power to ensure the 'free flow' of Hollywood cinema to theatres in Latin America. In the late 1960s and early 1970s, theorists, activists and filmmakers criticised this unequal power dynamic, which they saw as unfair competition. Communication theorists described it as an extension of the logic of 'cultural imperialism'; part of a larger Hollywood/governmental/military complex, char-acterised most famously by Herbert Schiller (1969).

Free trade agreements negotiated during the 1990s enabled the MPA from 1997 on to devise a new strategy to penetrate Latin American markets. While the neoliberal shifts of the 1990s enticed large national and transnational corporations to invest in national cinemas, these policies prompted concerns for the protection of national and regional cultural industries. By responding to these concerns – and, seemingly, to the criticisms of the 1960s – the MPA veiled its investments under the guise of 'cooperation', as it sought to demon-strate how 'the production and distribution decisions of MPA member countries also reflect[ed] this commitment to cultural diversity' (MPA, 2003). This new rhetoric emerged from lobbying on the part of Latin American, Canadian, European, Asian and African film producers for specific language in relevant multilateral trade agreements (General Agreements on Tariffs and Trade [GATT], Free Trade of the Americas Agreement [FTAA], etc.) that would grant 'cultural exceptionalism' status to cultural goods such as film in the name of cultural diversity. The MPA responded to this request by investing in Latin American co-productions to demonstrate their commitment to 'supporting' and cooperating with the very same industries they had always sought to dominate.

If the MPA studios' more subtle form of 'cooperation' seemed to signal a shift in their approach to Latin American films – typically viewed as competition – they began to invest in the most developed film industries in Latin America in the form of co-production funding and distribution deals. These investments allowed the studios to diversify their portfolios by investing in glossy entertainment fare while gaining valuable tax credits. Moreover, by investing in films that were officially classified as 'national films', they successfully circumvented screen quotas enforced in countries like Argentina and Brazil.

The MPA-backed studios have produced, co-produced and distributed film and TV programmes throughout the Americas. In general, the films co-produced with Hollywood studio money have very low budgets by Hollywood standards, typically between US$1 million and US$2 million, though the numbers have increased depending on the level of CGI or animation, as in the case of the US$22 million Argentine film *Metegol* (*Underdogs*, dir. Juan José Campanella, Argentina/Spain, 2013). Still, most films that receive co-production funding from Hollywood studios are relatively expensive by Latin American standards, and, rather than typical 'film festival films', they are more likely to be popular movies appealing to younger, upwardly mobile, upper-middle-class audiences. This audience tends to enjoy comedies and films focusing on trendy urban youth culture, movies that make money at the box office even though they are not necessarily exported abroad. In the Argentine context, the MPA's film investments generally went to films made by production companies partially owned by MPA members, such as Pol-Ka productions, an Argentine company owned in equal thirds by Artear (Channel 13), a national conglomerate owned by Grupo Clarín (Argentina) and Buena Vista International (Disney). In Hollywood parlance, these investments in non-English-language films are referred to as 'local language production' (Hoad, 2013).

Hollywood investments have prompted numerous debates about whether these ventures help or hurt local production. Sanford Panitch, president of Fox International Productions (FIP), argues that the types of films fostered are more commercial genre films in which local producers would be investing regardless (Hoad, 2013). In 2011, the MPA members participated in the production of over 100 films in various countries around the world, with Warner Bros. in particular making a long-term commitment to produce and distribute roughly 420 commercial foreign films abroad (Hoad, 2013). After interviews with various MPA studio executives, Hoad notes that these studio leaders would rather have a local film succeed at the box office at home, followed later by worldwide sales, than try to find the 'breakout hit' that might be a global phenomenon.

Though the MPA funds very little Latin American co-production or distribution in countries outside the 'Trinity' of Argentina, Brazil and Mexico,

Twentieth Century Fox domestically distributed one 2012 Chilean film that became the biggest box-office hit in the country's history. *Stefan v/s Kramer*, co-directed by Sebastián Freund, Stefan Kramer and Leonardo Prieto, was seen by over two million people and surpassed the US blockbusters *Avatar* (dir. James Cameron), *Ice Age 3* (dirs. Carlos Saldanha, Mike Thurmeier) and *Toy Story 3* (dir. Lee Unkrich) that year. Comedian Stefan Kramer stars in a comedy that centres around impersonations of nineteen well-known Chilean figures, including then-president Sebastián Piñera. The film was produced for US$1.6 million. While Hollywood studios are increasingly opting to diversify their portfolios and invest in lower-budget Latin American films, they are also continuing to engage in the studio practice of investing in 'runaway productions' whereby large film studios and smaller production houses find it economically advantageous to film in Latin American countries due to tax incentive policies in various countries, lower wages, skilled workers and lower infrastructural costs.

MPA CO-PRODUCTION IN MEXICO

Mexico is the number one Latin American market for the US audiovisual industry, and MPA member companies rank it tenth among all foreign markets, with Brazil ranked eleventh, and Argentina ranked seventeenth (MPAA, 2014). The MPA has played an important role in producing and distributing commercial films made in large part by 'industrial auteurs'. These directors work with multinational, corporate-owned production companies, and direct television commercials and shows in addition to film.

Mexican co-producers stand to benefit from Hollywood's involvement. In addition to the money invested, they also receive greater exposure from the wider distribution that the Hollywood studios command. For example, the Argentine remake, romcom *No eres tú, soy yo* (*It's Not You, It's Me*, dir. Alejandro Springall, 2010) was co-produced by Warner Bros. and remains the fifth highest-grossing domestic film of all time (Hoad, 2013). Three years later, *Nosotros los Nobles* (*The Noble Family*, dir. Gary Alazraki, 2013), a comedy hit also distributed nationally by Warner Bros., brought in US$15 million, taking in 6.8 million viewers. The debut director spent five years making the film, with Warner Bros. distributing it to 350 theatres and dedicating an undisclosed budget to publicising the film (Segoviano, 2013). Six months after that box-office record was reached, it was broken again by well-known television comedian Eugenio Derbez's film, *No se aceptan devoluciones* (*Instructions Not Included*, 2013), which surpassed the all-time record by selling 15.2 million tickets. This film was distributed by Pantelion Films, a company that arose from a partnership between Mexican-owned Televisa and the Canadian/US-owned Lionsgate films. Billing itself as the 'first major Latino studio', Pantelion credits its ongoing success to *No se aceptan devoluciones*.

Derbez's film also became the all-time top-grossing Spanish-language film and the all-time fourth highest-grossing foreign-language film in the US (Pantelion Films, 2017). This and *Nosotros los Nobles* combined accounted for 12 per cent of the total attendance for Mexican films for the year, representing the biggest increase from previous years. Mexican films accounted for 9 per cent of total movie-going attendance in 2011, and 4 per cent in 2012 (IMCINE, 2013). Collaborations between large Mexican commercial production companies and their US studio counterparts have therefore seen some commercial success.

The MPA in Brazil

Investigating linkages between Globo Filmes and the MPA companies, Randal Johnson observes that the Audiovisual Law stipulates that only independent film producers are eligible to apply for state funds, thus making Globo ineligible to apply for those funds or get tax breaks. Globo nevertheless circumvented this law by developing productive relationships with production companies that *are* entitled to raise funds under the law. At the same time, Globo Filmes established good working relations with several of the MPA members responsible for the distribution of many box-office hits during 2010 (2005, 24). Globo's virtual domination of Brazilian film production became a double-edged sword that exposed tensions between film as an artistic product and the commercial facet of cinema. Globo was responsible for revitalising Brazilian cinema by creating a higher 'standard of quality' and investing much larger sums of money than others were able to (Rêgo, 2005, 91). For example, it was one of the few Brazilian companies able to make the US$4.1 million investment in *Carandiru* (dir. Hector Babenco, 2003) (Pires, 2003). But if Globo helped raise technical standards, its omnipresence created an outcry in the independent film community, who argued that these televisual films were nothing but eye candy or, in the words of famed Cinema Novo director Carlos Diegues, that the televisual aesthetic embodied 'an audio-visual fast-food store' compared to film which is more 'personalised' and a 'unique event' (2003, 31).

Setting aside criticisms of the kinds of films produced by Globo and co-produced with US film studios, the reality is that comedies such as *Até que a Sorte nos Separe* (*Till Luck Do Us Part*, 2012) and *Até que a Sorte nos Separe 2* (*Till Luck Do Us Part 2*, 2013), both directed by Roberto Santucci, have accounted for a significant percentage of the Brazilian box-office gross. Produced by Gullane, in association with Globo Filmes and Rio Filmes, this franchise had the highest box-office impact in 2013, the sequel grossing US$16.3 million (Hopewell, 2013e). In 2015, a third film in the franchise was released, *Até que a Sorte nos Separe 3: A Falência Final* (*Till Luck Do Us Part 3*), co-directed by Marcelo Antunez and Roberto Santucci, and grossed US$10.5 million. Much of this success can be attributed to the well-established star system that includes revered comic actor Leandro Hassum, known for his long career working at Globo TV. He is the main protagonist in the sequel set in Las Vegas, in which a nouveau riche family try their luck at gambling, and interact with veteran US actor Jerry Lewis, who makes a cameo appearance as a bellboy. The fact that the sequel is set in the US is a commentary on the aspirations of the Brazilian upper middle classes.

In a study on contemporary Brazilian blockbuster films in Brazil, Courtney Brannon Donoghue notes that Hollywood studios such as Fox 'may invest up to R$1 million to a R$4 or R$5 million budget. Fox also will pay for print and advertising costs for theatrical distribution' (Donoghue, 2014, 542). She notes that two of Fox's most successful co-productions, *Nosso Lar* (*Astral City*, dir. Wagner de Assis, 2010) and *Se Eu Fosse Você 2* (*If I Were You 2*, dir. Daniel Filho, 2009), cost between R$5 and R$12 million to produce. Ultimately, the films grossed R$36 and R$50 million respectively, thus making Fox's minor investment quite a lucrative one for a local-language co-production (Donoghue, 2014, 542). For a Hollywood studio, this investment is a small outlay on their part but has the potential to reap larger rewards. This investment mechanism directly influences the kinds of films now being produced, and the fact that more movie theatres are being built since the 2000s (though still not enough in the case of Brazil), making it possible for costs to be amortised and profits made.

Despite the many criticisms lodged by cultural critics, academics and independent filmmakers against the collaborations between Globo, the Brazilian film industry and the MPA, these initiatives have yielded very positive benefits in furthering investment and promoting the film sector. Clearly, the kinds of national films produced by Globo Filmes are similar to Hollywood fare in terms of aesthetics, budgets and commercial appeal. Rather than single out Globo as a multimedia conglomerate that has financed a particular vision of mainstream Brazilian cinema, however, it is important to point out that other large companies have entered the field in the past decade, making 2012 the most successful year for Brazilian cinema at the box office since the 1970s. That year, nine out of ten Brazilian films were financed by a new alliance of companies, such as RT Filmes, Conspiração Filmes Entretenimento Ltda, LC Barreto, Filmes do Equador Ltda., Diler & Associados, Total Entertainment and Videofilmes Produções Artísticas Ltda, which are some of the most successful Brazilian production houses.

To bifurcate the Latin American state from the market would therefore be a false dichotomy, as it is often state legislation that promotes and incentivises the private sector into participating in film production. Below are some examples of state–private partnerships.

[Figure 3.1 Filming on the set at Hoover Dam, near Las Vegas, Nevada, *Até que a Sorte nos Separe 2* (*Till Luck Do Us Part 2*, 2013). Directed by Roberto Santucci, © Gullane with Paris Filmes, Globo Filmes, Riofilme and Telecine 2013. All rights reserved.]

STATE–PRIVATE PARTNERSHIPS

Case Study: Colombian Cinema and the Private Sector, 64-A Films, Bogotá
64-A Films, an award-winning production company based in Bogotá, Colombia, is emblematic of those throughout the region that offer multiple-platform services, including advertising, television, film, webisodes and digital media. Their work within the film sector has been surprisingly varied. In an interview, founder and owner Diego Ramírez discussed how he would like to make films that are festival-worthy, dramatic, well acted and that represent a diverse mix of different genres (2015). *Todo tus muertos* (*All of Your Dead Ones*, dir. Carlos Moreno, 2011) is a dark comedy that offers a commentary on the senseless violence that Colombia was undergoing at the time. Its searing indictment of ineffectual bureaucracy earned it entrée into the Sundance Film Festival, as well as Rotterdam. *Perro come perro* (*Dog Eat Dog*, dir. Carlos Moreno, 2008), a movie involving two hit men who try to double-cross their boss, was also successful at the national box office.

A more recent production, *Ciudad delirio* (dir. Chus Gutiérrez, 2014), filmed in Cali and featuring the famed regional salsa performance (*espectáculo*), received critical acclaim and screened at various film festivals, including Busan (South Korea), Cartagena (Colombia) and Trinidad and Tobago. Colombian company Cineplex (profiled in Chapter 4) picked it up for distribution and purchased the theatrical screening rights throughout Latin America.

Another example of 64-A Films' innovative projects is the *Madremonte Project*, co-produced with Los Angeles-based Jason Gurvitz's Green Dog Films and Deborah Del Prete's Coronet Films, which was launched in 2013. Ramírez and his co-producers put out a call in the trade paper *Variety* asking for original, feature-length screenplays in suspense, thriller or horror genres. They planned to select five scripts and shoot the films back to back in Colombia. Setting a maximum of thirty pages, the producers defined specific constraints, limiting the budget to US$1 million per project, thus curtailing expensive special effects and highly paid star actors. They also placed restrictions on the scripts' locations and number of actors: in each case, the cast could include a maximum of three actors, and the plot must unfold in no more than three locations. The producers selected a rainforest two or three hours away from Bogotá as a cost-saving measure. The call for scripts attracted 482 submissions, 20 of which made the shortlist (Ramírez, 2015). The five scripts selected represented writers from Vietnam, Spain, Colombia, Australia and the United States. The films would be shot consecutively, thereby possibly sharing locations (Gurvitz in Hopewell, 2014). The five films were slated to be English-language productions, filmed in Colombia to take advantage of Law 1556, which allows foreign producers 20–40 per cent cash rebates. Gurvitz added that 'we are creating a structure that is economically appealing', and pointed out that 'choosing artistic horror films from writers and directors from different countries, ensures the projects' artistic pedigree' (Hopewell, 2014). This project was indicative of how a familiar formula such as the horror genre could be made more participatory via crowdsourcing, and later become part of a special series that, if made well, may capture worldwide interest. In 2018, the project ceased production for indeterminate reasons.

[Figure 3.2 *Ciudad delirio* (2014) poster. Directed by Chus Gutiérrez, © 64-A Films and Film Fatal 2014. All rights reserved.]

PRIVATE TELEVISION FINANCE: TELEFÓNICA

The television sector in its various incarnations has been a long-time strong supporter of Spanish film funding. As mentioned in the previous chapter, since the 1960s, television legislation has allotted 6 per cent of revenue from public television (namely Television Española [TVE]) towards the development and broadcast distribution of Latin American films and Spanish co-productions. Spanish television has clearly been an unsung hero in the ever-increasing quest for funding. While TV funding was cut back in the wake of the financial crisis in the early twenty-first century, it should be acknowledged that Spanish television has been a major pillar of Latin American film funding. In more recent years, private sector television stations have taken on some of the financial responsibilities abandoned by public channels.

Since 2013, Spain's Telefónica conglomerate has emerged as one of the 'new kids on the block' with deep pockets. Even if, to date, it has invested exclusively in Argentine productions, this multimedia conglomerate owns not only television systems throughout the region, but also multiple television channels such as Telefe in Argentina, telephone landlines and mobile phone companies throughout the region. According to *Variety*'s John Hopewell, Telefónica Studios has one of the biggest production slates of any film company in Spain or Latin America, producing at least fifteen films a year. Moreover, the studio began collaborating with Argentina's Telefe television channel, to produce twenty-five films (Hopewell and de Pablos, 2013). In both Spain and Argentina, Telefónica is required by law to invest in or buy at least eight local movies a year (Hopewell and de Pablos, 2013). In recent years, they have been investing mainly in Argentine and Spanish higher-budget films with recognisable directors, though there are exceptions. In 2014, Telefónica invested in thirty films, including blockbuster hits such as Damián Szifron's *Relatos salvajes*. The year before, Telefe purchased equity and free-to-air rights for the five highest-grossing Argentine films of 2013 (in which it had invested), and whose total Argentine box-office gross added up to US$38.9 million: Juan José Campanella's *Metegol* (US$14.3 million); *Corazón de león* (*Lion Heart*, dir. Marcos Carnavale), starring Guillermo Francella (US$10.6 million); *Tesis sobre un homocidio* (*Thesis on a Homicide*, dir. Hernán Golfrid) (US$6.1 million) and *Séptimo* (*7th Floor*, dir. Patxi Amezcua) (US$7.1 million), both starring Ricardo Darín; and *Wakolda* (*The German Doctor*), Lucía Puenzo's Argentine Oscar entry (US$2.3 million). In all, in 2013 Telefe co-productions sold 6.3 million tickets in Argentina, with Argentine films hitting a high of 17.6 per cent domestic market share. Telefe films represented 89 per cent of Argentine cinema's box-office gross that year (Hopewell and de Pablos, 2013).

PRIVATE SECTOR CO-PRODUCTIONS

From the 1990s to the present, private equity companies from Latin America and the United States have started to take notice of the investment possibilities that Latin American films might hold for them. While co-production is indubitably one of the crucial intergovernmental policies to promote filming in Latin America, this strategy has also been utilised by private companies from the United States, Europe and Latin America itself to take advantage of the creative momentum and widespread popularity of the regional industry (Alvaray, 2013, 70).

Beginning in the 2000s, many large markets and film festivals have established co-production forums, meetings and 'speed dating' to encourage connections between producers who attend their events. In the United States, during 2010, the Producers Guild of America held an International Film Co-production showcase (CoProShow) at the Twentieth Century Fox studios, expanding it the following year to include US producers, who could also compete for financing via story pitches and meetings with film executives, though this programme was short-lived (Sedeño Valdellós, 2013, 304). In the independent film world, however, the Independent Filmmaker Project (IFP) has organised a multi-tiered programme called No Borders International Co-production Market, which annually seeks to pair US producers with their international counterparts.

At a time when investment by private companies is inequitable across the board, why are certain individuals and companies choosing to invest in Latin American films? Cristina Garza, vice-president of Mundial Films (Mexico), a former sales agent now investing in and distributing Latin American films, observes that the quality of available directors and actors is prompting companies to take notice (Hopewell, 2013c). While investors recognise the ever-increasing diversification of the contemporary Latin American film industry in the inclusion of more hybrid films of various genres, and observe that 'audiences want to see more of [these genres] in Latin America', they are also aware of what Ibero-American producer Elena Manrique calls an 'elevated genre' when referring to genres directed by well-respected auteurs (Manrique, 2015). Moreover, Cristina Garza defines auteur genre films as films that 'deliver social commentary with genre'. In this category, she names directors such as Adrián García Bogliano (Argentina), Dennison Ramalho (Brazil), Gustavo Hernández (Venezuela) and Jorge Michel Grau (Mexico) (Hopewell, 2013c).

Firms such as D Street Media Group (based in New York and Berlin), Costa Films (located in Buenos Aires) and Dynamo Capital (based in Colombia) have become 'important players in the Latin American media landscape, with capitalisation ranging between US$10 million and US$50 million each' (Schroeder, 2012, 89). While US investors are interested in distributing these films in the United States, they are not only eyeing local, but also global markets. As D Street chief Dexter Davis puts it, 'our aim is to make commercially viable stories in Latin America for the world, not just the US market' (de la Fuente, 2011a).

CASE STUDY: *METEGOL* (2013)

While the increase in investment is a relatively new phenomenon, it is important to acknowledge that private investment from Spain has been part of the fabric of Latin American film production for decades. Other than during the 2008 worldwide economic debacle, which forced the state to slash cultural funding, this support has continued, albeit perhaps more limited than in the past. Argentine/Spanish 3D animated film *Metegol* (*Underdogs*, 2013) was both the most expensive Argentine film ever made and the most expensive animated film ever made in Latin America. Directed by Juan José Campanella, *Metegol* required an unprecedented US$22 million budget. The film broke the record for the biggest opening-day gross in Argentine box-office history, taking in US$774,000 (Hopewell, 2013d). Examining this box-office smash hit, journalist Ian Mount has mused about whether Latin American animation is now ready to compete with Hollywood animated films, given the skilled workforce and availability of lower-cost technology. In his estimation, the answer is yes, as, despite the major differences in investment funding, the production values are made to look the same. Mount notes the following differences in the production values between a Latin American production and its US counterpart: 'Even though the twenty-two-million-dollar production meant leaving out details in hair, grass, and water, which would have been expensive to animate, the quality of the animation is indistinguishable, to the average movie-goer, from major US studio films' (Mount, 2013).

Even if *Metegol* was an incredibly high-budget investment for Argentina, US$22 million is a paltry sum compared to the US$200 million budget of Hollywood studio films *Cars 2* (dir. John Lasseter, 2011) and *Toy Story 3* (Mount, 2013). A significant amount of the capital needed to make *Metegol* was raised by Campanella, a famed industrial auteur trained at NYU who worked in US network television before returning to Argentina and who made various successful features (typically comedies). Campanella identifies the financial advantages of working within the framework of a Spanish/Argentina co-production: seeking to keep costs down, he and his producers contracted a small number of top Spanish animators and paired them with young Argentine computer animators whose rates were affordable; they also worked with technology companies to secure discount deals and avoided Hollywood's practice of hiring the costly services of executives or consultants (Mount, 2013).

[Figure 3.3 *Metegol* (*Underdogs*, 2013) poster. Directed by Juan José Campanella, © 100 Bares, 369 Prods., Antena 3 Films, Catmandu Branded Entertainment, JEMPSA, Canal Plus, Prana Studios, Telefe and Universal Pictures 2013. All rights reserved.]

In the United States, some companies have shown an increased interest in participating in Latin American film production. For instance, in 2006, independent film entrepreneurs, brothers Bob and (now deposed) Harvey Weinstein, formed a Latin American film fund with Argentine entrepreneur and arts patron Eduardo Constantini Jr. This fund has financed the production and acquisition of about fourteen Latin American movies between 2006 and 2010. Sources say the fund was worth approximately US$50 million. The portfolio included the noteworthy box-office smash *Tropa de elite* (*Elite Squad*, dir. José Padilha, 2007), whose success in movie theatres allowed its producers to recoup costs, despite the film being leaked through pirate channels (Mohr and Hopewell, 2006, 10) (see Chapter 6 for this specific case study). Constantini now runs Costa Films, which helped produce Mexican Amat Escalante's *Heli* (2013).

In 2015, media mogul Alex García was considered the largest independent film producer and financier in Latin America. García is the founder of the Mexican equity-backed fund AG Capital, which aims to fully finance films in the US$5–US$25 million range and to co-produce films above US$25 million. García stated in an interview that his strategy consists of exclusively investing in projects with low- to medium-sized budgets so that he can recoup costs at a reasonable pace as the film travels through a gamut of distribution platforms, from theatrical to DVD, television and online streaming services such as Netflix (de la Fuente, 2014a).

ITINERANT DIRECTORS IN SEARCH OF A BUDGET

The investment of finance capital has compelled commercial directors to search for higher-budget work. The migration of skilled labour has been a constant throughout different historical periods, and has recently manifested itself in the tendency among US and European production companies to select creative personnel to direct films, particularly A-list directors from Mexico, Brazil and Argentina. In 2006, Brazilian director Fernando Meirelles signed a three-year deal with Universal Pictures and its Focus Features unit to bring to the studio Brazilian-made films, in English as well as Portuguese. While the contract stipulates that Universal will have a first look at new Brazilian film projects, this clause only increases the likelihood that Universal will produce these films, without guaranteeing that it will. The contract does not cover Meirelles' personal projects or his work for O2 Filmes, Brazil's biggest independent studio at the time (Muello, 2006). This contract yielded the production of four films whose budgets ranged from US$2 million to US$10 million: *Blindness* (dir. Fernando Meirelles, 2008), *Xingu* (dir. Cao Hamburger, 2011), *We 3* (dir. Nando Olival, 2011) and *VIPS* (dir. Toniko Melo, 2010). Universal's participation was instrumental in the initial phases of these film projects as development departments were fairly new in Brazil (Muello, 2006).

At present, the most world-renowned Latin American directors are arguably the Mexican directors known variously as the 'Three Caballeros', the 'Three Mosqueteros' (The Three Musketeers) or the 'Three Amigos': Alfonso Cuarón (*Roma*, 2018; *Gravity*, 2013; *Great Expectations*, 1998; *Y tu mamá también*, 2001); Alejandro G. Iñárritu (*Birdman*, 2014; *Babel*, 2006; *21 Grams, 2003; Amores perros* [*Love's a Bitch*], 2000); and Guillermo del Toro (*The Shape of Water*, 2017; *Crimson Peak*, 2015; *Pacific Rim*, 2013; *El laberinto del fauno* [*Pan's Labyrinth*], 2006; *El espinazo del diablo* [*The Devil's Backbone*], 2001; and *Cronos*, 1993). Two out of three directors have not filmed in Mexico since 2001, instead directing films in Spain, the US, UK and Canada (Shaw, 2013), as well as other European countries. By winning prestigious Academy Awards, they have recently broken the 'White Hollywood Barrier': Cuarón won Best Director for *Gravity* (as well as Best Director awards at BAFTA and the Golden Globes), and Iñárritu won the same top Oscar prize one year later with *Birdman* and again with *The Revenant* (2015). With *Birdman*, he was the first Mexican to win three Academy Awards (Best Picture, Best Screenplay and Best Director). Del Toro won three Oscars for *Pan's Labyrinth*. When Iñárritu gave his 2015 Oscar acceptance speech, he called attention to the newest wave of immigration to the United States and publicly urged audiences to treat all immigrants (including Mexicans and Central Americans) with respect and not as second-class citizens. Deborah Shaw and Dolores Tierney (2009) have each examined how these directors have succeeded at so effortlessly crossing borders (principally) between Mexico and the United States. They attribute this fluidity to the way they have established themselves as 'transnational auteurs', and to the 'transnational modes of narration' they have adopted when working abroad. Shaw uses this expression to refer to globally inflected film languages that can be understood in international markets, making the product desirable to producers, distributors and audiences (Shaw, 2013, 11).

Focusing on Guillermo del Toro, Misha MacLaird notes that the director's higher-budget transnational productions such as *Mimic* (1997), *Blade 2* (2002), *Hellboy* (2004) and *Hellboy II: The Golden Army* (2008), among others, were shot in European and 'foreign location' studios where costs are lower (Prague, Canada and Ireland, for example). The trajectory of del Toro's career has followed a similar path to the handful of successful Latin Americans in the entertainment industry who have migrated to wherever they have found opportunities to make big-budget projects, in the tradition of Hollywood émigrés (2013, 163–4).

CREATIVE FINANCING: THERE IS NO 'ONE-SIZE-FITS-ALL' APPROACH

While these world-renowned auteurs travel abroad to complete their films, most filmmakers must rely on local and national financing opportunities. Some Central American filmmakers have relied on community support by using creative forms of fundraising. Executives at other companies have been bolder in supporting filmmakers from countries such as Nicaragua, Guatemala and Paraguay by investing production funds through non-established, legal channels. Such diversified forms of fundraising are illustrated in the case studies below. They include a range of possibilities. For example, when members of an artistic community create opportunities for film financing, such as raffles, auctions or benefit galas; when filmmakers or producers approach a business that does not typically invest in film, such as a telecoms company, or a business finances a film in which it is featured, akin to product placement; finally, crowdsourcing platforms that appeal to the general populace and can turn reaching budget goals into a collective endeavour.

Determined directors and producers in Latin America have found many innovative ways to fund their films, especially if they are from countries without a film institute or film funding infrastructure that assists directors in obtaining state or international grants. Guatemalan director Julio Hernández Cordón has directed seven films, quite a feat in a country where filmmaking is still an artisanal form. His sixth film, *Te prometo anarquia*, was one of eight feature-length films funded by Mexican IMCINE's FOPROCINE fund in 2014. Though Hernández Cordón is based in Guatemala, his dual citizenship as a Mexican makes him eligible to apply for Mexican funds, provided he film in that country. Moreover, he was awarded a US$40,000 grant from the Berlin Film Festival's

World Cinema Fund for this project, and was selected for the Panama Film Festival's Primera Mirada (First Look) post-production competition, where it won the top prize.

For one of his earlier projects, Hernández Cordón asked his sculptor friends to each donate a piece of artwork to auction off. After amassing a group of sculptures for his auction, a wealthy art patron bought the entire collection for US$20,000 (Hernández Cordón, 2015). This 'kickstarted' his career, with *Las marimbas del infierno* and *Gasolina* both premiering at the Cannes Film Festival. His latest film, *Atrás hay relampagos* (*Lightning Falls Behind*, 2017), premiered at the Rotterdam Film Festival.

Monociclo Cine, a production company based in Medellín, Colombia, is composed of university students who met studying communication at the University of Antioquia in 2009 and formed a film collective two years later. The company uses what they deem 'alternative production processes' to make films, mainly through pooling equipment, labour and other resources to complete short and feature films. Monociclo Cine's Facebook page states that in addition to production they are also helping to cultivate viewing publics and new exhibition spaces, such as organising the first three editions of the Festival de Cine del Suroeste (Southeast Film Festival) in Pueblorrico, Antioquia, Colombia.

The following two case studies are indicative of the entrepreneurial spirit that Latin American directors have demonstrated in finding ways to finance films within the private sector.

Case Studies: *La Pantalla Desnuda* (2014) and *7 Cajas* (2012)

Director Florence Jaugey's second film, *La pantalla desnuda* (*The Naked Screen*, Nicaragua, 2014), was produced four years after her debut film, *La Yuma* (2010). Her *ópera prima* had the distinction of being the first film to be produced in Nicaragua in two decades. Nicaragua's paucity of film production was partly due to a lack of funding infrastructure and film legislation.

La pantalla desnuda centres on an amorous relationship between Esperanza (French actress Paola Baldion) and Alex (Spanish actor Oscar Sinela), which spirals out of control when Alex decides to film their lovemaking on a smartphone. The conceit of the film is that the young man's phone is stolen soon after and the video goes viral within hours. The sex act leaked on video turns their relationship upside down and does irreparable damage to their families' lives. The US$500,000 budget was financed from various sources, including a grant from the Swiss fund Vision Sud Est, local television channel Channel 13, the Nicaraguan Tourism Institute (Intur), Movistar (Telefónica's mobile phone wing) and the Mexico-based cable channel Moviecity (Anon., 2014d). Jaugey explained how she had to be strategic in appealing to companies who might support her

[Figure 3.4 *La pantalla desnuda* (*The Naked Screen*, 2014) poster. Directed by Florence Jaugey, © Camila Films 2014. All rights reserved.]

project, and thus approached Movistar for finance. The company finally agreed, but was concerned that a viral sex video might somehow be perceived as problematic. As a negotiating tactic, the director agreed to make a public service announcement (PSA) to warn young people about the dangers stemming from the virilisation of videos, as this could taint their public image (Jaugey, 2015).

7 cajas was a first-time feature film directed by two directors who came from the advertising sector. They created a low-budget film that had far-reaching effects. With its high-paced mix of thriller and noir that incorporates local accents and locales, Paraguayan film *7 cajas* (*7 Boxes*, dirs. Juan Carlos Maneglia and Tana Schémbori, 2012, Paraguay) quickly became the biggest box-office hit in the history of Paraguayan cinema. With over 270,000 spectators, *7 cajas* beat the previous record holder, *Titanic*, at 150,000 viewers. *7 cajas* was commercially successful at home given its generic nature, excellent cinematography, script and setting highlighting a dynamic, bustling marketplace. At the same time, the novelty and originality of its formal qualities allowed it to successfully enter and thrive on the international film festival circuit (see Falicov, 2013a). In addition to its remarkable success in Argentina, where it sold 70,000 tickets, *7 cajas* travelled to 135 film festivals and won over twenty-nine awards.

7 cajas competed in the 2011 edition of Cine en Construcción (Films in Progress) a post-production finishing fund competition held at the San Sebastián Film Festival in Spain. Competing against contenders from Argentina, Brazil, Colombia, Mexico and Chile, the film won the industry award of US$35,000 to complete aspects such as the colour correction, sound mixing, subtitling and other elements which comprise the post-production phase, an often costly component of producing a film. *7 cajas* was clearly the underdog in the competition,

[Figure 3.5 *7 cajas* (*7 Boxes*, 2012) English-language poster. Directed by Juan Carlos Maneglia and Tana Schémbori, © Maneglia-Schémbori Realizadores, Synchro Image and Nephilim Producciones 2012. All rights reserved.]

as Paraguayan cinema had a limited exposure in film festival circulation, and particularly in a prestigious competition in Spain. This is in part attributable to the lack of a national film institute in Paraguay or any enacted film legislation to support and stimulate a national film industry. As the country has no film schools and only a few movie theatres, Paraguayan filmmakers such as Juan Carlos Maneglia and Tana Schémbori have had to struggle to find private sources of funding to make films in the absence of state support. Producer Estefanía Ortiz has stated the film cost at least US$435,000, and therefore she had to appeal to the private sector by approaching sponsors that included Brazil-based multinational bank Itaú, national gas companies and an Argentine/Paraguayan private dam corporation Yacretá. Additionally, the completion of the film was made possible by a small grant from the city of Asunción.

THE EMERGENCE OF CROWDFUNDING: HOW FRIENDS AND ASSOCIATES BRIDGE THE GAP

Crowdfunding or crowdsourcing has recently provided a model for funding low- to medium-budget projects via specific platforms started by Latin American entrepreneurs. These internet appeals help small- and medium-sized productions raise funds from friends, family and international investors via social media campaigns. In the United States, the phenomenon of crowdfunding has become commonplace in the independent film world. Platforms such as Kickstarter, IndieGoGo and GoFundMe have been successful in pooling together resources for any individual, professional or otherwise, to make films or other creative works. This funding method is also gaining traction in Latin America, for

example, the Brazilian site Catarse (which is the largest Latin American platform in the region), the Argentine site Ideame, whose scope is regional, featuring
projects from Uruguay, Colombia, Chile, Mexico and the US, and the Mexican
site Fondeadora.mx (now defunct). These sites not only help fund film but other
creative work as well. Fondeadora.mx, Mexico's first and largest crowdfunding
platform, stated that the company's objective was to 'generate [a] positive impact
in Mexico' (Catarse, 2017). The monetary scope of projects profiled on these
websites varies enormously, ranging from very small amounts (less than US$100)
to tens of thousands of dollars. Many of the films appealing for funds are documentaries, and a large majority are successfully funded. However, in the case of
Kickstarter (which is typical of these websites), no funding is forthcoming if
the target is not achieved, and so filmmakers appeal to their backers to mobilise
others to help reach their goals. On Fondeadora, the founders stated that the
purpose of the platform was not to 'sell an idea' or to 'look for investors' but rather
to create something that will reap great social benefit for each project's supporters
(Vertiz de la Fuente, 2013). Examples of awardees include the 12th edition of
the annual Macabro: Festival Internacional de Cine de Horror de la Ciudad de
México (Macabro: Mexico City International Horror Film Festival) in 2013, and
the documentary *Llévate mis amores* (*All of Me*, dir. Arturo González Villaseñor,
2014) about the Patronas, women from the Mexican state of Veracruz who
prepare food and then package and distribute it with water to the hundreds of
migrants who ride on top of dangerous trains (collectively known as 'The Beast')
from Central America to the United States (Vertiz de la Fuente, 2013). Not
only was this film successfully funded, it also played at many festivals throughout
Mexico, winning an award at the Los Cabos International Film Festival, and was
part of the official selection at IDFA (International Documentary Film Festival
Amsterdam). In 2015, Fondeadora featured twenty-eight film projects in various
states of funding support, as well as some short films, documentaries and web
series. Fondeadora boasted that over 500 projects have been funded since its
founding, with US$4.5 million invested in projects. In 2016, Fondeadora shut-
tered its doors to crowdfunding campaigns, and recommended Kickstarter for
those in search of a platform (Fondeadora.mx, 2016).

Kickstarter is the best-known and largest crowdfunding platform in the world.
Many Latin American filmmakers have utilised Kickstarter to call attention to
their film projects, seeking funding and supporters who will continue to act as
'boosters' for the film after it is completed and looking for distribution. While
the majority of projects emanate from the United States, a handful of Latin
American ventures have been listed on Kickstarter, with some ultimately funded
through crowdsourcing and enjoying critical or box-office success. At the time
of its release, the Costa Rican film *El regreso* (*The Return*, dir. Hernán Jiménez,

2012) was the most successful Kickstarter campaign ever attempted in Latin America (Pragda, 2017). While the film was directed by a well-known Costa Rican television and theatre actor and stand-up comedian, it is nonetheless important to note that public support was a crucial factor in the successful completion of the project and for its subsequent release in theatres. *El regreso* ultimately became the all-time highest-grossing Costa Rican film (Pragda, 2017). According to the Costa Rican cultural blog RedCultura.com, Jiménez had also received fan support outside the Kickstarter platform through donations made at Costa Rican banks (Báez Sánchez, 2011).

Having already directed his first film, *A ojos cerrados* (*Eyes Closed*, 2010), Jiménez mentions in his Kickstarter appeal video that if the 35,000 backers for his first film could each donate US$1 to his campaign, this would amount to a significant sum that could be dedicated towards expenses associated with post-production. In April 2011, Jiménez set a goal of US$40,000 and raised US$57,341 from 1,742 backers through Kickstarter. In addition to his viable track record, another explanation for why he exceeded his target is that he had already shot the film and simply needed finishing funds, thus diminishing the risk that it might never be completed. When making a compelling case for backers to fund this project, Jiménez noted in his video appeal that he was 'completing a film in a country where state funding for filmmaking is non-existent'.

Jiménez's avoidance of traditional channels for securing funding and ensuring circulation is noteworthy. In the video, he stresses that he is not interested in obtaining funds from investors, and that he does not submit his films to festivals since they are generally not accepted, possibly because they are more 'crowd pleasing' than 'serious art films'. Moreover, he directly states that 'he doesn't have the patience to spend time on this aspect of filmmaking and that [he] simply wants to make films for a national audience' (Jiménez, 2011). He decided to seek funding through a crowdfunding campaign because he felt that it was the 'most consequential and wonderful way to complete a film in a country without a film industry'.

CONCLUSION

To conclude, the private sector is slowly investing in contemporary Latin American film production to realise its potential, in much the same way as it did during the studio system phases in Argentina, Mexico and Brazil from the 1930s to 1950s. Clearly, policies such as film legislation which incentivises companies to invest in cinema (as the case of Brazil illustrates) are effective to a certain extent, but the debates continue about the kinds of cinema that dominate exhibition spaces and whether they do so at the expense of independent producers. Mixed models of funding, such as those in Colombia, have been proven to boost the production sector. Countries such as Panama and the Dominican Republic are working in this direction to improve their production output and to draw outside companies to film there. The models discussed in this chapter demonstrate there is no one way to make films in Latin America using private money. Indeed, fiscal limitations sometimes lead filmmakers or producers to ask small or large businesses to form non-traditional partnerships to utilise crowdfunding and other mechanisms. Executives at other companies have been bolder in supporting filmmakers from countries such as Nicaragua, Guatemala and Paraguay by investing production funds through non-established, legal channels in the quest to make films. Though these models are not systematised in any general sense, they are a testament to the ways independent filmmakers are realising their completed projects in economically challenging times.

4

Distribution

This chapter will explore the ways in which Latin American films are distributed to movie theatres and to homes, domestically, regionally and globally. While this includes Latin American distributors, its main focus is on US movie studio distributors who distribute Latin American films both in the region as well as in the US. Different scales of distribution will be profiled, including large film distribution companies owned by Hollywood studios, as well as nationally owned multimedia conglomerates (Mexico's Televisa, Brazil's Globo and Venezuela's Venevisión). The nationally owned conglomerates are Predominantly television companies that have branched out into distributing films that they have typically also co-produced with a US studio (see Chapter 3). While most of these films are destined for the regional market, in some cases they have been co-produced for the US market. For example, Televisa Cine attempted to distribute Mexican films in the US but shut down in 2006 after failures at the box office (Hecht, 2006). However, some of their films, such as *No se aceptan devoluciones*, case study profiled below, were co-distributed with a Hollywood studio, and were successful both in Mexico and in the United States.

Finally, there are many small, independent distributors who typically self-distribute their own or other independent films. Due to their small size and the type of film distributed, this sector makes up approximately 10 per cent or less of a country's national distribution. These companies usually distribute arthouse and low-budget productions; their market share is further compounded by their limited capacity to compete against large companies that have the advertising muscle of television and other forms of cross-promotion. The chapter includes a profile of one of these companies, Cineplex, an independent Colombian distribution company. Also examined will be small niche distributors in the US who distribute Latin American cinema such as Cinema Tropical, Global Film Initiative (currently suspended) and Pragda.

Other platforms for distributing cinema will be explored, starting with home video, which proliferated in the 1980s, and moving to newer systems such as Over the Top (OTT) video streaming, Video on Demand (VOD) and the more recent phenomenon of internet video distribution throughout the region. An example of the latter is Retina Latina, which offers free Latin American films streamed online for six participating countries.

Case studies of national films in the region and different examples of how they negotiate domestic releases, marketing, festival circulation and international sales will be discussed. This will enable the reader to pinpoint the various trajectories films have taken in order to be sold and distributed throughout the region and abroad. The importance that national, regional and international film festivals play in giving films exposure will be discussed as part of a larger strategy that arthouse films use to obtain distribution deals.

FILM DISTRIBUTION ON A GLOBAL SCALE

US distribution companies dominate all other countries' distribution channels worldwide, including Latin American countries. Although Argentina does have a number of companies who compete with the major US distributors, in 2013 Argentina's distribution market mirrored the international landscape, in that the five major distributors (UIP Universal Paramount, Buena Vista-Disney, Warner Bros., Fox and Columbia Tri-Star) shared 66 per cent of the market, which it had done consistently from 2000 to 2015 (Lima, 2015). In contrast, larger Argentine distributors (Artistas Argentinos Asociados [or AAA], Argentina Sono Film S.A., Cinema Group SRL, Eurocine S.A., Primer Plano Films Group S.A. and Pramer S.C.A) shared only 15 per cent of the market, with smaller, national independent distributors (Diamond Films, Alfa Films, Distribution Company, Energía and CDI) holding the remaining 10 per cent share (Friedlander, 2015).

A similar situation exists in Brazil. According to a 2013 study, the companies with the largest market share were Disney (16.3 per cent), Fox (12.4 per cent), Sony (9.5 per cent), Warner Bros. (10.7 per cent), Universal (10.1 per cent) and Paramount (7.3 per cent). National distribution companies (Downtown, Paris, Imagem and Rio Filmes) totalled 30.7 per cent of the market share (ANCINE, 2014). Thus, the United States' distribution companies, owned by the major studios, dominate the entire region. The smaller the national film industry, the larger the portion of the distribution 'pie' taken by the US majors.

Therefore, US companies will have a disproportionate distribution presence in smaller nations with very limited local film production. In Costa Rica, however, while 95 per cent of films distributed are of US origin, a national company, Distribuidora Romaly, does distribute three-quarters of these films, with the remainder distributed by national companies Discine and Sala Garbo (Getino, 2006, 239).

HOLLYWOOD DISTRIBUTORS OR NATIONAL ONES: WHAT ARE THE IMPLICATIONS FOR NATIONAL CINEMA?

As Toby Miller et al. point out, 'World film distribution is dominated by the US via arrangements that would be illegal domestically because of their threat to competition. UIP, Fox, Warner Bros., Buena Vista (Disney) and Columbia (Sony) all operate in this manner' (2004, 296). Whether distribution is by national companies (Globo is owned by the Brazilian Marinho family) or multinational corporations based in the United States or Japan, the objectives remain the same: buying distribution rights to films with appealing stars, bigger budgets and 'name' directors (or 'industrial auteurs' as some critics have dubbed them). These are typically genre films that appeal to a younger, wider, audience. Often these corporations have spun off successful television dramas or star vehicles to cross-promote content and advertise programmes on television stations they own.

The largest of Latin America's established television companies, such as Mexico's Televisa (owned by Emilio Azcárraga Jean), Venevisión (part of Venezuelan billionaire Gustavo Cisneros's business empire) and Globo Filmes (the distribution arm of Brazilian media giant Globo), are involved in distributing Latin American movies both at home and abroad. For instance, Televisa opened a Los Angeles office in 2003 to distribute Mexican films in the US. Televisa was the sole distributor (O'Brien and Ibars, 2004) for the May 2004 release of *A Day Without a Mexican* (dir. Sergio Arau), produced by Altavista Films. Because of financial difficulties, Globo Filmes, which helped distribute *City of God* (*Cidade de Deus*), was less able to pursue overseas expansion aggressively. Its financing arm, GloboPar, defaulted on a debt of more than US$1.5 billion in 2004 and underwent financial restructuring until mid-2005 when it successfully restructured US$1.3 billion of this debt (Gross et al., 2006). Engaging large media conglomerates to distribute films, whether national, such as Argentina's Grupo Clarín, or transnational, like Sony, has helped normally commercial filmmakers gain access to wider circulation channels. Because these conglomerates are also linked to television companies and other media outlets, a film can benefit from cross-promotion by actors who publicise the film on their network talk shows. These cross-media outlets are part of the 'windowing' process that a film goes though in its life trajectory. A case in point is the Argentine action film *Comodines* (*Cops*, dirs. Jorge Nisco, Daniel Barone, 1997), where Pol-Ka, a film, television and commercial production house owned partially by Grupo Clarín, and partially by Buena Vista International (Disney), made a popular television series into a 'blockbuster' movie using cross-promotion across media outlets, visual effects, high production values and product placement (see Falicov, 2003).

As in the United States and elsewhere, the norm is that privately owned distribution companies, either national (Zeta films in Mexico) or multinational (Buena Vista International or Disney), distribute primarily entertainment-oriented films. In some cases, however, Hollywood studios such as Warner Bros., Fox and Sony have co-produced and distributed other Brazilian films they deem 'less risky'. An example is children's pop sensation Xuxa's films in Brazil that were co-produced and distributed by Warner Bros.

What are the differences between a Latin American film selected to be distributed locally by a US 'major' and those distributed by a national company? In most cases, if a film is made with a higher production budget and has a more commercial, less 'arthouse' aesthetic (e.g. a genre film, or a star vehicle), there is a better chance that a Latin American film will be picked up for distribution by a multinational studio operating in large film producing countries such as Brazil, Mexico or Argentina. Occasionally, there are exceptions, such as *Secuestro Express* (dir. Jonathan Jakubowicz): an action thriller first seen by Bob Weinstein at the Los Angeles International Film Festival, it was the first-ever Venezuelan film to gain distribution by a large US independent studio, the Weinstein Company, in 2005. Not only was the film picked up for international distribution, but *Secuestro Express* was Venezuela's top-grossing film in 2005 (surpassing US blockbusters in that country such as *Titanic* and *Avatar*) (Finley, 2005). While these distribution models are found throughout most of Latin America, they differ in the socialist countries, to which we now turn.

SOCIALIST DISTRIBUTION MODELS: ICAIC

In contrast to the usual private sector model of distribution in non-socialist countries, both Cuba and Venezuela have nationalised distribution arms. In the case of Venezuela, Amazonia Films acts as the distributor of films from Latin America, Europe and Asia as well as domestic fare. They not only circulate films produced in the largest film studio, state-owned Villa del Cine (see Chapter 1), but also produce and distribute more than 200 hours of television programming (Rolfe, 2006).

In Cuba, as mentioned in Chapter 1, the ICAIC (in 1959, when the institute was founded) took charge of production, training, exhibition and distribution. However, after the fall of the Soviet Union in 1991, Cuba underwent an intense period of austerity (dubbed 'The Special Period in Times of Peace'), and the ICAIC was unable to fund cinema as it had in the past. Production was practically halted and only two films were released that year. Belt-tightening measures continued through the 1990s and the Cuban state had to obtain sources of revenue in the form of international co-productions in order to survive. Cristina Venegas specifies that these co-productions consisted of a foreign partner paying the ICAIC to organise the shooting of a foreign film, including identifying locations, hiring actors, providing stock footage and/or coordinating related research (2010, 41).

Ann Marie Stock (2009) explores the case of Cuban director Juan Carlos Cremata, who attempted to produce a film with the ICAIC during the Special Period. His proposal for a musical entitled *Candela* was rejected due to a lack of resources. In 2005, Cremata was the first to produce a feature-length film, *Viva Cuba*, outside of the ICAIC's production funding or equipment lending structure. He accomplished this by appealing to various funders, including Fundación de Nuevo Cine Latinoamericano, TVC Casa Productora (which typically funded televised telenovelas), La Colmenita, a children's theatre company (the film starred two children), and Quad Productions from France. He also sourced state-run tourist companies based in Cuba, such as Gran Caribe, Palmares and others. *Viva Cuba* played to great success abroad, gaining entrée to the Cannes Film Festival. It won thirty-four national and international awards, including the Grand Prix Écrans Juniors at Cannes (2005). The film also won awards from the UNEAC, the Union of Writers and Artists in Cuba. In response, ICAIC executives contacted Cremata and offered to distribute his film on the island. As Cremata acknowledges, to have the ICAIC there to help with distribution was key, as it 'would increase the odds of this film reaching a broad audience' (Stock, 2009, 280). Thus was born the process of making a Cuban film outside the typical channels (see also the case of Alejandro Brugués mentioned on p. 32 in Chapter 1). This system continues as the most prevalent mode, less for political reasons than for economic imperatives. Other directors opt to produce outside the ICAIC structure so they can improvise with actors without a structured, pre-approved script. *Venecia* (*Venice*, 2014), directed by Kikí Álvarez, is another example; the film was funded partially through a Kickstarter campaign, and then distributed by the ICAIC after completion (Álvarez, 2016).

These options have allowed Cuban cinema to reinvent itself by using more affordable digital technologies, and by finding new ways to disseminate its films. Stock documents how some filmmakers are aiding and abetting movie piracy by willingly uploading their films for free to guarantee some viewership and film circulation, given that these films are rarely shown on television or in movie theatres (Stock, 2009, 244).

In the twenty-first century, a new generation of Cuban filmmakers, armed with a variety of digital technologies, have found ways to make films outside of official channels. The ICAIC has responded to these new channels by sponsoring a successful annual film showcase called the Muestra Jóven (National Showcase of Young Directors), which has helped foment a newer, more ebullient movement of what Ann Marie Stock calls 'street filmmakers' (akin to the Argentine group known as the Nuevo Cine Argentino, which started in the mid-1990s and provides exposure to a new generation).

REVIVING PAN-LATIN AMERICAN DISTRIBUTION NETWORKS

The idea of pan-Latin American distribution as a network is not new; it first appeared when Latin America and Spain established a distribution network in the 1930s; again in the late 1970s, during seminal Latin American film festival meetings (in Viña del Mar, Chile, Mérida, Venezuela and Havana); and in the 1990s, when meetings were called with the goal of creating a regional distribution network using the Mercosur trade bloc framework. Despite all these attempts to resist the hegemony of US distribution networks, a solid network has never emerged that managed to function outside the dominant film distribution pipelines. Thus, state-run distribution wings (such as EMBRAFILME in Brazil during the 1970s), along with small, private sector distribution companies, have competed against a historically well-oiled machine. An additional impediment is that these large US companies typically work with privately owned movie theatres, which are less interested in providing a diversity of films (there are a few notable exceptions, such as Argentina's INCAA-run movie theatres, funded by the state [see Chapter 5]).

In 2011, a group of film distributors from various Latin American countries gathered at the Valdivia International Film Festival in Chile to discuss the possibility of forming a network for Latin American film circulation among themselves, without accessing the help of a European intermediary distribution company. Called LARED, the founding companies were Mexico (Interior 13), Ecuador (Trópico Cine), Argentina (LAT-E), Costa Rica (Pacifica Grey), Colombia (Interior 13, Colombia office), Brazil (Descoloniza Films) and Chile (LARED). The discussions focused on the traditional problems associated with distributing Latin American cinema regionally (de la Fuente, 2011b). LARED's website, which is connected to Australab, a consortium of film festivals (Valdivia, BAFICI and the support of the Rotterdam International Film Festival), outlines their purpose:

> Each one of the companies that make up this group has their own self-managed catalog, but they come together to make joint purchases when films imply a larger financial risk, due to the director's radical approach, when the costs are high, or simply to offer a film larger regional coverage, when all or several LARED members are interested in its distribution. The idea for this networking is to increase competitiveness for rights purchasing, to join economic forces, and to diminish the costs associated with film distribution. (Australab website, 2018)

This more cooperative model, in which independent distribution companies support each other rather than compete with or ignore one another, is based on the earlier 1970s pan-Latin American solidarity model. Another example is Latinopolis; it collaborates between companies in Brazil, Bolivia and Mexico, with support from an executive producer in Uruguay and a film marketer in Barcelona. A final example of an alliance between distributors and exhibitors is Aldea: formed in 2017, it organises a series of films representing each of the nine participating countries in a sidebar 'Aldea Presents'. The sidebar was launched first at Lima International Film Festival, Peru, and will travel the film festival circuit (de la Fuente, 2017b).

Another prominent presence, valued at over US$500 million, is a large corporate entity called LatAm Distribution, a division of AG Studio headed by Alex García, who teamed up with various production companies throughout Latin America (BN Films with US$150 million financing; US and Mexico-based Lemon Films, Mexico City's Itaca Films, Bazooka Films, Anima Estudios and Eduardo Costantini's Costa Films in Argentina and others) valued at over $500 million. LatAm Distribution is responsible for circulating films in Mexico, the United States' Latino market and throughout Latin America (Hopewell, 2013g) (see LatAmPictures.com).

INDEPENDENT FILM DISTRIBUTORS: CINEPLEX, COLOMBIA

Cineplex is an independent film distribution company, founded in 1993, and based in Bogotá, Colombia. In 1993, only the Hollywood distributors were importing mainstream commercial productions into the country. According to Cineplex CEO Elba McAllister, she and her husband decided to create a space for an alternative, arthouse and independent cinema in Bogotá, Medellín and Cali, Colombia's largest cities. Some films are also distributed throughout Central America, Ecuador, Venezuela, Peru, Bolivia, Chile, Mexico and Argentina. Cineplex has also purchased the rights to sell films on DVD on their website (McAllister, 2015).

In a homage video celebrating twenty years, many Colombian film critics lauded Cineplex for giving them the opportunity to view such classic films as *The Crying Game* (dir. Neil Jordan, UK, 1992), *The Scent of Green Papaya* (dir. Tran Anh Hung, France/Vietnam, 1993) and the *Three Colours* trilogy by Krzysztof Kieślowski (France/Switzerland/Poland, 1993–4). Cineplex representatives, usually Elba McAllister herself, attend international film festivals all over the world. In addition to important Latin American festivals such as Panama and Cartagena, Colombia, the emphasis is placed on attending the largest ones with markets (Cannes, Berlin, Toronto) in order to scout out films and purchase the territorial rights to screen them in Colombia and other parts of Latin America.

Moreover, Cineplex also works as a sales agent in supporting contemporary Colombian cinema. The company has assumed that role for various Colombian film directors, with the aim of obtaining international distribution deals at film festivals. McAllister detailed how she entered an arena fraught with power dynamics where European sales agents, at different times, tried to buy Colombian films for an absurdly low price. As an example, McAllister recounted her experience with a European agent who bid a high price for a Colombian film that garnered the coveted 'world premiere' status at a prestigious film festival. He threatened to pull the film at another prominent European film festival if Cineplex chose to go with different distributor (2015).

In 2005, Cineplex organised a six-month tour of ten recent Colombian films on 35 mm prints to promote and market Colombia's image abroad. They selected the Spanish-speaking Central American countries (Costa Rica, Panama, Guatemala, El Salvador, Honduras and Nicaragua), which historically have had limited opportunities to view Latin American cinema in theatres. The tour was organised with financial support from several sources: the 'Mixed Fund for Film Promotion' Proimágenes initiative, which contributed 50 per cent of the total budget; the Colombian Ministry of Foreign Affairs, which covered the costs of the 35 mm film copies and shipping; and by Cineplex, which underwrote the travel costs for the directors, producers and actors who accompanied their films and attended post-screening discussions in each country. A sample of films screened included *La sombra del caminante* (*The Wandering Shadows*, dir. Ciro Guerra, 2004), *The First Night* (dir. Luis Alberto Restrepo, 2003), *Sin Amaparo* (*Without Amparo*, dir. Jaime Osorio Gómez, 2005), *Sumas y restas* (*Addictions and Subtractions*, dir. Víctor Gaviria, 2004) and others (Jiménez Hinestrosa, 2005).

The examples above illustrate the range of film distribution: from large, US distributors whose roles are to screen mainly US or US/Latin American co-produced films in a domestic market, to smaller, local independent and arthouse distributors. The smaller model has taken on multiple roles to help buoy national film industries, at the same time forging distribution networks to screen films at arthouse cinemas and multiplex theatres worldwide.

WINDOWING PLATFORMS: HOME VIDEO, DVD, OTT (OVER THE TOP SERVICES), VOD (VIDEO ON DEMAND)

According to Henry Puente's definition, film 'windowing' is a process by which additional revenue is gained after a film's theatrical release. This revenue includes a series of windows or exhibition points such as foreign theatrical release, video rental and sell-through, DVD, pay-per-view (PPV), VOD, premium and basic cable television licensing, network television licensing and digital downloading

(Puente, 2011, 8). The following section explores various windowing channels for national films.

Home video technologies, including Betamax, VHS and DVD formats started in the 1980s, but really became popularised in early 1990s with the rise of video rental stores. Over that decade, between 7 and 8 million videocassettes were sold in the region, including 3.5–4 million in Brazil, 1.2–1.5 million in Argentina, 1.5 to 2 million in Mexico and 800,000–1 million in Venezuela. The price of one videocassette at the time was between US$30 and US$50 (Getino, 2007, 280). While in 1993 there were 15,000 video rental stories in the region, with approximately ten million members, by 2000 the number had dropped to 12,000, and there were only five countries with video clubs (Argentina, Brazil, Chile, Paraguay and Uruguay). Eighty per cent of the video content was from Hollywood studios, with national films only accounting for between 2 and 8 per cent of the total, varying with the size of a country's film output and capacity to sell videotapes (Getino, 2007, 281). By 2006, the region had switched to DVD format and forty million people, comprising 90 per cent of households with televisions, purchased DVD players for their homes. Latin American home video viewers were watching fifteen to twenty times more films in their homes than in movie theatres (Getino, 2007, 276).

The decline of DVD sales in Latin America developed concurrently with the rise in internet connectivity and larger broadband widths, and with the prevalence of platforms such as YouTube. The increased use of these formats occurred especially in the larger, wealthier countries with sizable middle-class populations. The countries with the highest internet penetration, in 2013, were Chile, Brazil, Mexico and Argentina; in all of these countries, the practice of streaming videos, both legally and illegally, grew. Latin America had the fastest-growing internet population, increasing 12 per cent by 2013, to more than 147 million individual visitors (Fosk, 2013). Consumers spent ten hours online per month on social networking sites, double the global average time (Gruenwedel, 2014). Indeed, approximately 11.5 million online videos were viewed every month in Argentina, Brazil, Chile and Mexico. Online video consumption had the deepest penetration in Argentina (93 per cent or higher), followed by Chile (92 per cent of the online population), Brazil (84 per cent) and Mexico (81 per cent) (Gruenwedel, 2014). In 2018, 55 per cent of the Latin American population has access to the internet, with the majority using smartphones (Statista, 2018). In 2018, Uruguay is currently the country with the highest broadband penetration (79 per cent), followed by Chile at 54 per cent, Argentina at 49 per cent, Mexico and Colombia at 48 per cent, and Brazil at 43 per cent (Anon., 2017).

While movie piracy will be discussed fully in Chapter 6, its prevalence in the region for many decades has not deterred middle-class consumers from subscribing to PPV digital television streaming services not tied to cable channels, known as OTT services.

Digital distribution platforms such as OTT services are some of the fastest-growing innovations in the film distribution sector in Latin America, delivering film and TV content via the internet, without the need to subscribe to a traditional cable or satellite pay-TV service. The myriad forms of viewing films and television shows outside of broadcast and cable channels facilitates a higher degree of film circulation for those consumers without access to cable television, but with access to other digital devices. While the overall penetration rate for cable television in Latin America was 53 per cent in 2014 (Bernardo, 2014), by 2016, there were over ninety different OTT digital video platforms which make it possible to stream national films at home for a monthly charge. Currently, Mexico is in the lead, with the largest penetration of households who purchase these services, but Brazil is projected to surpass Mexico by 2018, with nearly half a billion dollars in fees (Anon., 2016a). Brazil's OTT providers also organised an OTT association, Abott, which was the first of its kind in Latin America to assist these companies in lobbying the government and Congress to defend their interests (Ozores, 2018).

Brazil's OTT landscape consists of smaller US and Brazilian companies, such as Looke, launched in 2014 and owned by Brazilian bookstore franchise Saraiva, Brazilian service Netmovies and Esporte Interativo Plus, the sports-focused broadcasting and streaming video platform; these companies are vying for market share against the dominant force in Latin America, US-based Netflix. Brazil stands at the forefront of OTT providers who are presenting more local content to audiences nationwide, thus competing with market rivals (Gruenwedel, 2014).

Netflix has attracted five million subscribers since 2015, and customers pay either monthly credit card subscriptions or monthly bundled subscriptions (billed along with cable). In 2011, Netflix announced the expansion of its business to forty-three countries in Latin America. Thus far, the results are mixed. When Netflix was rolled out in Brazil at the end of September 2011, potential customers complained that the catalogue was outdated and not extensive enough. *Narcos* (2015–17), Netflix original programming set in Colombia, has been a success story in the United States, but proved controversial with Colombian audiences (Peña, 2016).

In the case of Mexico, in order to provide sufficient national content, Netflix made a deal, in 2011, with megamedia broadcaster Grupo Televisa. A partnership was established whereby Netflix would distribute up to 3,000 hours of shows per year of Televisa-provided soap operas and other programmes (Prescott, 2011). By 2016, however, Televisa had removed its content in order to populate Blim, their OTT competitor.

To capture the more 'independent' film aficionado, Mexican independent distributor Canana (founded by Pablo Cruz with actors Gael García Bernal and Diego Luna) partnered with Netflix in 2011 to run episodes of the television show *Soy tu fan* (*I'm Your Fan*, 2010–). *Soy tu fan*'s first season had previously been shown on Once TV, a smaller, maverick channel competing with television mega-giants Televisa and TV Azteca, who occupied 90 per cent of the marketplace (Young, 2011). Reed Hastings, the CEO of Netflix, Inc., predicted that the company would lose money in Mexico for two years until it could build a big enough subscriber base (Fritz, 2011). Beginning in 2012 with roughly 1.96 million subscribers, Netflix has enjoyed the largest share of OTT VOD services. In 2014, the number rose to 4.85 million subscribers (Anon., 2014b). Still, in the case of Mexico, while Netflix holds the largest market share of the streaming market (with Claro Video and Blim commanding second and third spots), Pacheco notes that, overall, Netflix occupies 20 per cent of internet time in Mexico, with YouTube accounting for 90 per cent (Pacheco, 2017).

In the spirit of 'Any device, anytime, anywhere', which is now the 'ubiquitous network' for digital entertainment, Netflix expanded its platform offerings by updating smartphone applications (such as iOS and Apple TV) which support unlimited TV and movie streaming for Latin American customers. While the price for monthly service in Latin America (in 2018) is US$5.25 for basic service in Mexico and Colombia, 'snail' mail service is not available. Netflix took a surprising risk in entering the Cuban market, which has a very low internet penetration (less than 5 per cent access). Despite having access to underwater cable lines from Venezuela, which have been slow and inconsistent, Irish telecommunications company Deep Blue has pledged to install a high-speed fibreoptic cable system valued at $US350 million throughout the Carribean, including Cuba, to be functional in 2020 (Cubanet, 2017).

In 2014, the entire region of Latin America had a downstream Netflix traffic rate of 5.5 per cent, compared to 2.2 per cent the year before, which is to say that the region's internet usage is growing exponentially, especially in the larger countries (Roettgers, 2014). According to *Variety*, the 2011 launch of Netflix throughout the region helped galvanise prices paid for pay-TV rights in Latin America (Hopewell, 2011), resulting in the launch of new companies or the rebooting of OTT services such as Televisa's Blim, Mexico's América Móvil's Clarovideo and Globo. The end of 2016 saw the launch of HBO GO in Colombia, Mexico, Argentina and Brazil (Hopewell, 2016). Other regional players such as Mexico's Klic (Cinépolis) and Grupo Salinas's Totalmovies were short-lived efforts (Cornelio-Marí, 2017, 217). Grupo Televisa's Veo claimed that their content was the most watched in Mexico (NexTV Latam, 2013). In February 2016, Televisa announced that Blim would be a regional SVOD service throughout

Latin America, and later that trimester, Blim replaced Veo as the sole Televisa provider (Cornelio-Marí, 2017, 220). In 2016, it was predicted that these newer services such as Blim, HBO Go and a service launched by Telefónica, Movistar Play SVOD (which had expanded to twelve countries by the end of the year) (O'Neill, 2016a), could surpass Netflix's hegemonic position after 2020. In the ever-greater quest for content, Movistar Play reached an agreement with the large US multimedia conglomerate Viacom to include additional streaming content such as live feeds of Comedy Central, MTV, Nickelodeon, Nick Jr and Paramount Channel TV channels in 2018 (Aguilera and Brannon, 2018). Another advantage that national providers have over Netflix is that only a quarter of Latin Americans use credit cards (required for Netflix), whereas national companies are finding ways to include subscription costs in bundled services which can be paid for with cash (O'Neill, 2016b).

Another, perhaps more ominous, threat to online streaming and VOD services is the high prevalence of movie piracy in Latin America. One website which has been very popular for video streaming is Cuevana (now Cuevana2 and Cuevana3), which operates out of Argentina. While these websites solely provide web links to illegally downloadable movies, they actually deliver good-quality programming. Indeed, some would argue that the catalogue is more extensive than Netflix. However, Cuevana is not a legal company and does not have to comply with the same standards that govern legal businesses such as Netflix, which must compete financially with file-sharing companies in the region. Even though Cuevana is one of the most trafficked sites online for streaming videos, it may not pose a threat to Netflix, given that the latter is a constantly expanding multimillion-dollar business, reaching out to not only Latin America, but to Spain and other parts of Europe as well (González, 2012).

Two issues – video piracy online and the general distrust in Latin America about providing credit card information over the internet – probably mean that more VOD will be accessed via cable television rather than streaming on the computer. This is evidenced in Argentina by the expansion of VOD services by traditional telecoms companies such as Telefónica Argentina and Telecom Argentina, which stream video distribution nationally, and, in Brazil, by satellite broadcaster Sky and cable company Net (Hopewell, 2011).

As mentioned in Chapter 2, distributor Leopoldo Jímenez, head of Nueva Era distribution, cites that over 100 films were produced in Mexico in 2015, but not enough distributors were picking them up (de la Fuente, 2015). Thus, in 2014, when only 10 per cent of Mexican films were shown in cinemas (down 2 per cent from the national box-office figures a year earlier), film institute IMCINE devised a digital distribution online platform called Filminlatino, ensuring that more Mexican films would reach an audience. Filminlatino was created in partnership with the Spanish VOD service Filmin, which has a catalogue of 1,900 titles, 600 of them from Mexico and Latin America. While 300 Mexican films (90 features, the remaining shorts) on the website are free under the GratisMx programme, there is also a subscription service for viewing a larger selection of cinema from all over the world. These films, both free and paid, may only be accessed by those living in Mexico. In 2018, there were over 70,000 subscribers, according to their website.

In an era where digital video streaming services are outpacing DVD sales and are projected to surpass movie theatre sales in the United States by 2017 (Huddleston, Jr, 2015), this was a timely move by IMCINE, assuming that US trends are eventually adopted by middle- to upper-middle-class audiences throughout Latin America. Finally, this platform also seeks to join forces with film festivals throughout Mexico so that simultaneous premieres occur, creating more access to audiences, and aiding in the commercialisation of these films via digital platforms (IMCINE, 2015).

NEW REGIONAL MODELS: RETINA LATINA

In March, 2016, a new digital online platform was officially launched at two film festivals: on 4 March at the Festival de Cine Internacional Cartagena de Indias (Cartagena International Film Festival), Colombia (FICCI), and four days later at the Festival de Cine Internacional Guadalajara (Guadalajara International Film Festival), Mexico (FICG). Retina Latina (www.retinalatina.com) is an online streaming platform which screens national films sponsored by six film institutes (Bolivia, Ecuador, Colombia, Mexico, Peru and Uruguay). The players worked collaboratively to reach intellectual property agreements, allowing viewers in the region to obtain, free of charge, web access to a library of feature-length films and documentaries. This website is available only in other Latin American countries, not in the US due to intellectual property restrictions. Jaime Rodríguez, who runs the platform, said that films from the region faced too many bottlenecks when trying to screen films in predominantly US-owned movie theatres, and were also obstructed by national theatre chains more interested in high-budget, light entertainment fare (Rodríguez, 2016). These independent arthouse films are typically lower budget. It is difficult to view them outside their home countries, and to screen at the occasional film festival. This way, through agreements mainly with film producers but also with state film institutes, Retina Latina films find an optimal, digital space in which to circulate outside of movie theatres. Other countries in Latin America such as Argentina and Brazil may join the network later, if agreements between agents in the two countries can be resolved.

CANAL O CUBO

Brazil currently has an independent online distribution platform, Canal O Cubo (http://www.canalocubo.com/). Co-founded in 2014 by filmmaker Fariano Cafure, who, frustrated with the reality that most independent filmmakers were never being shown on the big screen, estimated that 90 per cent of films do not get the audience they would like (Brown, 2014). Cafure and co-founder Thiago Fraga offer this free service to any filmmaker who would like to upload their short or feature-length film, provided it is licensed under one of the six licenses available from Creative Commons. The filmmaker retains the rights and the movie does not need to be brand new (Brown, 2014).

One reason that this model works well is that Brazil is one of the Latin American countries with the greatest number of internet users, accounting for one-third of all users in the region (Anon., 2014c). Chile, in contrast, has the highest per capita internet penetration, with two-thirds of the population having access to the internet in 2016. Argentina follows, with 70 per cent penetration (Anon., 2016c).

FILM DISTRIBUTORS IN LATIN AMERICA AND THE UNITED STATES: CASE STUDIES

Latin American films are distributed throughout Latin America and the US, or Latin America and elsewhere, using various marketing strategies. The following case studies examine the different distribution trajectories of two films, each characterised by varying funding mechanisms and distribution. One, *No se aceptan devoluciones*, a Mexican blockbuster hit, broke records in both Mexico and the United States. The other, Argentine/Spanish/Norwegian/French co-production *Wakolda* targeted European distribution and has been studied by film market analyst and journalist Sydney Levine for her blog SydneysBuzz.com.

No Se Aceptan Devoluciones (Instructions Not Included 2013)

This film was written by and stars Eugenio Derbez, a well-known comedian, Televisa television star and voiceover artist (known as the voice of the donkey in the Latin American version of *Shrek* [2001] and *Shrek 2* [2004]). Derbez has a loyal audience following, and his wit captured the hearts and minds of a significant number of Mexican moviegoers. The film broke the record for the biggest opening weekend with proceeds of US$11.6 million. Televisa-owned Videocine released the film with 1,500 prints, an enormous investment; Mexican films are usually released with 300 film prints (Hecht, 2013b). Videocine worked with the Mexican theatre chain Cinépolis's satellite system, which increased the capacity of the 1,500 prints onto 2,500 screens. This represents a new release pattern for Mexican film (Levine, 2014a). The film, spoken in Spanish and English, focuses on Mexican–US migration, making it ripe material for a cross-border hit. The distribution company, Pantelion, is itself a cross-border collaboration between Televisa and Lionsgate. The film became one of the biggest hits in Mexico for 2013, and was the most watched Spanish-language film of all time in the United States.

To promote *No se aceptan devoluciones* in the US, Derbez was featured on Univision morning and evening talk shows the week before its release; the film travelled to five cities in major US Hispanic markets to reach its demographic. In hopes of targeting Latinx families, the marketing strategy also included outdoor media, radio and promotional tie-ins with Jarritos soda. In total, about US$5 million was spent on marketing a movie which cost about the same amount to produce (Erazo, 2014). *Instructions* went on to earn US$44.5 million, making it the highest-grossing Spanish-language film ever in the US, topping Guillermo del Toro's *Pan's Labyrinth* and the adaptation of Laura Esquivel's popular novel *Like Water for Chocolate* (dir. Alfonso Arau, 1992) (Erazo, 2014). It began its run for a medium-sized film (under 1,000 screens) with 348 theatres; after twenty-four days, it had expanded its reach to 978 theatres (Anon., 2013c).

US Latinx audiences are known to be moviegoers. In 2013, Latino/as comprised 17 per cent of the general population but 32 per cent of movie audiences (Nevarez, 2014). While, in 2016, the numbers were slightly lower (16 per cent of the general population and 19 per cent of moviegoers), the fact remains that US Latinxs are overrepresented in theatre audiences (MPAA, 2015b).

This demographic tends to 'turn out in outsized proportions for animated films and studio pics with Latino actors like the *Fast and Furious* franchise more than Latin American films brought to the US' (Stewart, 2013). According to Andrew Stewart, many previous attempts to directly target this substantial audience with Spanish-language films or with Latino talent have stumbled, possibly because these modestly budgeted efforts looked too much like art films and lacked family appeal (2013). *Instructions* was successful because it was a Spanish-language, family-friendly comedy with mass appeal, as well as a big-name talent with a large following (Erazo, 2014). Distributor Pantelion continues to seek Latin American films that could potentially cross over to the United States. In 2017, after a number of box-office disappointments, Derbez's *How to Be a Latin Lover* (dir. Ken Marino), starring an ensemble cast of Mexican and US actors (including Raquel Welch, Rob Lowe, Salma Hayek and Kristen Bell), performed better than expected in the United States, taking US$32 million in box-office receipts after playing in 1,118 theatres. The audience demographics were noteworthy in that 50 per cent were over 35 years old, and 89 per cent identified as Latinx moviegoers (Anderson, 2017). In Mexico, the film was an overnight box-office sensation, earning US$7 million over its opening weekend.

[Figure 4.1 Eugenio Derbez in *No se aceptan devoluciones* (*Instructions Not Included*, 2013) poster. Directed by Eugenio Derbez, © Pantelion Films 2013. Photo by Marcia Perskie. All rights reserved.]

Wakolda (The German Doctor 2013), by Sydney J. Levine from SydneysBuzz.com

Wakolda was produced by Historias Cinematograficas, owned by director-producer Luis Puenzo (*La historia oficial* [*The Official Story*, 1985]), and the father of the director-writer Lucía Puenzo. Historias Cinematograficas financed *Wakolda* as a Spanish/French/Norwegian co-production with Argentina and was shot in Spanish and German. The film was funded in part by the INCAA, ICAA, Aide aux cinémas du monde, Le Centre national du cinéma et de l'image animée, Ministère des Affaires Étrangères (France), Institut Français, Sørfond Norwegian South Film Fund, Programa Ibermedia and TVE. Its French co-producer, Pyramide International, was also the international sales agent (ISA), and Wanda Vision of Spain its Spanish distributor. Hummelfilm of Norway came on board as part of the Sørfond Norwegian South Film Fund's €100,000 grant requirement. Stan Jakubowicz, a producer from Venezuela, also participated. Argentine television channel Telefe was a co-producer, as were Moviecity/LAPTV. The Argentine distributor was Distribution Company Sudamericana.

The film was made in association with P&P Endemol Argentina and Cine.Ar. The television advertising budget invested by Telefe in its TV campaign was exceptionally large with 893 TV spots broadcast in ten markets in a five-week span.

The German Doctor, based on the director's own novel Walkolda published in 2011, explores Nazi doctor Joseph Mengele's life spent in hiding in Patagonia during the 1960s. Mengele gets involved with a family of two adults and three children; the mother is pregnant with twins and the eldest daughter, age 12, has stunted growth. The protagonist, the German doctor, conforming to a Nazi Aryan worldview, offers to experiment on the girl using growth hormone, and Mengele's nefarious fascination with twins also comes through in the film. European distributors Pyramide International of France and Wanda Vision of Spain signed on after Cannes selected the film for the Un Certain Regard section in 2013. *The German Doctor* was released on 24 April 2014 in the US by Samuel Goldwyn Films, who acquired the film after its Cannes premiere. Pyramide International licensed the film to over thirty countries, including Distribution Company (Argentina), Madman Entertainment (Australia and New Zealand), Los Filmes de la Arcadia (Bolivia and Chile), Imovision (Brazil), Cine Colombia (Colombia), Palmera International (Costa Rica and Panama), Wiesner Distribution (Dominican Republic and Puerto Rico), among others.

In Argentina, by its fifth week on screen, *Wakolda* had reached 400,000 spectators and held strong on seventy-five screens. It maintained an average of close to 100,000 spectators per week. Even though its release was much smaller than many other films, *Wakolda*'s spectator average per copy was higher than films such as *Séptimo, Corazón de León* and *Metegol* (which released with Disney on about 250 screens). *Séptimo* was released by Twenty-first Century Fox, *Corazon de león* was released by Disney and *Metegol* by Universal. This outstanding performance allowed the distribution company to increase the number of screens to eighty-five in the second week. It is worth noting that *Wakolda* was distributed in Argentina by an independent company, Bernardo Zupnik's Distribution Company, which also distributed *El secreto de sus ojos* (*The Secret of Their Eyes*, dir. Juan José Campanella, 2009). In the US, *Wakolda* grossed US$418,392 in eight weeks, showing in thirty-nine theatres. It has grossed US$2,600,000 in thirteen countries outside of the US. In August 2014, it was among the top twenty films on iTunes, an unprecedented event for a non-English-language film; it was the only foreign-language film in the top fifty that month. *Wakolda*'s release in Spain (with forty copies) garnered excellent reviews and an average of over €1,500 per copy. Its French release was with sixty copies (eight in Paris); its Russian release with forty copies. *Wakolda* was Argentina's submission for the 2013 Academy Award Nomination for Best Foreign Language Film; it won many prizes, includ-

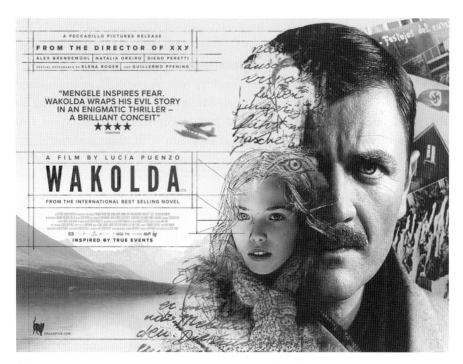

[Figure 4.2 *Wakolda* (*The German Doctor*, 2013) English-language poster. Directed by Lucía Puenzo, © Historias Cinematograficas Cinemania, Telefe, Distribution Company, The Stan Jakubowicz Co., Hummelfilm, Wanda Visión, Pyramide Prods., Moviecity and Peccadillo Pictures 2013. All rights reserved.]

ing the Camilo Vives Platinum Award for Best Iberoamerican Co-production at the Panama International Film Festival.

The case studies above highlight how some films cross borders with private or state film co-production agreements. Some circulate more easily than others because of transnational film stars, veteran producers and/or the support of large national or US film distributors. Others, after playing the film festival circuit and winning prestigious awards, with the accompanying networking, manage to disseminate their work via international distribution.

LATIN AMERICAN CINEMA DISTRIBUTED IN THE US: COMPANY PROFILES

This section describes various companies, many of them non-profit, tasked with bringing Latin American films, features, documentaries and shorts to various venues throughout the United States, including theatrical releases in commercial theatres and museums, films for the educational market and community screenings.

Cinema Tropical

In the United States, there are a handful of distributors who purchase the rights to distribute Latin American films theatrically and on DVD. Some of these companies are small arthouse ventures such as First Run Icarus Films, Women Make Movies and Menemsha Films. The largest and best-known US Latin American distribution company for theatrical distribution and educational sales of Latin American cinema is the non-profit venture Cinema Tropical, co-founded by Carlos Gutiérrez and Monika Wagenberg in 2001, and now run by Carlos Gutiérrez. Cinema Tropical's aim has been to bring Latin American films to US audiences in small arthouse venues throughout the country, in university classrooms and in modern art museums such as the Museum of Modern Art (MoMa) in New York City. Cinema Tropical has an educational mission as well, involving curatorial work, a blog and a Facebook presence which provides the latest news about Latin American cinema. The Cinema Tropical Awards, established in 2010, honours the year's best Latin American films. A selected group of film critics judge and praise the merits of each nominated film in an effort to lend more visibility to cinema from the region. Other award ceremonies have a similar goal; these include the Premios Platino, created in 2013 by EGEDA, the Spanish Producers' Association, and the Fénix Film Awards, created by the Mexican-based promotion organisation Cinema 23, which started in 2014.

Pragda and the Spanish Film Club

Pragda, the Spanish film club, is another distributor for the educational market. Funded by the Spanish government, this non-profit organisation exhibits Spanish and Latin American films to universities around the US. Founder Marta Sánchez explained that, in 2015, the four sources of funding upon which the organisation depends were grants from the Spanish Ministry of Education, Culture and Sports, the Spanish Ministry of Foreign Affairs, a private donor in the United States and through revenue streams (Rodríguez Sánchez, 2015). In addition to distributing films to screen on campus, Pragda also provides, for a fee, campus visits or Skype sessions by film directors. According to director Florence Jaguey, this model has given new life to films released in prior years. She observes that her 2010 Nicaraguan film *La Yuma*, about a female boxer, continued to be distributed to universities five years after it was released, thanks to Pragda (Jaguey, 2015).

Global Film Initiative

While the majority of film funding initiatives for Latin American filmmakers are European, Global Film Initiative, a US-based, non-profit organisation founded in 2003, distributed Latin American films (and those from other Global South countries) in the United States. The Global Film Initiative played a vital role in the so-called 'closed market' in the United States, in terms of theatrical and home exhibition and distribution. Although the organisation has had to pause its operations, it is worth discussing here because of the model it presents in the acquisition, distribution and support for filmmakers from developing countries, helping them gain entrée into the US market. The origin of Global Film Initiative, according to Susan Weeks Coulter, co-founder and chair of the board, began when she and Noah Cowan of the Toronto International Film Festival learned about the Hubert Bals Fund. Coulter and Cowan felt that this type of financial support to 'up and coming filmmakers' from Africa, Asia, the Middle East and Latin America was critical (Coulter, 2011). With no state funding from the United States, this fledgling organisation sought the support of private donors. The organisation's principal focus was purchasing the distribution rights from Latin American filmmakers with the goal of releasing the films in the US, either in theatres or on DVD. If a larger distributor, after seeing one of these films shortly after release in the US, wished to distribute the film worldwide, the Global Film Initiative would ask the filmmaker to reimburse them for the rights. Some film titles featured under this programme included *Una vida útil* (*A Useful Life*, dir. Federico Veiroj, Uruguay, 2010); *La mirada invisible* (*The Invisible Eye*, dir. Diego Lerman, Argentina, 2010); and *Cinema, aspirinas e urubus* (*Cinema, Aspirins and Vultures*, dir. Marcelo Gomes, Brazil, 2005). Furthermore, the organisation created study guides for educators who screen and discuss films in a classroom setting. Annual tour packages of Global Film Initiative movies circulated in various college campuses, thereby exposing college students to films that may not yet have been seen theatrically. Since the Initiative remains on the organisation's website, it is hoped that funding will be found in the future to continue this excellent programme.

THE ROLE OF FILM FESTIVALS IN DISTRIBUTION

The film festival circuit is an additional, important platform to encourage independent film distribution. Film marketing scholars observe that independent distributors have much smaller budgets for prints and advertising (P&A), fewer distribution outlets and rely on positive word of mouth, leading to limited release and presentation in film festival circuits (Mingant, Tirtaine and Augros, 2015, 5).

Indeed, film festivals have become a crucial vehicle for small, low-budget, independent and/or arthouse films, both for the opportunity of being viewed in a privileged space, and hopefully, as a result of that viewing, to secure distribution of the film within the global marketplace. This section will detail how, for independent filmmakers, film festivals operate as markets, educational seminars, funding platforms and exhibition circuits, allowing Latin American films, both developed and emerging, to access European and US middle-class audiences.

Film festivals, because they attract more independent, 'arthouse' films, have created a unique opportunity for film directors and producers to sell their work in a 'marketplace' that recognises this niche market. Marijke de Valck notes the counterhegemonic potential of circulating films outside the dominant commercial system of large movie theatre chains: 'In addition, festivals offered opportunities for national film industries to circumvent the American grip on the market at commercial movie houses … film festivals bypassed distribution, which served as a bottleneck for European film industries that were not cartelized' (De Valck, 2007, 92–3). However, it is also true that Hollywood studios, always looking for ways to diversify their portfolios and manage risk, have created their own speciality, 'independent' labels which also buy films through the festival circuit.

Filmmakers from the Global South, in order to facilitate access to European markets, apply for European film funds; many of these funding organisations stipulate that filmmakers also partner with a European producer. For example, the Berlinale's World Cinema Fund stipulates working with a German producer. According to French film producer Marc Irmer, this partnering is quite valuable for both parties. For Latin American producers, it facilitates access to exhibition and distribution in another country. For European producers, it can provide access to state funding schemes in Latin America, as well as to cash flow from national film institutes that offer credits or later subsidies. How well this works is debatable, but what it does demonstrate is that the Europeans view some Latin American countries as funding sources, where they may not have in the past.

According to De Valck's (2007) research on the history and theory of film festivals, their role is increasingly to elevate their 'brand identity' by producing films from the developing world. The aim is twofold: assisting with the development of a film culture in Latin America (for example), and also having the opportunity to screen these new works when completed. For example, with the competition Cine en Construcción at San Sebastián (Spain) and Toulouse (France), both festivals select winners who have access to finishing funds, and some of them are chosen for the sidebars such as 'Horizontes Latinos' (San Sebastián) or in the open competition the following year.

Film festivals have now become fundamental vehicles for nourishing the health and survival of at least some Latin American films on various funding levels. It may be on the production end, with the chance of gaining script development or finishing funds; it may be the opportunity to give the completed work an initial screening. Resulting awards and critical praise could lead to a distribution deal for circulation of these films in the global market. This process applies to both standard arthouse fare, and to the occasional higher-budget films which have become showcases for Latin American directors, and may be programmed at Toronto or Cannes, or elsewhere. According to Octavio Nadal (commercial manager for Patagonik Productions), before his company struck a deal with Sony in 2001, attending film festivals was his best hope of enlisting a distributor. For example, Patagonik struck its distribution deal with Sony Pictures Classics when the company screened *El hijo de la novia* (*Son of the Bride*, dir. Juan José Campanella) in Toronto (O'Brien and Ibars, 2004, 42).

CONCLUSION

This chapter sought to bring together the myriad ways in which Latin American films are distributed throughout the region and the world, which necessarily includes the large companies, both national and US. A case study of Colombia's Cineplex, an independent film distributor, was profiled. Latin American films have been distributed theatrically within the region and in the United States through large and independent distribution companies. In recent decades, however, newer digital platforms are working to make Latin American cinema more accessible though OTT services that are similar to VOD.

Two film case studies – one a Mexican production funded by Mexican, Canadian and US investment, the other an Argentine/European co-production – were examined in terms of their industrial profile, their funding and the resulting distribution strategy. Free, accessible digital platforms such as those spearheaded by IMCINE and others such as Retina Latina (which is comprised of a network of film institutes that have collaborated to make national films accessible to all within those participating countries) work on various scales to create pan-Latin American distribution chains to circumvent the US distribution companies that continue to dominate the whole region.

5

Contemporary Exhibition

Across the region, there is great diversity among exhibition spaces. Corporate movie theatre construction is growing rapidly, especially in privately owned contemporary multiplex theatres. At the same time, alternative, lower-cost viewing spaces and venues are being established, lending greater opportunities for screening of national cinema. One example of this is Espacios INCAA (INCAA Spaces) a state-owned theatre run by the Argentine Film Institute. Similarly, *cines móviles* (mobile cinemas launched in Cuba in the 1960s), under the auspices of Ambulante, a non-profit founded by a team that includes Mexican actors Gael García Bernal and Diego Luna, have more recently flourished in Mexico, Colombia and the United States. Given the dearth of venues in rural and smaller urban locations, these newer exhibition spaces are crucial for overcoming barriers (including high ticket cost) to access films. These venues increase citizen-moviegoers' access to a diversity of film offerings. They can now choose from commercial blockbusters typically offered at multiplexes; national cinema in venues open throughout the year; and film festivals, which showcase national and foreign independent films.

These different modes of exhibition demonstrate how the ownership of movie theatres can impact film offerings. Movie theatre exhibitors have historically opted to screen dependable Hollywood fare, which benefits from a significantly greater investment in marketing than its national cinema counterpart. This chapter will continue with an overview of how ownership underpins the expansion of the major multiplex chains across the region, and then focus on Cinépolis, a relatively new player in the movie theatre business that became the dominant theatre chain in Latin America. While the chain's owners – the Ramírez family – contribute to the democratisation of movie culture in some respects (for example, by underwriting the Morelia International Film Festival), Cinépolis's film offerings mostly comprise the same predominantly Hollywood fare, despite the large number of screens (sixteen or more) available in the multiplex or megaplex configuration. Responding to this Hollywood film hegemony, the Argentine government has passed screen quota legislation which helps support and promote national cinema by mandating that these films be screened in theatres for a prescribed amount of time. Guiding this measure is the concern that the films made throughout the region are not always given an opportunity to screen in predominantly privatised exhibition spaces. Similar government initiatives are occurring in Brazil, Venezuela and elsewhere.

REGIONAL MULTIPLEX CINEMAS

Over the past fifty years, theatre exhibition ownership has predominantly been a mixture of international and national privately owned chains. Until the twenty-first century, the main operators were located in the United States, with a few from Australia. However, today, the major Latin American chains are Mexican. While nationally owned movie theatre chains have always functioned side by side with foreign-owned chains, the national chains have succeeded at obtaining the majority market share only in Colombia and Argentina.

Cinépolis is the largest chain in the region, and Cinemex became the second-largest chain in Mexico following the 2013 purchase of the US chain Cinemark, which constitutes the most geographically diverse circuit in Latin America with 178 theatres and 1,289 screens in fourteen countries. It is the largest theatre chain in Brazil, Colombia, Costa Rica, Honduras, Bolivia and Panama, among others. In Argentina, Cine Hoyts is the second-largest theatre chain. Until it was purchased by Cinépolis in 2015, Cine Hoyts was owned, for five years, by a Chilean company, and held a 40 per cent market share of Chilean movie theatres (von Sychowski, 2015).

Major Theatre Ownership

The following section will describe the major exhibition players, highlighting some of the consumption trends among international, national and independent theatre chains. In Latin America, national and international corporations typically own exhibition venues; small independent chains make up a very small percentage of ownership. In Mexico, for example, independent and small family-owned theatres account for only 3 per cent of ownership (Hecht, 2013a). Brazil, however, is a bit of an anomaly; although the five largest theatre owners represent 44.6 per cent of all theatre ownership (Cinemark, Cinépolis, GSR, Araujo and Cinesystem), the majority of the market share is comprised of small, independently owned theatres (ANCINE, 2014).

In Argentina, Mexican, US and Australian movie theatre chains capture the minority market share, yet draw the highest percentage of moviegoers. In 2014, 37 per cent of the movie screens, attracting 59 per cent of moviegoers, were owned by the four largest chains: Hoyts (Mexican), Village (Australian), Cinemark (Mexican) and Showcase (National Amusement Inc., US) (Rodríguez Sánchez, 2015, 7). The remaining 63 per cent of the screens, attracting 41 per cent of box-office receipts, were national chains – Riocin, Cinema Centre and Sunstar. The national chains operate only in the interior of the country, apart from large cities such as Buenos Aires, and 80 per cent of their theatres are digitised (Rodríguez Sánchez, 2015, 7).

In Colombia, the five largest movie theatre chains are Cine Colombia, Cinemark, Procinal, Cinépolis and Royal Films. The largest, with a 49 per cent market share, is Cine Colombia, founded in 1927. In 2016, it was operating in eleven cities with eighteen theatres throughout the country. This chain was the first 'early adopter' of digital technology (in 2007), and by 2010 its cinemas were entirely digital. Colombia also has various independent arthouse venues, such as Babilla Cine, as well as a theatre in the Cinematheque in Bogotá.

MULTIPLEX MOVIE THEATRE CONSTRUCTION
In 2011, Paramount's senior vice-president for Latin America, Jorge Peregrino, stated that the theatrical market was rapidly expanding, both in Brazil, with the fastest growth in theatre construction in the region, and across Latin America as a whole. This expansion continued, from 2,679 screens in 2013 to 2,830 screens in 2014 (Statista, 2014a). The growth in Brazil was justified by the country's relatively low proportion of movie theatres in the early 2000s, in comparison to other countries with sizable film industries. According to Xin Zhang, the top fifty circuits throughout six territories (Mexico, Brazil, Argentina, Chile, Colombia and Venezuela) had 9,185 screens across 1,252 sites in 2014, with 393 screens added in 2015 (2015). Growth has been steady, with total box-office returns in Latin American countries increasing from US$1.14 billion in 2005 to US$2.2 billion in 2010 (Cajueiro, 2011). However, in 2013, UNESCO researcher Roque González painted a less rosy picture of this same scenario. Speaking in terms of box-office growth, González stated that while 'there was significant growth in Brazil, Colombia, Mexico and Peru, others such as Chile and Venezuela saw only modest increases while Argentina and Uruguay experienced relative stagnation' (2013, 30). Both Zhang and González point out that even though box-office sales had increased in Brazil, this was due to higher ticket prices, affordable by an expanding middle class, and also to paying premium prices to attend 3D movie theatres (Cajueiro, 2010), an area of significant growth.

In 2015, box-office revenue increased in Latin America by 13 per cent overall, with Argentina accounting for the majority of this growth, at a rate of 38 per cent that year (MPAA figures). Though this bodes well for a burgeoning exhibition sector, journalists from the *Hollywood Reporter* observed that the vast majority of films being shown and garnering box-office revenue are big-budget spectacle films from Hollywood studios, rather than rarely screened home-grown fare (Mango and Hecht, 2016). There are an ever-broader number of options available for home viewing (television, cable and internet), on a variety of platforms (tablets, smartphones, laptops etc.). With this awareness, Hollywood studios are attempting to counter the home viewing trend by continuing to produce big-budget blockbuster movies, with the express intention of drawing in viewers enticed to a palpable, visceral experience on a large screen (González, Barnes and Borello, 2014, 58).

In 2014, Mexico boasted 5,678 movie theatres, which put it head and shoulders above the other countries in the region. Only 565 of these theatres are analogue, making Mexico one of the region's most developed digital theatre sectors. Other countries with large digital movie theatre concentration include Brazil with 2,830 screens, and Argentina and Colombia at 867 and 879 theatres respectively (Statista, 2014b). The proportion of digital screens shows that, in general, in comparison to analogue, they make up more than 50 per cent of all theatres. Colombia is the exception, as 879 theatres, or 96 per cent, are digital.

Compared to past decades, digital theatre growth in large- and medium-sized cities is expanding. The question is whether or not there is a correlation between increasing Latin American theatre chain ownership and the diversity of film offerings.

Does Latin American Ownership Benefit Regional Cinema Exhibition?

Even though Cinépolis, the largest movie theatre chain in Latin America, is Mexican rather than US-owned, the majority of multiplex theatres screen predominantly big-budget Hollywood films. Thus, despite the increasing number of regionally owned screens, it is still difficult to get lower-budget national films screened. Indeed, in Brazil, where a large number of theatres are owned by Latin American companies (mostly Mexican and Brazilian), national theatre ownership has not led to an increased screening of national cinema in theatres. Foreign productions, particularly those from the United States, continue to dominate film screenings in Latin America, while domestic film screenings make up less than 12 per cent in all countries in the region (Piva et al., 2011, 18). Much of the popularity of Hollywood cinema stems from the high-budget productions and the accompanying star system, so carefully cultivated for decades. Economic inequality is evident in the disparities in budgets for theatre exhibition film copies. A 2012 Argentine study reported that US films had an average of 62.5 print copies per film, whereas Argentine films had 11.8 copies on average (DEISICA, 2012, quoted in González, Barnes and Borello, 2014).

In her study of shopping mall culture in Latin America, Arlene Dávila interviewed Mauricio Vaca, CFO of Cinépolis, regarding the predominance of Hollywood films in movie theatres owned by Latin American companies:

The problem is that few films from the national cinema are rentable [profitable]. When programming films, you know what will work with Hollywood fare. You know how many films will be produced and the specifics of their release dates. But it is very difficult to calculate and determine which national movies will be released or have demand. With US films there's a lot more information. You also have franchises and sequels, proven formulas and well-known stars. (quoted in Dávila, 2016, 85)

As it stands, competition is very unequal between US films imported into Latin American theatres, on the one hand, and their national counterparts, on the other. Occasionally, a national hit will capture the imagination, but this is more likely to occur when the production company has a US distributor such as Disney, Warner Bros. or Sony Entertainment (a US subsidiary of a Japanese parent company). The distributor will spend considerable funds on P&A and have access to many movie theatre copies to recoup costs.

González, Barnes and Borello compare the biggest film hit for 2010 in Argentina, *Toy Story 3* (a US/Japanese co-production) with the biggest Argentine hit of the year, the romantic comedy *Igualita a mí* (*Just Like Me*, dir. Diego Kaplan, Argentina, 2010). *Igualita a mí* was produced by Patagonik, a large production company partially owned by Disney and Grupo Clarín, and distributed by Buena Vista International (Disney). Whereas *Toy Story 3* sold three million tickets, *Igualita a mí* sold 855,854 tickets, attracting the highest number of spectators for an Argentine film, and placing it eighth out of all films in 2010. Additionally, when the US films were also offered in 3D, a feature that Argentine films often lacked, they tended to generate higher ticket sales (2014, 71). Thus, nationally or regionally owned movie theatres may bring financial gains to their countries, but they do not necessarily translate into more opportunities for national cinema exhibition.

Case Study: Cinépolis

Mexico stands out in the area of film exhibition infrastructure. According to MPAA global box-office statistics, in 2015 Mexico ranked eleventh in the world and had the largest market in Latin America with US$900 million ticket sales; this was followed, regionally, by Brazil with US$800 million, and Argentina with US$200 million (MPAA, 2015b). Owned and operated by the Ramírez family, the Mexican chain Cinépolis is the largest in Latin America and the fourth largest in the world. The chain consists of 205 theatres in sixty-five cities across Mexico, and more than 230 movie theatres and 3,000 screens worldwide, with a presence in Guatemala, El Salvador, Costa Rica, Panama, Colombia, Brazil, Peru, India and the US (2014 figures).

The history of Cinépolis began in 1949 when Enrique Ramírez Miguel entered the exhibition business in the city of Morelia. By 1956, he had built the Cinema Morelia and would team up soon thereafter with his father and another family, the Alarcóns, in the construction of twenty-three widescreen movie theatres. This group became the first independent cinema operator in Mexico, and remained so until 1971, when the company was sold to the Mexican government (Fuchs, 2013). The business went through various configurations until it became the Morelia-based family operation known as Cinépolis or 'Cinema City'. The founder's grandson, Alejandro Ramírez Magaña, is the current CEO; Alejandro's father is the chairman of the board. Due to the company's involvement in various philanthropic causes in a manner akin to the Bill Gates family foundation, Alejandro's brother and board member, Enrique Ramírez Magaña, has become a public figure in film festival circles. As well as making large contributions to medical research, the family is the main sponsor of the Festival Internacional de Cine en Morelia (The Morelia International Film Festival).

In addition to its fame as the largest chain of theatres in Latin America, Cinépolis is also distinctive for offering high-end movie-viewing experiences; they were the first to open VIP luxury theatres and are now the largest owner of such venues in the world. Cinépolis is also known for its quest for technological innovation. In 2017, the company owned 4,973 theatres spread across twenty-two countries, including the United States, and has most recently opened venues in India and Brazil. In the same year, Cinépolis opened 601 theatres in twenty-two countries around the world.

As previously mentioned, one of Cinépolis' hallmarks is its high concentration of investment in theatres, both in large cities but also in urban areas with populations of 50,000 to 100,000, usually conurbations with a moviegoing population but few theatres (Tucker, 2013). According to the company's CEO, 'it took us 31 years to reach 1,000 screens' by 2003, 'only six to reach another 1,000, and another short three years to get to 3,000 screens just last year [2012]' (Fuchs, 2013). The rapid expansion of movie theatres across Mexico is in large part the result of Cinépolis' efforts to appeal to higher-income filmgoers. Part of this strategy involves providing a luxury experience (fewer seats and more legroom) and being an early adopter of cutting-edge technology. Cinépolis was the first company to introduce the multiplex format to Mexico; in the 1990s, to install stadium seating; and in the early 2000s, to introduce the first IMAX screens in commercial multiplexes, at the same time developing their own large-format screen concept, Cinépolis Macro XE. Cinépolis also operates digital cinemas and was the first to bring 3D to Mexico. By 2013, it was still the only cinema chain in Latin America featuring 4D, a technology similar to 3D but with the addition of enhanced sensory experiences such as wind and dry ice.

3D Technology

3D movie exhibition is a relatively recent addition to digital theatre offerings. At the time of writing, this technology, despite elevated ticket prices (costs range from an extra US$2 to US$5 per ticket), has been successful at drawing in moviegoers in the United States and Europe. In the US, the number of 3D-capable screens increased tenfold over four years (2008–14) (MPAA, 2012). In contrast, in Latin America, because the upgrading of screens can cost roughly US$200,000, the change has been much slower. To help subsidise the transition to digital 3D, digital theatre owners are seeking out corporate partnerships. Coca-Cola sponsored Cinemark's first 3D screen in Buenos Aires, and cellphone operator Movistar teamed up with Hoyts General Cinemas to sponsor a screen in Santiago (Newbery, 2008). In 2009, six Guatemalan movie theatres with 3D technology were unveiled to the tune of US$2.5 million (Anon., 2009a). One year later, Cinépolis and national theatre circuit Alba teamed up to open new businesses in Guatemala by taking advantage of the relative lack of entertainment centres outside the metropolitan areas. (Anon., 2010c).

The conversion of a 2D film into 3D is a technological process which adds an additional 5–25 per cent to film production costs. Moreover, viewers must wear dark polarised glasses in the theatres. By 2008, when theatres in most of the industrialised world had 3D capability, Latin American theatres did not. At that time, with only some fifty movie screens converted to 3D-capable projectors, critics predicted that a proliferation of adapted screens would not be forthcoming. According to US studio executives, 'currency fluctuations and regional economics remain the overriding factors shaping Latin American box office territory by territory' (DiOrio, 2008). Four years later, with an improved economic landscape in countries such as Brazil and Mexico, investors were rethinking the negative 2008 forecast for 3D theatres. By 2011, Brazil had the most number of 3D theatres at 467, while Argentina had a meagre 80. In 2012, a total of 2,600 out of 10,315 throughout the region were 3D-capable (MPAA, 2012). In terms of Latin American 3D film production, film industries scholar Roque González noted that the first Latin American 3D full-length animated movie, *Piratas en el Callao* (*Pirates of Callao*), was made in 2004 by the Peruvian director Eduardo Shuldt. A wave of 3D films was later released between the end of 2009 and 2011. Examples include *Brasil animado* (*Animated Brazil*, dir. Mariana Caltabiano, Brazil, 2011), *Brijes* (*Guardians of the Lost Code*, dir. Benito Fernández, Mexico, 2010) and *Pequeñas voces* (*Little Voices*, dirs. Jairo Eduardo Carrillo, Óscar Andrade, Colombia, 2011); There have also been Mexican/Argentine co-productions such as *Top Cat* (dir. Alberto Mar, 2011) (a remake of the very popular Hanna-Barbera cartoon), *Boogie el aceitoso* (*Boogie*, dir. Gustavo Cova, 2009) and *Gaturro* (dir. Gustavo Cova, 2010), both adaptations of

Argentine comics (González, 2011). Exemplifying the transnational crossings and circulation typically part of the production and circulation of Latin American cinema, the Mexican 3D animated feature film *El gran milagro* (*The Greatest Miracle*) about Catholic mass, produced by Dos Corazones Films, travelled to El Paso, Texas, and select cities in December 2011. The film's director Bruce Morris had also worked on some of Disney's well-known animated movies, including *Finding Nemo* (dirs. Andrew Stanton, Lee Unkrich, 2003), *The Little Mermaid* (dirs. Ron Clements, John Musker, 1989) and *Pocahontas* (dirs. Mike Gabriel, Eric Goldberg, 1995) (Anon., 2011). Thus, while the film was produced solely with Mexican funds, it was exhibited with great success in both the domestic market and later in the United States.

4DX Technology

The emergence of 4DX technology constitutes an additional attempt to draw moviegoers into theatres. Developed by the South Korean company CJ Group, 4D combines 3D visuals with a range of bodily and sensorial effects designed to enhance the viewer's experience. These special features – moving and vibrating seats; strobe lighting; jets of air or water, mist, wind, fog or smoke; bubbles and aromas drawn from a collection of 1,000 different scents – are programmed into a 4DX track which controls their timed release while the film is playing (Tucker, 2013). In addition to Cinépolis' 28 4DX theatres (2017 figures) in Guatemala, Costa Rica, Brazil, Colombia, Peru and even India, theatre chains such as Cine Colombia, Venezuela's Cinex and Mexico's Cinemex installed this technology in 2015 (Giardina, 2015).

DIGITAL INITIATIVES

Converting theatres to digital technology has been far more prevalent than the installation of 4DX equipment. Cinépolis' management successfully completed the process of converting all of its movie screens in Latin America from analogue to digital exhibition, investing US$300 million in 2013 (Young, 2013). Converting screens to digital allowed the company to downlink films to theatres, thus speeding up access to films throughout the region. The first film to be distributed via satellite was *Despicable Me 2* (dirs. Pierre Coffin, Chris Renaud, 2013), which was delivered simultaneously via the satellite network to 281 theatres in Mexico. Rather than taking the usual three to four days to make and deliver hard copies throughout the country, the downlink took a matter of hours (Dager, 2013).

While Cinépolis is an example of a large movie-theatre chain that has converted fully to the digital exhibition format, there are other independent, arthouse and smaller-scale digital initiatives, such as the Brazilian digital Rain Network, which created an innovative digital exhibition format.

Rain Network

Brazil is the most populous nation in Latin America, but it is very challenging to distribute films to remote areas because of the country's vast terrain and complex topography. Distributing films the traditional way involved printing expensive celluloid copies and delivering them to cinemas, posing a problem for those film distributors in Brazil who did not have the funds to strike many copies. For example, in Brazil in 2003, each print cost about US$1,350. Therefore, to launch a big film such as *The Matrix: Reloaded* (dirs. Lilly and Lana Wachowski, 2003) on 500 screens (modest by the standards of many markets), distributors would have to spend US$675,000 on prints alone (Anon., 2003). Enter digital video and satellite technology capable of downlinking films to digital theatres, and the software developer and founder of Rain Network, Fabio Lima, who used this process to implement digital technology on more than 140 screens across Brazil, making Rain the largest digital video theatre chain in the world in 2002.

Lima, one of the pioneers of digital cinema networks, worked with a team to develop computer technology that could transfer large files and download them onto a server. This technology, called MPEG-4, downloads digital films quickly and is less expensive to operate than earlier digital video download technology. The films were then beamed by satellite from Rain's central computer in São Paulo to cinemas across the country. Depending on bandwidth, it could take as little as twenty minutes to send a ninety-minute film to a theatre (Downie, 2004). Rain paid approximately US$43,500 for the total cost of a digital theatre, which included computer, projector and satellite receiver, as well as conversion expenses that participating theatres would otherwise have to assume. Rain and its partners built and owned 25 per cent of the screens, while the rest belonged to independent cinema owners (Anon., 2003). These networks provided access to cinema in more remote places and concurrently contributed to technological modernisation.[1]

Lima's system, called Kinocast, was used to distribute and exhibit digital films throughout the country, as it was able to reach more remote areas like Manaus, in the Amazon. With Kinocast, Rain thus attempted to bridge the gap between the metropolis and outlying areas. The Rain Network downloaded films to cinemas via satellite and then controlled projection through a central computer working remotely on a virtual private network (VPN). This method saved distributors hundreds of thousands of dollars in printing and transportation costs (Bellos, 2003). Nevertheless, the Hollywood majors rejected this model because they saw the format as being too susceptible to piracy. They preferred the earlier software model, MPEG-2, whose higher resolution and longer download speeds prevented piracy. For this reason, Rain was able to distribute only art cinema and Brazilian films. The Rain Network prided itself on being a low-cost way of 'democratising culture' and allowing access to films throughout the country. During its existence (2002–9), this model expanded to twenty-six venues in the UK, Puerto Rico, Argentina and other countries in Latin America (Anon., 2008a).

By October 2008, Rain was operating in 108 theatres throughout the country, the largest number in São Paulo, which had thirty theatres. Rio de Janeiro had sixteen theatres, and the remainder were spread out among twelve other states (González, 2009). As Christofoli's research suggests, national films made up a significant proportion of the art films exhibited between 2004 and 2009. In 2008, for example, out of the 114 films screened via Rain Network, sixty-eight of them (77 per cent) were Brazilian. The following year, out of 104 films, seventy (73 per cent) were national (Christofoli, 2010, 227). In 2008, Rain partnered with Marco Aurélio Marcondes (former director of the state film distributor EMBRA-FILME, founder of Globo Filmes and, more recently, of Europa Filmes). They created a new VOD distribution concept called MovieMobz, which included an interactive component as well as a blog where users could register their requests for films they wanted to see in a theatre (Luca, 2009).

For Lima, digital theatres were not in competition with large-scale theatres. He stated: 'We don't want to replace the modern multiplexes. They already make money with celluloid. We want to serve audiences who do not normally go to the cinema, people who want to see films that reflect their own culture. Globalization is for the middle classes. The masses want local content' (Anon., 2003).

In the realm of television, this idea has borne itself out. Latin American communication scholar Joseph Straubhaar and others have taken note of the 'asymmetrical interdependence and (differences in) cultural proximity' between upper-middle-class and working-class Brazilian viewers and the television programmes they watch. The upper-middle classes prefer imported programming, which is also subtitled into Portuguese (depending on the medium), while working-class viewers prefer local comedies, dramas and other stories told in the native language (Straubhaar, 1991). Though Lima's statement connected working-class audiences to national cinema, some of these national films may have been more humorous and commercial, utilising the star system in a way that appealed to a broader audience than the more experimental, arthouse or 'slow cinema', which are not as readily enjoyed by diverse audiences stratified along socio-economic class lines.

By 2009, the Rain Network had disbanded. Despite its relatively brief run, the Rain Network remains an important example of the first and, for a time, largest digital film network in Latin America, and noteworthy because it did not seek to compete with the 'majors'. Rain was also unique in its time in that it attempted to provide access to affordable digital arthouse and Brazilian cinema for more geographically isolated viewers in Brazil.

The politics of film exhibition invariably expose the disparities between larger big-budget blockbusters, typically produced in Hollywood or Europe, and national fare, either of the arthouse variety or, sometimes, of a more commercial nature (although there are fewer of these than their Hollywood counterparts, and with much smaller production budgets). These disparities influence the daily choices that film exhibitors make when they select what to screen. Since Latin American films are given less screen time than US films, various countries enacted screen quota legislation to counter this bias (an area that will be examined in the following chapter).

EXHIBITION ALTERNATIVES IN URBAN CORE AND RURAL AREAS

While they can increasingly be found throughout large metropolises in Latin America, luxury cinemas target the aspiring socio-economic classes who want to experience the technological innovations typically found in advanced industrialised countries. As these cinemas are generally inaccessible for most people in the region, initiatives have taken shape to respond to the dearth of theatres, such the Argentine INCAA's programme designed to battle the 'occupied screen' effect in multiplex cinemas. The INCAA runs theatres which show exclusively Argentine cinema in older movie houses in downtown cores and other locales where theatres once thrived. The city of Rio de Janeiro has developed another model by constructing urban movie theatres in *favelas* (low-income neighbourhoods) in order to facilitate low-cost access to film culture and entertainment. Other initiatives, principally undertaken by socialist countries such as Cuba, Nicaragua and Venezuela, have brought mobile movie theatres to rural areas since the 1960s, and, more recently, the Mexican group Ambulante has successfully used mobile cinemas to create film festivals in Mexico City and rural spaces throughout the country and in the United States. In Peru, Grupo Chaski has a decades-long history of organising travelling cinemas throughout the rural parts of the country.

Film Institute-Owned Movie Theatres (Espacios INCAA, Argentina)

In 2006, Argentina's Instituto Nacional de Cine y Artes Audiovisuales (National Film and Audiovisual Institute) (INCAA) created state-sponsored movie theatres called Espacios INCAA, mandated through the federal legislative bill 1582/06, requiring the creation and renovation of national film exhibition spaces throughout the country. Exhibition bottlenecks for national cinema were addressed to a limited extent, beginning in the mid-1990s, when the INCAA invested in a few urban movie theatres to create a dedicated space for Argentine cinema. To date, INCAA theatres in Buenos Aires include the Sala Tita Merello complex on Calle Suipacha (site of a once-popular downtown theatre), the more gentrified Teatro de la Comedia on Avenida Santa Fe, as well as the Espacio INCAA Km 0, the site of the Gaumont movie theatre. The idea behind these theatres is to promote further autonomy in the screening of national cinema, as per the INCAA's purview, and not to be beholden to the whims of exhibitors, who by and large consider national films to be more risky and less profitable than Hollywood films. Additionally, the INCAA has tried to remedy the many closures of provincial movie theatres by opening them in various areas across the country. For example, in addition to theatres in Rawson and Trelew in Argentina, and Comodoro Rivadavia in Patagonia, the INCAA inaugurated a long-awaited theatre in the city of Mendoza in 2011, which was officially dedicated by former INCAA head Lilliana Mazure. In 2015, thirteen new screening rooms were built or renovated, bringing the total up to sixty-nine state-run movie screens. Many recent openings are restored theatres in rural parts of the country where neighbourhood theatres were abandoned. For example, the Atlas theatre in Termas de Río Hondo, Santiago del Estero, was refurbished as a cinema for local citizenry, and the Gran Rivadavia theatre, a picture palace of 1,400 seats was reopened in the Greater Buenos Aires suburb, having been shuttered for over a decade. These state-wide cultural initiatives support the exhibition of national cinema. In so doing, they also create a dedicated space for film culture to flourish, and for job creation. As of 2015, the INCAA runs fifty-five theatres throughout the country, with more than 18,000 seats, ninety film festivals, mobile cinemas and film competitions (INCAA, 2016). In 2018, the number of theatres dropped to forty-seven, still a significant number in light of impending budget cuts to the INCAA.

Urban Cinemas Built with City Funds

In 2010, the city of Rio de Janeiro funded the production company RioFilme for the risky undertaking of building a state-of-the-art 3D movie theatre in a low-income Rio *favela*. Concomitant with efforts to prepare the city for both the 2014 World Cup and the 2016 Olympics, RioFilme opened its first theatre in the Complexo do Alemão, a neighbourhood that had been the scene of clashes between police and drug dealers in 2010 (de la Fuente, 2011c). The ninety-three-seat 3D theatre has an admission price of four reals (US$2.80), half of the regular price in the rest of the city. Based on volume, their market strategy seems to have paid off: CineCarioca Nova Brasilia opened to 85 per cent audience capacity, which far exceeded their counterparts at middle-class malls. Selling over 160,000 tickets in 2010–11, it averaged a 67 per cent occupancy rate, and 91 per cent of the moviegoers had never seen a movie in a theatre before (Hopewell, 2013b). Two years later, the city renovated a once-classic movie theatre originally built in the 1950s, the CineCarioca Meier, housed in the Centro Cultural João

Nogueira, o Imperator, featuring three screens and a 400-seat capacity. Unlike its Argentine counterparts, this theatre screens mainly Hollywood fare, with the occasional national film.

Mobile Cinema Traditions

Mobile cinemas are an alternative form of film exhibition created to reach populations in both rural and remote areas who have no access to movie theatres. Whether by train, truck or, in some cases, boat or mule, mobile cinemas originated with colonial governments (in Ghana, Tanzania and South Africa) but also have socialist roots in the agitprop trains run by Alexander Medvedkin in the Soviet Union. The model for *cines móviles* was later adopted by Cubans after the Revolution of 1959, and subsequently by the Nicaraguan government in the late 1970s, continuing up to the 1990s. This form of ambulatory exhibition maintains its trajectory today in Venezuela, Mexico and Peru.

Cuban Mobile Cinemas

In 1961, the ICAIC created the Department of Film Dissemination, which was in charge of running the mobile cinemas. This department oversaw the process of training projectionists in the provinces, teaching them, as part of this process, how to think critically about media. In addition, the department would organise a seminar with filmmakers and film technicians every three months, allowing all of the mobile cinema workers to watch films and learn about the history, theory and production practices. These seminars enabled participants to gain and develop a level of education and expertise that they could then pass on in their screenings.

According to José Manuel Pardo, who oversaw the implementation of mobile cinemas from their inception until the 1980s (when they were replaced by video-theques or small video theatres), the first mobile cinema truck began operating in the province of Havana, projecting films at local schools (1971). This history is famously recounted in Octavio Cortázar's documentary *Por primera vez* (*For the First Time*, 1967). The film depicts how a Cuban mobile cinema van came to the geographically isolated community of Los Mulos, near the Guantanamo-Baracoa region, and showed films to residents for the first time in their lives. In Cuba, the mobile cinema vans were also used to entertain groups that could not afford to attend movie theatres. By 1962, the ICAIC's mobile cinemas had organised 4,603 screenings for 1.2 million spectators. By 1971, this figure had surpassed 25 million viewers, many of them first-time spectators. In a 1971 article for *Cine Cubano* magazine, José Manuel Pardo states that 106 mobile cinema trucks were in circulation, many of them Soviet-made, and some of them jeeps. The drivers were also the projectionists, and every vehicle carried a 16 mm projector,

[Figure 5.1 *Por primera vez* (*For the First Time*, 1967). Directed by Octavio Cortázar, © ICAIC and Warner Home Video 1967. All rights reserved. Courtesy of BFI Stills Library.]

a vinyl screen, speakers and other equipment. The driver/projectionists typically organised 80 to 140 screenings per month, working twenty-five days in a row, with five days off (1971).

Nicaraguan Mobile Cinemas in the 1980s

After the triumph of the Nicaraguan Revolution in 1979, the Nicaraguans adopted many of the cultural programmes that the Cubans had started, adapting them to meet Nicaragua's goals of national cultural integration and democratisation of the arts. A fleet of twenty-five mobile cinemas circulated throughout the countryside every twenty-eight days; they screened films such as Buñuel's 1949 comedy *El gran calavera* (*The Great Madcap*) to audiences like the coffee-growing community of Tepayac in 1987 (Lenti, 1987, 71). By 1981, the two million spectators reached by this mobile cinema project were viewing mostly Latin American cinema (Getino, 2006, 263).

Peru's Grupo Chaski

In recent years, there has been a resurgence in mobile or itinerant cinema projects, funded both privately and publicly. Given the relative accessibility of DVDs, DVD players and computers, efforts have been taken to further democratise exhibition. In 2004, the Peruvian film collective Grupo Chaski, together with producer Stefan Kaspar, launched a micro-cinema network to enable Peruvians to view films outside the film circuits in the capital, Lima. Kaspar, along with other members of Grupo Chaski, began the project by travelling to remote villages with a small screen and a DVD player (Ross, 2008). This initiative led to the establishment of thirty-two permanent micro-cinemas (www.Grupo-Chaski. org) consisting of a room full of chairs, a video projector, a DVD player, a sound system and a screen, at a total cost of US$2,500 (down from US$5,000 a few years earlier) (Acosta, 2005). Prior to each screening, Stefan Kaspar gives an introduction and then discusses the films with the villagers. The Grupo Chaski project was made possible with the advent of digital technology, and made necessary by the lack of movie theatres. In 1985, there were 230 cinemas in Peru; by 2005, there were thirty-three multiplex cinemas, thirty-one of which are concentrated in just five, mainly upper-middle-class neighbourhoods in Lima (Acosta, 2005). Average Peruvians have stopped attending movie theatres due to the availability of home video, but also because of a dearth of neighbourhood theatres. The average Peruvian is able to afford the micro-cinemas because the charge, the equivalent of 60 US cents per admission, is a fraction (seven times less) of the average price of a movie ticket at a Peruvian multiplex theatre.

Mobile Cinemas in Venezuela

In 2007, the city of Caracas began fiscally supporting the *Cine móvil popular* (Popular Mobile Cinema project), founded in 1996 (Circuito Grande Cine website, 2014). Spearheaded with US$250,000 in funding from the city government, and supported by the movie chain Circuito Gran Cine, a local bank, a supermarket chain and the Swiss Embassy, *Cine móvil popular* aimed to create, in the city squares of seven low-income neighbourhoods in the capital, a gathering space where people could see alternative and independent films (Marquez, 2006). In 2014, the programme was still active, and, with the support of other non-profit organisations, had the potential to expand to other towns and cities throughout Venezuela. Similarly, established in 1986, the Cine Móvil Huayra, directed by Juan Manuel Hernández, has had a meaningful trajectory, screening films from Africa, Asia and Latin America for the past three decades (Hernández Castillo, 2016).

Ambulante (Mexico, El Salvador, Colombia and the United States)

The non-profit organisation Ambulante exemplifies a more recent type of mobile cinema project. In 2005, Ambulante launched a mobile documentary film tour that has travelled to cities throughout Mexico (with a special tour to Nicaragua in 2011) with the aim of taking documentary filmmaking beyond elite venues and bringing it to everyday citizens. Ambulante's three-month tour consisted of exhibiting roughly 150 international documentary titles to more than 100 spectators, in venues with a capacity of 200 seats. The tour offered more than 60 per cent of its programming for free. This project was launched by co-founders Gael García Bernal, Diego Luna, producer Pablo Cruz (who formed the production company Canana) and Elena Fortes after the Mexican documentary *Tropic of Cancer* (dir. Eugenio Polgovsky, 2005) won many prizes at international film festivals without even a single screening in Mexico (Eguigure, 2010). They clearly saw a need to project films that were denied access in Mexican movie theatres. In 2013, Ambulante crossed the border and travelled to Los Angeles, where it screened films throughout the following year with the objective of 'promot[ing] social change and cultural transformation' (Johnson, 2013). Mobile cinema initiatives play an increasingly important role, both at the level of these non-profit initiatives, and also in the form of film festivals, which offer free outdoor screenings (on wheels) in various neighbourhoods, especially those without close access to movie theatres. Ambulante has grown to include spin-off organisations in El Salvador and Colombia. In Mexico, it has become the documentary film festival with the greatest reach throughout the country. Ambulante has also sponsored multiple educational initiatives, which include Ambulante Más Allá, a film production workshop for young people where they receive mentoring from filmmakers.

FILM FESTIVALS AS EXHIBITION SITES

The final topic explored in this chapter is the major exhibition and distribution role of the film festivals, especially when today's large, world-renowned festivals (Cannes, Toronto, Sundance, Berlin) have film markets and sales agents whose sole function is to buy the latest, most critically acclaimed films, or those with the most box-office potential.

Films are vetted by programmers and screened at film festivals all over the world: from national festivals showcasing national cinema, to the most prestigious festivals and their important film markets (such as those mentioned above, Cannes being the largest and most influential). These international film festivals deploy a bevy of film programmers to attend smaller festivals around the world and hand-pick films to screen at their larger venues. Thus, the film festival circuit is composed of multiple nodes with interconnected linkages, offering the possibility that films from around the world can wind up at prestigious events, where they will be exhibited, and potentially purchased for distribution worldwide.

Another function of film festivals is their local reach into non-traditional exhibition spaces. Film festivals are another mode of ephemeral exhibition as they offer a short-term venue for screening work, creating alternative spaces and constituting another circuit outside of the multiplex establishment. The

Colombian Cine en los Barrios project ('Movies in the Neighbourhoods') has a fifteen-year history as part of the Festival Internacional de Cine de Cartagena de Indias (Cartagena International Film Festival) (FICCI). In 2016, the festival featured forty-six films in free outdoor screenings, held in various neighbourhoods. These films were often documentaries filmed in poorer districts of the city, and the sites acted as a 'meeting place and communion between neighbours of all ages that, in the very act of viewing a film together, strengthens ties as a community' (Andrade, 2016). The most lauded Colombian film of the year, *El abrazo de la serpiente* (*Embrace of the Serpent*, dir. Ciro Guerra, 2015) was screened, as part of the festival, in the municipal women's prison in the city's San Diego neighbourhood. Other festivals with a similar outreach mission include Trinidad and Tobago, Panama and the BAFICI (Buenos Aires) festival, which offered interested moviegoers a selection of ten films free of charge at the Parque Centenario amphitheatre.

CONCLUSION

This chapter explored the current trends in movie exhibition in Latin America, comparing the largest chains (Cinépolis, Cinemex, Cinemark and Cine Colombia, among others) to the smaller national and independent chains. Digital cinema projection, which accounts for more than half of theatres region-wide, is a growing trend. In an effort to draw consumers away from their smaller home screens and into the super-sensory experiences of the movie theatre, new technologies, including 3D and 4DX, are increasingly being incorporated by upscale venues. A look at the now-defunct digital cinema Brazilian network Rain Network illustrated a historical experiment in digital downlinking theatre systems, a process that attempted to mitigate geographic borders in remote terrain where there are obstacles to accessing cultural products such as films.

The final section examined a response by various mobile cinemas to the trend of building luxury theatres prevalent in metropolitan cities such as São Paulo, Mexico City, Lima, Buenos Aires, Santiago and others. These luxury cinemas are becoming fully digitised and equipped with 3D and 4DX technology for middle-class and upper-middle-class patrons to enjoy. This new development has summarily excluded people who live in rural areas and therefore lack both the access to multiplex cinema, and the means to afford such a facility. The response has been a proliferation, throughout the region, of various mobile cinema projects, with the aims of democratising culture and offering residents an opportunity to see national and international cinema, both fiction and documentary. These mobile cinema projects, including Ambulante, the largest such initiative, provide temporary, free outdoor screening events at film festivals, and function as a form of education and community building.

6

Film Legislation, Screen Quotas and Piracy

FILM LEGISLATION

Many countries in Latin America have passed film laws to support and protect their film industries. Some of the industries legislate protectionist policies in the name of preserving their cultural heritage (for example, Argentina's policies are not far removed from those of a *dirigiste* state such as France). Others justify such legislation on the basis of economic development, grounded in the need to protect an 'infant industry' against larger film industries such as Hollywood. Chile, for example, channels funding from the business development sector to support its national film industry. As mentioned in Chapter 3, some film industries (Brazil and Mexico, among others) provide tax incentives to encourage the private sector to invest in film production. Emerging industries such as those of Panama, Puerto Rico and the Dominican Republic have followed suit. Colombia's legislation will be the case study for this chapter, with discussion centring on both a 2003 film law known as '814', and Law 1556, passed almost decade later, which provided additional incentives and cash rebates for foreign companies shooting in Colombian locations.

In addition to politicians who lobby on behalf of a film sector constituency, many other important players help make these laws a reality, including directors, producers, actors and union workers, who band together to create professional associations and put pressure on legislators and others for help in sustaining the industry. These groups have played a fundamental part in raising awareness of various causes. For example, in 2003, a group of Uruguayan producers, the Asociación de Productores del Uruguay (Uruguayan Film Producers Association) (ASOPROD), were outraged that the government would not pay the mandatory US$100,000 membership fee to the Programa Ibermedia film finance pool. The association claimed that they had thus far received Ibermedia funds that added up to triple the basic required contribution (amounting to a US$300,000 return on their investment). In response to the payment default, the directors staged a hunger strike to draw attention to how vitally important participation was in the Programa Ibermedia fund for the country's film production landscape

(Noticine, 2003). Though the strike was effective and the quota was paid, this financial instability continued on an annual basis. Finally, in 2008, the Instituto del Cine y el Audiovisual del Uruguay (Uruguayan Film Institute) (ICAU) was launched with a fund of 25,000 Uruguayan pesos, with a firm commitment to pay the annual membership fee to Ibermedia. This commitment was still being kept in 2017, when Uruguay contributed US$150,000.

Historically, film legislation has had a dual thrust: it has both supported the production of domestic film through state funding mechanisms, and has facilitated transnational links as early as the 1930s, when some Latin American countries created co-production treaties with Spain and other Latin American nations. In the 1990s, to help facilitate film production across borders, accords were signed between Latin American, European and other countries, such as Canada and China.

As discussed in Chapter 2, the state plays a fundamental role in maintaining film industries, given the unequal competition from the north. Film industries in the region form part of a national patrimony and cultural expression. Randal Johnson observes that cultural policies such as film legislation also help 'lessen the consequences of the presence of commercial mass media and the privately owned culture industry' (Johnson in Martínez, 2008, 34), and thus preserve a space for arthouse cinema, documentary and other less mass-mediated genres.

Though some film industries have enjoyed long periods of commercial success at various historical junctures, beginning in the 1960s, they have not traditionally had a long history of investment by the private sector. (Information on country-specific film legislation is available on the various national film institute websites.[1]) As Randal Johnson observes, 'film policies have developed over time and with different configurations – depending on the specificities of the national context and the structure of the industry – in order to guarantee at least a modicum of stability for future development and to ensure the production of culturally serious or aesthetically experimental filmmaking which might not survive if subject to exclusively commercial measurements' (1996, 129).

As discussed in earlier chapters, state bodies have approved film laws to help guarantee production funding and, in some cases, assist with distribution and exhibition. Brazil, Mexico and Colombia have put film policies in place, including domestic tax incentive laws, to encourage the private sector to invest in national cinema. In other cases, protectionist policies can include 'the compulsory exhibition of short films before each feature, the establishment of a certain number of days per year of mandatory national film exhibition … and the setting of a proportion of national films to be exhibited in relation to numbers of foreign films released' (Johnson, 1996, 136).

In her study of the politics of Latin American film legislation, Marta Fuertes lists three types of film laws passed in the region: '1. Laws that govern public institutions in charge of financing the film sector; 2. Financial mechanisms for production, distribution and exhibition available to partially assist these sectors; 3. Protectionist policies which regulate partially financed film produc- tions' (2014, 40).

Therefore, general legislation typically governs film institutes in charge of overseeing financial mechanisms, budgeting and otherwise. Other kinds of legislation can be passed to mandate how the state will oversee exhibitors and distributors' compliance with laws – for example, regulating the tax on movie tickets sold in theatres. Finally, film institutes adopt protectionist policies to act as a bulwark against the Hollywood behemoth. Screen quota legislation has been most forcefully adopted in Argentina, the latest legislation enacted in 2004. This chapter will also examine the politics of the screen quota policy and its effectiveness. Using the Argentine case study, it explores how film institutes either do or cannot enforce screen quota compliance, and how legislation has provided incentives for the private sector to invest in the film industry.

As changes in technology enable greater exhibition and distribution flows of films via the internet, satellite and other digital outlets, governments have been at pains to design legislation to combat film and media piracy. This chapter explores the pervasive practice of film piracy throughout Latin America, emphasising how some countries have been labelled more egregious offenders than others. This has been documented in reports published by powerful government copyright pro- tection organisations backed by the MPAA and other US industry trade groups. A case study of the Brazilian film *Tropa de elite* illustrates the effects of internet piracy on newly released commercial films.

Legislation in Colombia

Colombia's initial steps towards film legislation date back as far as 1938, when the government created a film branch within the Ministry of Education. It was not, however, until President Alfonso López Pumarejo's second term in office in 1942 that a law was promulgated for the protection and promotion of Colombia's film industry (Araújo Castro, 2005, cited in Martínez, 2008, 7). Ley 9 (Law 9) was created to formalise the sector and help filmmakers and investors create production companies in compliance with the law – that is, with at least 80 per cent domestic capital. This law aimed at building a commercial film industry similar to those developed in Mexico, Argentina and Brazil during the 1930s and 1940s. Film legislation was updated in 1972 when the Ley de Sobreprecio (Law of the Surcharge) was levied. This added a fee to the cost of each movie ticket to support the production and mandatory exhibition of short films (*cortometrajes*) in addition to features (Martínez, 2008, 7).

In 1978, Colombia passed a law creating the Companía de Fomento Cinematográfica (The Film Development Company) (FOCINE), housed in the Ministry of Communications. During the state-run company's ten years of operation, more than 600 short films were produced and distributed in theatres (Martínez, 2008, 8). FOCINE was not without its flaws, however. Critics such as Luis Alberto Álvarez (cited in Martínez, 2008, 8) felt that, even if the films funded 'deal[t] with important social topics or ha[d] entertainment value', their technical quality and calibre of acting left much to be desired. Discussions were held later about how to more adequately address technical training and preparation before supporting film production.

In 2003, legislation dubbed 'La Nueva Ley del Cine' (The New Film Law) was passed that led to the creation of the Fondo para el Desarrollo Cinematográfico (Film Development Fund) (FDC). The law stipulated that no less than 70 per cent of the funds must be awarded to productions selected through a competitive application process, while the remainder was dedicated to supporting training programmes, film preservation and the distribution of national cinema (Reina, 2014). This second law authorised tax incentives used for film investments, or donations to national film projects, helping investors and donors recoup some of the costs by reducing some of their tax burden. The Ministry of Culture regulates all private sector investment (both national and international) by means of investment certificates (Suárez, 2012, 187)

Furthermore, the 2003 Nueva Ley del Cine established revenue streams for film production in Colombia, mandating that 10 per cent of all movie theatre tickets are taxed, with this amount going into the FDC film fund, which is overseen by the state. While this 10 per cent tax has been in effect since 1932, other constituencies have also been obligated to pay into the fund. For example, film exhibitors must pay an 8.5 per cent tax on foreign (specifically, US) movie revenues. The amount of this tax is reduced to 6.25 per cent for exhibitors who screen national *cortometrajes* prior to feature films. Distributors pay a 7.5 per cent tax on their earnings, and producers must remit 5 per cent of their revenues to the FDC. These funding streams contribute US$14 million to a film fund and complement the 2003 film law, which offered subsidies and tax savings of up to 41.23 per cent to resident producers (de la Fuente, 2013).

Ley 1556 (Law 1556), which was passed in 2012, was specifically designed to entice foreign producers. It provided tax incentive policies for foreign shoots of feature films and TV movies where more than US$600,000 was invested in Colombia. As long as the foreign producers use a Colombian film services company to assist them, they can receive cash rebates of 40 per cent on qualifying local film spending, and cash rebates of 20 per cent on lodging, catering and transportation expenses (Mitchell, 2013). Moreover, the city of Medellín created a municipal film commission, which passed an incentive granting producers a reimbursement of up to 15 per cent of expenses incurred in the city, which may be combined with the national incentives (Proimágenes, 2015). Since 2013, some ten projects from different countries including the US, Argentina, Spain and France have taken advantage of Colombia's rebate, which the annual government budget funds up to US\$12.5 million (Thompson, 2015).

Law 1556 has helped to spur new partnerships, including the film *Cara oculta* (*The Hidden Face/Bunker*, dir. Andrés Baiz, 2011), the first-ever Colombian investment by Fox International Productions, produced in collaboration with Colombia's Dynamo Producciones, Spain's Cactus Flower and Avalon PC. To date, the country's only soundstages are housed in Bogotá, but the Colombian Film Commission, given their recent success in attracting foreign companies to the country, hopes to invest in cities such as Medellín. The Film Commission is targeting independent US producers, using as incentives the short three-hour plane ride from Miami and a well-developed infrastructure, including a well-trained technical crew, film lab and post-production facilities in Bogotá. Numerous trade magazines also allude to the fact that the Colombian Film Commission promotes 'film shooting' with the intent of supplanting the country's reputation during the 1980s as a site of armed conflict and drug war violence. Perhaps the recent peace talks in the country (though still not definitive at the time of writing) are one of the main factors in drawing such increased activity; other factors include the tax incentives and funding opportunities for filmmaking.

Ultimately, this newer landscape for film investment has proven to be a major incentive for film production culture to thrive, both locally and internationally. The Colombian film institute and its film marketing wing, Proimágenes, headed by Claudia Triana, have been successful at marketing the country as a value-added destination in which to film, as well as calling attention to its competitive incentives packages, which were unveiled in 2012 at various film

[Figure 6.1 Proimágenes Colombia logo.]

[Figure 6.2 Mickey Rourke stars in *Blunt Force Trauma* (2015). Directed by Ken Sanzel, © ETA Films and Voltage Pictures 2015. All rights reserved.]

trade events, including the American Film Market. Both producer Diego Ramírez and distributor Elba McAllister attribute the film institute's success to the organisation's transparency. In Ramírez's words, 'Proimágenes is reputable, free from corruption and cronyism, and current director Claudia Triana is well respected for her integrity and leadership' (Ramírez, 2015). These qualities are rare, as many other historical examples have demonstrated.

US actor Mickey Rourke became an advocate for filming in Colombia after he and several Australian actors starred in *Blunt Force Trauma* (dir. Ken Sanzel, 2015), which also featured Freida Pinto and Ryan Kwanten. In an attempt to 'brand' the country as a safe and suitable place to work, Rourke and Kwanten provided testimonials for short videos advertised on the Proimágenes Film Commission website. They extolled the high level of training and dedication of the mainly Colombian crew, praising the beauty of the landscape, as well as the solid and capable direction of the above-the-line crew, including the director and camera operator. These promotional videos operate on two levels: they advertise the upcoming film starring recognisable actors, and they promote the location where the film was shot, thereby giving the country some exposure while it circulates internationally.

We now turn to another form of film legislation known as the screen quota. The screen quota mandates that a certain percentage of national films must be screened in movie theatres throughout a country, thereby ensuring adequate screen time. Argentina has the strongest screen quota legislation and will serve as our case study.

SCREEN QUOTA POLICIES

Governments adopt screen quota legislation as part of a protectionist set of policies. Film industries scholar Jorge Schnitman characterises this type of quota legislation as part of an array of 'restrictive policies'. In his estimation, 'a purely restrictive state protectionist policy would concentrate on measures designed to impede a complete takeover of the domestic film market by foreign products by means including screen quotas, import quotas, high import taxes, and other measures' (Schnitman, 1984, 46). Schnitman specifies that a 'comprehensive' state production policy would include both restrictive and supportive policy measures, including production subsidies, bank loans and scholarships for training production crew etc. (Schnitman, 1984, 46). This terminology is useful in categorising the forms of support that various countries provide to their respective film industries, whether they resemble a European form of support that includes film loans and screen quota policies, or are less developed due to the absence of a film law, as is the case in some Latin American countries without legislation, including Paraguay (which is working diligently to pass a suitable law). Other state policies appeal to the private sector in a neoliberal fashion: for example, laws offer tax rebates to film companies, both on- and offshore.

The earliest form of a national screen quota appears in British legislation from 1927, mandating that movie theatres allot a certain percentage of screen time to national cinema. This protectionist policy was enacted to stymie the large influx of US product that was dominating British screens at the time and stifling the national industry – a trend which continues to this day. While the quota system resulted in more producers investing in films, this policy had some negative effects, as it prompted local producers and exhibitors to invest in some cheaply made 'B' movies known as 'quota quickies', taking advantage of the guaranteed venues in which these generally poorly made films were screened. In Brazil, during the 1970s, screen quota legislation led to the production of a large number of *chanchadas* (light, sexual comedies, mentioned in Chapter 1), which were made quickly and without much regard to quality. Yet the success of some of these comedies did provide the impetus for exhibitors to produce films destined for the silver screen. These exhibitors also successfully competed for viewers with television sets, as the screening of adult material of this kind was prohibited on TV (Schnitman, 1984, 67).

These examples serve to point out that, in some cases, screen quotas can actually be used to undermine national film industries when the films produced to fill a vacuum are of poor quality. But in other ways, screen quotas can be extremely valuable, as in Argentina's case.

A handful of Latin American countries currently have screen quota policies in place: Argentina, Brazil, Bolivia, Colombia, Mexico and Venezuela. Each country has its own laws on the statute books, but they are part of the same discourse: the quotas are created in reaction to the formidable competition that industries face from the large Hollywood studios. In Venezuela, for example, quotas aim to provide state support for Venezuelan directors and producers in ways that obligate distributors to pick up their work. The Venezuelan Nueva Ley del Cine (New Film Law) of 2005 therefore mandates that all film distributors in the country must distribute a minimum of 20 per cent of Venezuelan films out of the total number of films distributed (National Assembly document, 11, qtd. in Villazana, 2008, 168). A Mexican law passed in 1992 exposed its neoliberal underpinnings as it required that this quota shrink over time, thus weakening the state's commitment to protecting national cinema. The law stipulated that in 1993, 30 per cent of national films had to be screened in Mexican movie theatres throughout the year; this had dropped to 10 per cent by 1997 (Harvey, 2005, fn 265) and to 4.5 per cent by 2003 (Anon., 2009b). Argentina's screen quota law is one of the most stringent and comprehensive in Latin America. It serves as a case study to further understand the dialogues, debates and voices, both pro and con, in said legislation.

The Argentine Screen Quota of 2004

The earliest legislation mandating national film exhibition in Argentina was enacted in 1944 under the Perón government, when the 21.344 decree was passed to ensure that national cinema was screened in movie theatres (España, 1992, 48). After the founding of the Instituto Nacional de Cine (National Film Institute) (INC) in 1957, legislation was passed in 1961 to adopt a '6-to-1' rule which stipulated that for every six foreign films imported into Argentina, one domestic film had to be marketed and released in movie theatres. Enforcement of the law was delegated to Argentine distributors, who baulked at this proposal. Thus, when MPAA head Eric Johnson came to Argentina prior to his death in 1963, he persuaded the government to abandon the legislation (Schnitman, 1984, 39–40).

In June 2004, in part due to the leftist Peronist atmosphere generated by President Néstor Kirchner's administration, the INCAA (Instituto Nacional de Cine y Artes Audiovisuales) (which was renamed from the INC in 1995) spearheaded the passage of new screen quota legislation (Resolución No. 1076/12) to counter Hollywood's hegemony. It stated that movie theatres were required to show one national film per screen per quarter: so, for example, exhibitors of a sixteen-screen megaplex must screen sixty-four Argentine films per year. Another law, known as the 'continuity average', obligated film exhibitors to continue screening national films if these domestic productions garnered audience attendance of between 6 and 25 per cent of total attendance per theatre in a given week. This legislation ensured that exhibitors could neither arbitrarily drop national films nor change screening times midweek (Newbery, 2004).

This law was particularly crucial for smaller film industries because of the distinct disadvantages they faced in attracting audiences to their films. By and large, Argentine film producers do not have the necessary funds to effectively market their films. Whereas a Hollywood blockbuster relies on high-priced 'blitz' campaigns for a film's opening weekend, an Argentine film usually gains momentum more gradually, through word of mouth.

In 2004, a roundtable on Argentine cinema, focusing on the issue of screen quotas, was held at the Buenos Aires Festival de Cine Independiente (Buenos Aires International Independent Film Festival) (BAFICI). Participants who were uniquely positioned across the film industry revealed competing viewpoints regarding screen quotas. These included Bernardo Zupnik, head of the Argentine film distributor Distribution Company; Manuel Antín, former head of the INC, and founder of the prominent Universidad de Cine (FUC) film school; film director Juan Villegas; and David Blaustein, documentary filmmaker and then-director of the Museo del Cine Pablo C. Ducrós Hicken (Film Museum). Not surprisingly, the majority of filmmakers in the room felt that screen quotas contributed to ensuring better access to exhibition for national films, and to countering the 'occupied screen' effect. Of course, Zupnik, the lone distributor's voice, was adamantly opposed to the idea, stating that 'one cannot force exhibitors to screen films that are not good' (Zupnik, 2004). He framed this debate as an issue of quality rather than as a power dynamic or economic issue between Hollywood and the Argentine film industry. From a distributor's perspective, at least, a quota would hurt the industry as a whole. Former INCAA head Jorge Coscia, to counter opinions exemplified by distributor Zupnik that poorly made films are protected against consumer preferences, wrote in a polemical essay that the INCAA had no interest in forcing a film to be shown if there was little audience for it. Coscia deemed that doing so would contradict the spirit of the 1994 cinema law, which undergirds a system in which high box-office returns subsidise Argentine films. By forcing unpopular films to be shown, the INCAA would thereby 'destroy the cinema that it is trying to protect' (2004, 122).

In 2009, the cinema law was modified to guarantee Argentine films a minimum of two weeks' screening time in a movie theatre, allowing the films to build an audience. The earlier version of the law guaranteed only one week unless fewer than five copies of the national film were available for screening. The justification for this, according to INCAA account manager Mario Miranda, went as follows: 'We noticed that there was a type of discrimination going on. Out of 68 films released in 2008, more than half – 37 – were relegated to the "alternative circuit." On top of that, of the 31 local films that did reach commercial theatres, 30 per cent were removed from the marquee after the first week' (Miranda qtd. in García, 2009).

The INCAA enacted other measures; one involved subsidising those theatres whose exhibition of national films did not garner enough attendance
to reach the continuity average mentioned above (thus allotting more screen
time to more poorly performing films). A second was offering a cash prize
every three months to the movie theatre which sells the most tickets for an
Argentine film.

This programme has been effective to varying degrees. The most notable
challenge to its success is limited enforcement on the part of exhibitors, because
they generally favour screening US films since they usually draw more people
to the movie theatres and are more profitable. This tension illustrates differing
visions of the same cultural artefact: while movie theatre owners approach film
as a commodified form of entertainment, state and local filmmakers lobby to
enact legislative policies to help protect and stimulate national filmmaking as a
form of national patrimony.

The United Nations Educational, Scientific and Cultural Organisation
(UNESCO) has taken a formal stance on this issue by supporting governments'
uses of screen quotas in their efforts to resist Hollywood's hegemony. That the
effort of preserving and nurturing various cultural forms throughout the world is
characterised as a quest to protect 'cultural diversity' or as 'cultural exceptionalism'
implies that, even when inserted within a dynamic of trade, culture should be
exempted from being solely labelled as a trade good. Rather, it should be viewed
as a cultural product imbued with intangible properties that are crucial to the
cultural, racial, ethnic, social and local identity of a nation or people. Those who
support screen quotas have even coined the term the 'exceptionists' to refer to
themselves, appropriating this label from the rhetoric of 'cultural exceptionalism'
successfully championed by France and Canada against the United States during
the 1993 GATT negotiations. While the expression 'cultural exceptionalism' has
given way to the concept of 'cultural diversity' (see Frau-Meigs, 2003 and Moises,
2002), even organisations greatly influenced by the United States such as the
Organisation of American States (OAS) have supported UNESCO's declaration
to protect the diversity of cultures against globalising forces.

In his essay 'The Screen Quota: A Fundamental Step Forward', Jorge Coscia
concludes with the following statement:

> The screen quota is not a flag by itself; the real flag is the defence of our interests,
> our culture, our jobs, and our cinema, which is constantly cornered in our own
> market … Hence, policies are tools, they are not the ends but the means. The screen
> quota is a fundamental issue, because culture is essential to a country's project. But
> it is also relevant because debates and discussions continue to establish new means
> of development, sovereignty, and growth. (2004, 122)

While the screen quota may currently be functioning to the best of its ability, it is becoming ineffective, given that changes in technology are undercutting cultural policy tools, because direct satellite broadcasting, digital compression, VOD and distribution via internet streaming can result in even more porous borders, and open the floodgates to Hollywood's film and television industries. All of these processes 'undermine the state's effort to protect national culture' (Feigenbaum, 2004, 256). In the interest of preserving a national film industry such as Argentina's, communication scholar Harvey Feigenbaum recommends different kinds of subsidies to avoid overreliance on restrictive policies: individual subventions for production, an emphasis on distribution and marketing, and infrastructure funding for production facilities and training (260–1). The quota becomes irrelevant for wealthier film industries that use co-production agreements to circumvent quotas, such as those of the United States and Spain.

Other scholars are less hopeful in their findings. Entertainment lawyer and scholar Edwin Harvey cites various reasons to explain why the screen quota has not always been upheld. One example in Colombia concerns the 2002 law stipulating that national films had to be screened at each movie theatre screen for a minimum of thirty days per year (2005, 255). Problems, occurred, however, when the number of films produced diminished and was insufficient to fulfil the quota requirements. This resulted in the law being modified the following year to allow co-productions to count as Colombian films.

Other problems arose in Argentina when filmmakers expressed concern that their films were not screened as legally mandated. Rodolfo Durán, director of *Vecinos* (*Neighbours*, Argentina, 2010), wrote a lengthy report and complaint to the INCAA, documenting his problematic interaction with some movie theatre chains who chose not to screen his film. While this situation is not uncommon, the state-owned Espacios INCAA did comply with the law and screened Durán's film (Durán, 2013). Other researchers, including Banegas Flores and Quiroga San Martín, point out that Bolivian theatre owners do not uphold the screen quota laws because it is simply impossible to enforce them (2011, 34). In sum, while the notion of the screen quota is far from reaching full compliance, it remains an important tool in levelling the exhibition playing field for Latin American films.

THE INFORMAL ECONOMY: DIGITAL PIRACY IN THE REGION

Overview of Piracy

This book has centred thus far on the formal economy and legal 'above ground' aspects of the production, distribution and exhibition of both foreign and national films within and outside Latin America. Across the world, multiple reasons account for the coexistence of an informal economy alongside a formal one. Even if millions of people browse the stalls in the bootleg DVD sections of counterfeit markets, hidden in plain sight, these spaces are often considered to be 'underground' or part of a 'shadow economy'. There are other illegal means of accessing movies: viewing and downloading films and television shows online using download sites called 'cyberlockers' which require less bandwidth; or participating in 'peer-to-peer networks' (P2P), more common in advanced industrialised countries (Schoon, 2016), but also used, although in smaller numbers, throughout the region. Carolina Patino, in her study of Colombian documentary film distribution during the mid-2000s, characterises formal and informal economies as follows:

> From the point of view of government, the formal market belongs to the sector of the economy that has hosted the existing legislation to create enterprises which pay taxes and offer well-paid jobs that meet all requirements as well as follow government laws. On the contrary, the informal market has been seen as a sector with people who have businesses that do not meet the basic standards, who do not respect copyright legislation, and who do not pay taxes imposed by the law. (2014, 4)

This section will examine some of the ways in which films and television programmes are circulated within the informal economy, both as DVDs and online. It will also examine the response to this circulation by the anti-piracy forces, mainly the US film studios and US government, who pressure national governments to work harder to enforce laws prohibiting the production and circulation of pirated goods. As Paul McDonald succinctly phrases it, 'to combat video piracy, a range of legislative, enforcement, and technological measures have been implemented. Through authorising legislative frameworks to protect intellectual property, governments play a role in the fight against piracy, while police and other local or national enforcement bodies apply these regimes' (2007, 179).

If the term piracy is used to denote a negative poaching of copyrighted material, its meanings can vary: while industry groups in mainstream advanced industrialised culture view piracy as a criminal act, it can alternatively be considered as 'democratisation of culture' (González, 2009), especially for people with little access to movies, movie theatres or lacking disposable income. Regardless of whether one considers piracy an infringement of intellectual property rights (IPR) or simply as a way to gain access to a regionally or cost-prohibitive cultural product, it is a widespread practice that researchers and law enforcement officials have witnessed and documented. In some countries, allegedly stringent laws passed in Peru and Venezuela have been difficult to enforce due to budget cuts and a lack of political will. Brazil, in comparison, has tougher enforcement of video piracy. In 2004, the Decreto (Decree) No. 5.244 was passed creating the Conselho Nacional de Combate à Pirataria e Delitos contra a Propriedade Intelectual (National Council to Combat Piracy and Crimes Against Intellectual Property) (CNCP). The council's main tasks were educational campaigns such as 'Cool School', designed for youth; and, beginning in earnest in 2011, there were police raids on high-volume movie and music pirates (Anon., 2012b).

In 2010, UNESCO published a document, under the auspices of their World Anti-Piracy Observatory, listing the probable reasons that cause people to illegally obtain audiovisual goods. These explanations resonate with research on how Latin Americans perceive piracy. The piracy phenomenon stems from a diversity of social, economic and legal factors. Causes include:

1. A low level of public awareness of the laws.
2. A lack of negative social stigma that would make the public realise that piracy is a criminal activity. Members of the public often do not realise that by purchasing pirated products or engaging in infringing activities, they may be contributing to the spread of unlawful practices.
3. A high consumer demand for cultural products. The social demand for music, films, books and software is very high, which may encourage the development of an illegal market to cater to the needs of consumers.
4. Misconceptions about piracy. The public often views piracy as a means of having access to cheaper, just-as-good versions of works, ignoring the effects that piracy has on creativity, creative industries and related sectors.
5. Inefficient intellectual property protection and weak enforcement of rights.
6. Poorly drafted or incomplete laws, and weak enforcement thereof, directly contribute to the increase of piracy.
7. The high cost of cultural goods. Cultural goods are expensive to create, produce and distribute. The multiple costs involved before the product reaches the consumer add up to make the final product expensive. Consequently, poverty is identified as an important factor contributing to the spread of piracy. With such high prices for genuine products, there is a constant market for counterfeit, cheaper goods.
8. The difficulty of accessing legitimate works. Supplies of legitimate products in stores and libraries are often insufficient, particularly in developing countries. Technical protection measures in digital format products are also viewed as hindering access to certain copies and, therefore, as limiting the availability of legitimate works to the general public.

9. Considerable business profits for pirates. Pirates do not incur any of the costs related to the production of original cultural goods, and their upfront investment for illegal reproduction and distribution is minimal. Hence, the perspective of making, with little effort, substantial profits is another reason for the spread and persistence of piracy.

This analysis is clearly applicable to a large demographic of Latin Americans. For example, in a 2010 Mexican survey of piracy activities, researchers found that consumers aged 15–34 accounted for the highest percentage of 'illegal down-loaders' (30 per cent of those surveyed). The consumers were equally distributed between men and women and were educated (generally having completed high school or vocational school). The study also found that the prevailing attitude among that group was that it is justified downloading movies because 'it bene-fits me', and that, given the absence of national law enforcement on piracy, they would not be punished for their actions (Baz et. al, 2015, 41–2).

DIGITAL PIRACY FORMS AND PRACTICES
While industry analysts tend to lump together a wide range of practices in characterising piracy as a 'global scourge', it is actually a 'heterogeneous mix, where diverse agents with different objectives intervene … and where amateur practices coexist with small or medium-sized businesses, local or national, and transnational counterfeiting industries' (Mattelhart, 2012, 736). Piracy practi-ces vary throughout Latin America, depending on socio-economic class and geographic region. In wealthier countries such as Chile, Argentina, Brazil and Mexico, individuals download films from various websites on the internet either directly or interactively via P2P. In poorer countries, where there is lower broad-band internet penetration, physical copies (DVD and VCD) of pirated films are purchased in informal markets, on street corners and in bona fide shops in cities and towns.

In Latin America, the pay-TV group Alianza contra la Piratería de Televisión Paga (Alliance Against Pay Television Piracy) hired the British Company NetNames to study nine countries: Argentina, Brazil, Chile, Colombia, Ecuador, Peru, Paraguay, Uruguay and Venezuela. Their findings suggest that 789 petabytes (1 petabyte=1 million gigabytes) were consumed across three different audiovisual modalities of illegal streaming: Cyberlocker, P2P networks and IPTV (Internet Protocol TV). They concluded that, out of 220 million users in those countries, half of them were downloading illegal content from websites in 2015 (Peña, 2016).

Brazil is the consumer of the second-largest amount of pirated web content in the Americas with 1.2 billion downloads in 2014. Consulting firm Tru

Optik indicated that Brazil is only surpassed by the United States, which downloaded 2.1 billion files that year. Another consulting firm, SimilarWeb, reports that the top fifty film and TV series piracy sites received over 2 billion hits from Brazil – eight times more than the Brazilian Netflix site received in 2014 (Sawada, 2016).

While the majority of Brazilians are downloading material illegally, there is a growing group of former pirates cum middle-class consumers who are leaving behind digital piracy practices in favour of legal digital streaming platform services. For example, former internet pirate Fabio Pires, a 40-year-old from São Paulo who typically copied twenty movies per month to sell on DVD, ceased his activities because he felt that those who had the means to buy a monthly streaming plan should opt to do so. For 26-year-old former pirate Guilherme Toscano, from Goiânia, Brazil, convenience was a deciding factor in his decision to abandon pirating movies; he believes that by signing up for a monthly streaming service, he always 'has a library on hand, without having to search websites and possibly catch a virus on the computer'. He continues: 'The monthly fee is small and the content found on Netflix and other OTT services are incentives' (Sawada, 2016). These examples demonstrate how, theoretically, streaming services might assist in lowering the incidence of internet piracy among a small demographic with access to high bandwidth internet service. This phenomenon also supports the results of a multi-country research project on informal piracy markets in emerging economies led by communications scholar Tristan Mattelhart, who found that 'if piracy has caused the loss of potential revenues for Hollywood companies, it has also, to a large extent, enhanced the circulation of their contents in these markets – preparing, in a sense, the group for future legal exports' (2012, 747).

For those without ready access to broadband technology, unauthorised film copies are formatted and sold on DVD, or the less expensive VCD (which is often a cruder copy of the film without the additional 'making of' featurettes included in the DVD). In most cases, bootlegged DVDs and VCDs are sold at various outdoor marketplaces, on street corners and in stores; in some cases, such as in Costa Rica, these establishments are legitimate video stores. However, according to scholar María Lourdes Cortés, they carry both legitimate and counterfeit copies of DVDs. (Cortés, 2015). The spectrum of sellers is similar to the spectrum of buyers: some are college-educated young people downloading and selling illegal wares; others are street vendors selling many types of products, including counterfeit goods. And finally, there are larger, transnational counterfeiting rings, which have links in China and other countries where bootleg DVDs are produced in large volume. These DVDs are shipped to the United States as a transfer point between large markets such as Meave in Mexico, where sellers from Guatemala, Honduras and El Salvador travel by bus to purchase the DVDs and resell them in their home countries (Ramos, 2012).

Rather than focusing on the ethical question of whether combating piracy is warranted, this brief overview will discuss the piracy practices of various countries and analyse their varied effects. Bootleggers in Bolivia and Ecuador have cultivated strong circuits of distribution that are useful for national filmmakers. They have formed *sindicatos de piratería* (piracy unions) which give producers and directors a share of the profits when they collaborate with the union to disseminate physical DVDs, VCDs and online content. For national filmmakers, this means, in effect, that if they want their films to be disseminated throughout the country, they must negotiate with a group of people who pirate films but pay government taxes (Loayza, 2010, 160). This dynamic might suggest that the film sector in Bolivia condones piracy, yet this system has become a pragmatic, inexpensive and effective means of circulating films. This is a useful alternative, considering that filmmakers do not have large marketing budgets at their disposal and few distributors are willing to purchase the rights to their films.

While contemporary Bolivian films are distributed through the informal market via the pirate union, offerings of classic Bolivian cinema are limited and nearly impossible to find in the large open-air marketplaces in the city of El Alto (Jordan, 2008). According to the various illegal DVD vendors I spoke with in El Alto in 2010, the Cinemateca Boliviana (Bolivian Cinematheque) is responsible for this scarcity, as it has declared itself by law to be the official purveyor of these films, and has established fines for vendors caught selling classic Bolivian cinema. This dynamic therefore creates a dichotomy: most national filmmakers engage in business with a pirate union to exploit one of the few opportunities available to disseminate their work, yet the distribution of canonical Bolivian arthouse cinema is placed under the sole purview of the Cinemateca. Ecuador also has a piracy union which distributes domestic films, thus preventing the emergence of an 'official distributor' (Recktenwald, 2013).

In 2011, a team of researchers, led by Joe Karaganis from the US-based Social Science Research Council (SSRC), published a multi-country study entitled 'Media Piracy in Emerging Economies', which concluded that there were many reasons that explained why piracy was so rampant in the developing world. The study found that 'high prices for media goods, low incomes, and cheap digital technologies are the main ingredients of global media piracy' (Karaganis, 2011, i). Their findings suggest structural reasons account for why most people in Latin America choose to purchase a bootleg copy of a film on the street or download one on their personal computer, rather than purchase an official copy at a much higher retail price. Karaganis and his team found that 'relative to local incomes in Brazil, Russia, or South Africa, the price of a CD, DVD or copy of

Microsoft Office is five to ten times higher than in the United States or Europe' (Karaganis, 2011, i.). Given the fact that 'piracy' is 'a social practice that allows many members of the working classes across Latin America to gain access to consumption of a significant amount of cultural goods, which otherwise would be out of their reach' (Getino, 2012, 139), it is important to establish why formal institutions such as government, the private sector, the major film studios and technocrats insist on 'neglecting the social processes that operate around it' (139).

In Mexico, for example, illegal copies of DVDs were so prevalent in the streets of Mexico City and elsewhere that Mexican film distribution companies such as Videomax and arthouse distributor Quality Films teamed up with the MPAA to slash prices by more than 50 per cent and sell legitimate movies in the very barrios and public plazas that have served as Mexico's (and the hemisphere's) biggest bazaar for piracy (Bensinger, 2003). The studios had to concede that their DVD prices were prohibitive for the average person. Thus, rather than charge US$36 for a DVD in a store, they now sell the same DVD for a fraction of the price. Setting the price at US$4.50, these companies undercut by a full 10 pesos the typical bootleg's price of US$5.50 (Bensinger, 2003). These examples illustrate how the informal economy plays a grounding role in the Latin American formal economy.

Case Study: The Paradox of Piracy – *Tropa de elite* (2007)

Brazilian feature film *Tropa de elite* (*Elite Squad*, dir. José Padilha, 2007) was allegedly leaked onto the web by the titling house before it was released. Its trajectory is a testament to the ubiquitous nature of film piracy in Latin America. As the film became widely disseminated over P2P file-hosting sites, an estimated eleven million people (19 per cent of the population of São Paulo) watched it prior to its theatrical release (Novaes, 2007). As a result, the film's release date was moved up, making it impossible to schedule a television advertising campaign. Despite this, 180,000 people saw it in cinemas over the weekend (few Brazilian films are seen by more than 100,000 during their entire run). Moreover, its gross was 90 per cent higher than that of the opening weekend for the worldwide hit *Cidade de Deus* (Bollier, 2007). *Tropa de elite* became the highest-grossing Brazilian film for 2007, at 17,908,176 Brazilian reals (US$10,004,568), with 2.5 million people viewing it in theatres.

While some critics insinuated that this 'leakage' was a savvy marketing ploy on the part of the director and team, director José Padilha vigorously denied this allegation. In an angry missive published in the daily newspaper *O Globo*, Padilha explained how much potential damage had been wreaked on the film's release when it was made available for viewing and purchase months before the theatrical release. Despite Padilha's concerns, the leak, rather than having any

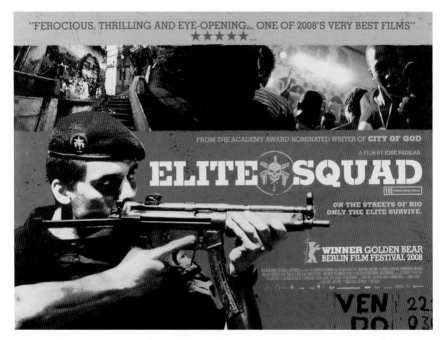

[Figure 6.3 *Tropa de elite* (*Elite Squad*, 2007) English-language poster. Directed by José Padilha, © Universal Pictures do Brasil, The Weinstein Co., Zazen Produções, Posto 9, Feijão Filmes and Costa Films 2007. All rights reserved. Courtesy of BFI Stills Library.]

negative repercussion on sales, actually worked as a form of advanced publicity. Furthermore, the hype over the film convinced exhibitors to double the numbers of screens throughout Brazil from 150 to 300. In this instance, the incredibly sophisticated informal network of disseminating *Tropa de elite* worked to its advantage. The film was also a critical success abroad, winning a Golden Bear at the 2008 Berlin Film Festival.[2]

Attempts to Combat Piracy

Piracy monitoring worldwide is principally undertaken by the International Intellectual Property Alliance (IIPA), an umbrella organisation comprised of five member trade associations (including the MPAA), and representing over 3,200 US companies which produce and distribute materials protected by copyright laws throughout the world (IIPA, 2017). Founded in 1984, the IIPA 'seeks to strengthen international copyright protection and enforcement by working with the US government, foreign governments, and private-sector representatives' (IIPA, 2017). Because of the high level of piracy throughout the world, this organisation earmarks resources for anti-piracy education workshops in various countries, and it lobbies foreign governments. Those efforts are conducted through the IIPA's work with the Office of the US Trade Representative (USTR), which is responsible for developing and coordinating US international trade, and for overseeing negotiations with other countries (USTR in McDonald, 2016, 694). According to McDonald, each year the IIPA makes submissions for consideration in the USTR's 'Special 301 Report', which is the annual assessment of foreign government compliance with effective IP standards and enforcement measures. The IIPA checks whether failure to meet such compliance obligations presents a market access barrier to trade, and, by creating a space for widespread infringement, impedes the growth of legal markets to US copyright industries (694). McDonald observes that 'although in many respects fighting piracy and liberalising trade remain distinct objectives in MPAA policy, equally they have become almost inextricably intertwined' (694). This is demonstrated in the way in which the IIPA was involved in the drafting of the Agreement on Trade-Related Aspects of Intellectual Property Rights (TRIPs), which is administered by the World Trade Organization (WTO) (694).

The 'Special 301 Report' is based on input from US embassies abroad and other government offices. After a review of more than one hundred countries, the USTR ranked thirty-four nations in two lists: some were placed on a Priority Watch List for violating IPR, while trading partners who have improved their status (in some cases from the previous year) were put on a Watch List or even removed entirely. Trading partners on the Priority Watch List present the most significant concerns, for the year, regarding insufficient IP protection, enforcement or actions that otherwise limited market access for individuals relying on intellectual property protection. In 2017, eleven countries including Argentina, Chile and Venezuela were on the Priority Watch List. These countries will be the subject of intense bilateral engagement during the coming year. Nine Latin American or Caribbean countries are included on the Watch List: Bolivia, Brazil, Colombia, Costa Rica, Dominican Republic, Ecuador, Guatemala, Mexico and Peru (USTR, 2017).

Whether on the Priority Watch List or the Watch List, these countries' governments and police forces were reprimanded by the USTR for not taking harsh enough actions against open-air markets which sell pirated and counterfeit goods. In the Argentine case, the government was criticised for not shutting down La Salada market on the outskirts of Buenos Aires, billed as the 'largest mall and black market in South America'. In 2015, the Cuevana website (discussed in Chapter 4) extended its reach when it launched an app called 'Cuevana movil', allowing users to illegally download movies from their smartphones. In 2016, the app was removed by the authorities (USTR, 2016a, 3).

In 2010, the Obama administration announced that, to increase public awareness and guide related trade and other enforcement actions, it would elevate the profile of the Notorious Markets List by publishing it separately from the Special 301 Report. The USTR published the first stand-alone Notorious Markets List in February 2011 as an 'Out-of-Cycle Review of Notorious Markets', and has published a list every year since (USTR, 2016b). In 2016, a special 301 Out-of-Cycle Review of Notorious Markets detailed how ten countries from across the world were listed as hosting the largest and 'most notorious' markets selling bootlegged goods. Latin America accounted for five of these countries: Argentina's Salada; Brazil's Galeria Pagé and Mercado Popular 25 de Março in São Paulo; Mexico's Tepito market in Mexico City and San Juan de Dios market in Guadalajara; and Paraguay's Ciudad del Este (USTR, 2016a, 18–20). These are monitored on trade and government watch lists each year, and annual reports single out various markets and online sites, taking note of those that have been shut down or penalised (USTR, 2016a).

Markets in the Ciudad del Este region near Paraguay have been associated with organised crime (USTR, 2016a), and have faced allegations linking them with terrorist activity (Mattelhart, 2012). By 2015, however, the Paraguayan government's cooperation with the USTR and IIPA authorities to combat illicit activity earned the country the removal of its name from both the Priority Watch List and the Watch List that year. A year before this shift, Paraguayan authorities, including La Dirección Nacional de Propiedad Intelectual (National Directorate of Intellectual Property) (DINAPI) took additional aggressive enforcement actions that included conducting raids, seizing merchandise from vendors and interdicting cargo at the international airport in Ciudad del Este (USTR, 2016a, 72).

Throughout the region, various anti-piracy groups have created mechanisms for combating piracy through their organisations, who work hand in hand with governments. One of these groups, Unidad Especializada en Investigación de Delitos contra los Derechos de Autor y la Propiedad Industrial (Specialised Entity for Crime Investigations Against Copyright and Industrial Intellectual Property) (UEIDDAPI) in Mexico, was formed by the government Office of the Inspector General to be a consortium of public and private sector organisations (including companies such as Grupo Televisa, Warner Bros. and Hanna-Barbera) that could lobby for added enforcement of IP infringement and other piracy-related activities. (UEIDDAPI, 2016). Unsurprisingly, some of these organisations have traditionally had the support of, or been sponsored by, the MPAA and the US Embassy.

In his research on piracy in Mexican informal markets, Mexican scholar José Carlos G. Aguiar argues that the incidence of piracy practices has grown, despite tighter IPR enforcement laws designed to penalise perpetrators for pirating films or television shows. Aguiar's conclusion is based on his study of anti-piracy measures taken during the 2000–6 *sexenio* (six-year term) when President Fox launched the 'war on piracy', involving more than 6,000 police operations per year until the end of his administration (Aguiar, 2010, 145). At a broader level, Aguiar argues that, after fifteen years of anti-piracy laws and programmes in Mexico, the sale of pirated and counterfeit items continues unabated (Aguiar, 2010, 145). He accounts for the failure of these laws by arguing that, as they are promoted by exogenous forces such as the IIPA (and, by extension, the MPAA), they stem from a legal structure that is based on global commerce and operates within a global neoliberal network of interests which are simply not a priority within the nation (145).

CONCLUSION

This chapter focused mainly on the legal structure regulating the film industry, including legislation to support film funds. Protectionist policies such as the screen quota were examined, using Argentina as a case study. The screen quota was instituted decades ago to help give Latin American productions an opportunity to exhibit and distribute their works, as these films tended to be at a disadvantage given exhibitor preferences for larger, less risky films typically originating from the United States. Though it is a system of laws that often lacks the financial resources to prosecute any violations of it, the screen quota has been most successfully revived in Argentina. The screen quota has been effective in some countries and contexts, depending on the amount of resources allocated to enforce the law. On the one hand, those countries with enough infrastructure and political will to institute screen quota policies have helped national filmmakers, such those in Argentina, secure adequate time on the theatre marquee. For the majority of other countries, however, there are issues ranging from limited supply of national films, thus making the screen quota hard to implement, to a lack of enforcement of various screen quota laws, thus rendering them an ineffective dead letter.

Informal practices such as film piracy, pervasive in the region, were discussed in ways that highlighted the United States' efforts to counter these practices, as well as different countries' approaches to the issue, approaches which often went hand in hand with the US trade group protocol. Considering recent changes in the film and media landscape, the integration of formal and informal networks in Bolivia and Ecuador illustrates how digital technologies help disseminate media (much to the chagrin of those who are attempting to contain or combat piracy), and facilitate lower-cost production.

Film piracy, in its myriad forms, is often discussed as a scourge to film industries. While official discourse on piracy maintains that it is an infringement of individual intellectual property, there are also examples where unauthorised circulation gave greater exposure to certain films, and also gave audiences wider access to films that perhaps they would not have been able to view in movie theatres or with official retail DVD purchases.

Conclusion: Latin American Film Industries

SUMMARY AND PROSPECT

Chapter 1 of this volume traced the history of Latin American film industries, beginning with the studio era in 1930s Brazil, Mexico and Argentina, where a private model of film production prevailed and the dominant narrative form was a mass cultural product aimed at an urban, wide audience. In the late 1950s and early 1960s, the rise of television and the increased dominance of the US Hollywood product exhibited in Latin America (which began during World War II, following the collapse of the European market) weakened the profitability of the studio system model, resulting in its decline.

Shortly thereafter, in response to Hollywood's dominance, national film institutes were founded across Latin America to help bolster the film industries. These institutions would assist in administering state legislation such as film funding laws which allocate monies from the federal budget imposed tax). Moreover, beginning in earnest in the mid-1990s, some of the institutes, such as in Argentina, would oversee the enforcement of protectionist measures such as screen quotas.

'Runaway productions', filmed in various Latin American locales, focused on the historic relationship between Hollywood and Mexico, with an assessment of the advantages and disadvantages of film commissions which promote offshore location shooting. Countries with newer film legislation, such as Panama, the Dominican Republic, Colombia and Puerto Rico, have offered tax incentives and cash rebates, resulting in increased traffic to their respective countries. However, the long-term effects have yet to be examined. Other state models of film production include a socialist model of filmmaking such as in Cuba and Venezuela. In Cuba, there was a shift in production funding strategies in the mid-1990s following the collapse of the USSR, marking the 'Special Period in Times of Peace'. As a result, the ICAIC transitioned from an autonomous model of funding (the film institute was essentially a wing of the state) to an international model, with international producers being courted from abroad to co-produce films. Additionally, the ICAIC also positioned Cuba as a low-cost site for foreign location shooting.

Chapter 2 showed how the state intervened to provide stability and continuity to a film production sector always in the formidable shadow of Hollywood. State governments throughout Latin America created film institutes charged both with managing and orchestrating film development funds, and also provided filmmakers with resources to, among other programmes, attend film festivals and screen films. Increasingly, it became necessary for film institutes to have a presence at film festivals, as they were tasked with not only managing their film brand, but also showcasing films that were invited to be screened at festivals abroad (and films would be screened internationally in coordinated effort with consulates and embassies abroad). The state also works transnationally in collaboration with other state film institutes, both within the region and, to a more limited extent, in Europe (such as Spain and Portugal), and more recently with other countries such as Canada and China. These cross-border ties help promote international co-productions between countries, with the additional advantage of spreading the costs between two or more film institutes.

Two pan-Latin American funds, Programa Ibermedia and Cinergia (the latter temporarily suspended due to a decline in grant funding), have assisted greatly in pooling together funds from various Latin American countries (and in the case of Ibermedia, European countries such as Spain, Portugal and most recently Italy). Fund loans are disbursed based on co-production competitions among the countries. These models, which have produced award-winning films, have helped strengthen ties between producers and the crews who work on them.

Though the state has been the lynchpin ensuring that Latin American film industries operate on a consistent basis in the face of economic and political fluctuations, it cannot always fulfil fiscal responsibilities towards the film sector. In certain cases, or in different historical periods, filmmakers have chosen to work outside the state for several reasons, among them high levels of bureaucracy, censorship or perception of a lack of transparency. In one instance, Mexican director Guillermo del Toro accused the Mexican film institute of outdated thinking, so that for him, a move towards the private sector signalled 'that whole fossilized approach has now been overturned, thank God' (Falicov, 2008, 267). As examined in Chapter 3, additional reasons, such as federal and state tax incentives for private investment, have led to the private sector playing a more active role in film production. Currently, the countries with the most private investment are Brazil, Colombia and Mexico; yet all of them display a paradox between criticism of state bureaucracy and inefficiency, and the fact that it was precisely state legislation and financial incentives which paved the way (beginning in the 1950s) for large companies to invest in a nation's cinema. Thus, the state is still relevant despite a neoliberal shift hailing the 'primacy of the market'.

Chapter 4 profiled various distribution companies throughout the region. These include the major US studios with a wide reach, such as UPI, Fox, Buena Vista (Disney), Sony and Warner Bros. The for-profit LatAm Films, formed by successful financier and media entrepreneur Alex García, both distributes as well as produces films for the Latin American and US markets. Beginning in the late 1970s and gaining momentum in the twenty-first century, small independent distribution companies have pooled resources and created pan-Latin American distribution networks; an example is LARED, whose member country distributors meet at film festivals to discuss combining resources in order to purchase films with expensive distribution rights. In 2016, the online distribution network Retina Latina began offering free online Latin American films to (currently) six Latin American countries who joined the network, enabling consumers with access to broadband internet to access these films free of charge. The chapter also highlighted the case of an independent film distributor from Colombia, Cineplex, to demonstrate how national films are distributed at home and abroad. Two case studies in distribution, one Mexican, the other an Argentine/European co-production, were discussed in terms of their industrial profile, how they were funded and how this helped determine their distribution strategy. A section of the chapter examined various distribution companies based in the United States (Cinema Tropical, Pragda and the Global Film Initiative) and charged with distributing Latin American cinema to cinemas, universities and museums in the US. Other forms of digital distribution include OTT (Over the Top) VOD (Video on Demand), platforms for accessing video on demand without subscribing to the digital cable packages currently gaining popularity in Mexico, Brazil, Argentina, Chile and other countries. Moreover, Latin American middle-class households increasingly have easy access to film and television shows via computers, tablets and television sets. However, in general, only a small percentage of the population in many Latin American countries have access to broadband video distribution.

Even so, access to digital technology is empowering more independent, low- to no-budget filmmakers than ever, as digital equipment becomes less expensive. New funding strategies which differ from the more traditional studio model are emerging, including crowdfunding through social media and the use of YouTube as a marketing strategy. Accessing international film festival funds, which are concentrated in Europe, is a competitive but advantageous manner of attaining funding, prestige and an opportunity to enter the global film festival circuit.

Chapter 5 explored various exhibition platforms, ranging from multinational brick-and-mortar movie theatre chains (such as Cinépolis, Cinemark and others) to smaller, independent chains. The larger ones, in an effort to keep drawing moviegoers to their venues, have incorporated more expensive entertainment technologies (e.g. 3D, 4DX), experiences usually affordable only by wealthier audiences. The smaller chains are more likely to screen arthouse cinema from their home countries, as well as from all over the world. Some of the theatres are state owned, such as Espacios INCAA from Argentina. Alternative forms of exhibition include mobile cinema screenings organised to provide movie access to rural communities.

Chapter 6 explored film legislation, one of the key factors in providing both stability and financial support for independent producers-directors, and in encouraging the private sector to invest in national film industries. Screen quotas, adopted by many Latin American countries but rarely enforced (save Argentina), are a means to utilise protectionist policies against the Hollywood 'tanques' (blockbusters) crowding the film landscape. The final section examined film piracy, ever-present in many forms throughout the region. Consumers clandestinely access films through website downloads, P2P, and DVD and VCD sales. There are various reasons for this widespread practice, and the chapter ended with a discussion of how US agencies and their Latin American partners are attempting to combat such activities.

FUTURE PROSPECTS: NEWER PRODUCTION STRATEGIES

The future of film industries depends on the continued support of the state in a number of areas, especially in sustaining a type of cinema which embodies and explores a nation's identity. This support can increasingly foster relationships with the private sector, as well as with international partners. International opportunities include co-production funding, training workshops abroad, access to international film funds such as the Hubert Bals Fund (the Netherlands) and the World Cinema Fund (Germany), and residencies at Cannes and Torino (Italy), as well as producing seminars at Produire au Sud (France). These funds from the Global North are essential, but can be problematic, given a colonial past that potentially plagues the North–South dynamic.

Horizontal Models of Funding

More recent, horizontal efforts through digital crowdsourcing platforms within Latin America are strategies which create more South–South linkages. Examples include Ideame from Argentina and Catatarse from Brazil, among others (in addition to US platforms such as Kickstarter and IndieGoGo). These grassroots crowdsourcing options are also social media platforms utilised by filmmakers at all stages of their careers: from the newly minted film school graduate to the veteran film director, and from large- to micro-budget fiction and documentary films. Newer film fund initiatives include Tres Puertos Cine (Three Ports Cinema), which is held at the Valdivia Film Festival in collaboration with other global initiatives (including CineMart from Rotterdam). This platform takes a more horizontal approach to working with film directors and producers (see Falicov, 2017).

These possibilities for funding, as well as cooperative production models (such as the 'Best Picture System' from Central America, and Monociclo Cine from Colombia), demonstrate how young people are pooling together equipment, labour and other resources in order to create independent, low-budget films with or without state support.

INCREASED VISIBILITY THROUGH AWARDS CEREMONIES

Latin American film industries have come together with Spain to form a regional bloc in terms of promoting and marketing, within the region, critically acclaimed movies of the year. Organisations such as the Spanish Producers Association (Entidad de Gestion del Derechos de los Productores Audiovisuales) (EGEDA), the New York-based distribution company Cinema Tropical and the Fénix Film Awards based in Mexico have independently established gala awards programmes to promote and recognise the achievements of Ibero-American filmmakers. Televised awards ceremonies, with films vetted by Latin America's top film critics, scholars and programmers, add to the prestige and fanfare that annual prizes confer on Ibero-American productions.

These sponsoring organisations understand how awards presentations, as well as individual film awards, can help increase awareness of the high-quality productions made in the region. They also create a space where auteurs, star actors, journalists and other film sector professionals can come together. Collectively, these activities fashion a public awareness campaign about films that receive accolades. Interestingly, these awards competitions, gala events and the publicity surrounding them might serve as the neoliberal version of the earlier iterations of film festival encounters of the 1960s–70s; it was there that radical filmmakers came together to create collective distribution platforms, solidarity bonds against imperialist cinema and other identity formations, all of which helped to solidify their New Latin American Cinema Movement. While these current film awards events are not necessarily seen as political gestures, they are important crossroads for filmmakers, producers and other professionals who must come together, and, rather than compete against one another, find ways to support and laud each other's achievements. This process, one that is necessary for the continuation of the industry, helps filmmakers from Latin America create more networks of circulation, visibility and sustainability.

Appendix A

Country	Institute	Est.	Founding Legislation	Purpose	Selected Services and Programmes
Argentina	INCAA: Instituto Nacional de Cine y Artes Audiovisuales (*National Institute of Cinema and Audiovisual Arts*)	1968	Law 17,714	The INCAA's function is to develop and regulate filmic activity throughout Argentina, and to promote national film production abroad.	• Film Development Fund – subsidises national production • ENERC – national film school, trains audiovisual professionals • Espacios INCAA – theatres dedicated solely to Argentine film • CAEC – rates Argentine films for exhibition • Management of International Affairs – supports Argentine films at international festivals and manages Ventana Sur film market
Brazil	ANCINE: Agência Nacional do Cinema (*National Cinema Agency*)	2001	Law 10,454	ANCINE is a regulatory agency whose responsibilities include the promotion, regulation and oversight of the cinema and audiovisual market in Brazil.	• Audiovisual Sector Fund – finances audiovisual programmes/products • Cinema Near You – funds construction of theatres across Brazil • Cooperation Protocols – facilitates international co-productions • Support for Brazilian Film Participation in International Festivals • Filming in Brazil – regulates international production in Brazil

Country		Year	Law	Description	Functions
Bolivia	CONACINE: Consejo Nacional del Cine (*National Film Council*)	1991	Law 1302	CONACINE's mission is to work within the framework of Bolivian social diversity to grow the audiovisual sector.	• Intellectual Property Registration • Filming Licensing – regulates international production • Business Registry – oversees national film production/distribution companies • Certifies nationality of film products for quota compliance
Chile	CAIA: Consejo del Arte y la Industria Audiovisual (*Audiovisual Art and Industry Council*)	2003	Law 19,981	CAIA's objective is the development, promotion, dissemination, protection and preservation of the national audiovisual industry, as well as research and development of new audiovisual works.	• Audiovisual Development Fund – funds a range of activities including film production, professional development, and research and education • Advises National Council for Culture and the Arts on audiovisual policy • Promotes preservation and dissemination of Chilean audiovisual heritage • Develops and maintains relationships with international governments and institutions to promote co-production and collaboration
Cuba	ICAIC: Instituto Cubano del Arte e Industria Cinematográficos (*Cuban Institute of Cinematographic Art and Industry*)	1959	Law 169	The ICAIC is the national film authority, the main producer of films in the country, and is responsible for the promotion and national and international distribution of Cuban cinema.	• National distribution – distributes Cuban films on the island • Produces feature films, animations and documentaries • Hosts International Festival of New Latin American Cinema (annual festival held in Havana)

Country	Institute	Est	Founding Legislation	Purpose	Selected Services and Programmes
Colombia	PROIMÁGENES: Fondo Mixto de Promoción Cinematográfica (*Joint Film Promotion Fund*)	1997	Law 397	Proimágenes seeks to strengthen the Colombian film industry through the development of legal tools that create favourable conditions for Colombian cinema at home and abroad.	• Film Development Fund – finances Colombian film projects, supports the development of film culture and audiovisual industry infrastructure • Colombian Film Commission – promotes Colombia as a production destination • Colombia Film Fund – offers financial incentives for foreign production • Bogotá Audiovisual Market – promotes Colombia's audiovisual industry and its products
Costa Rica	CCPC: Centro Costarricense de Producción Cinematográfica (*Costa Rican Film Production Centre*)	1977	Law 6158	The CCPC is responsible for promoting the Costa Rican audiovisual industry through four areas of focus: production and co-production, outreach, development and archiving.	• Costa Rica Audiovisual – supports production, fosters partnerships between the national audiovisual sector and public entities, promotes Costa Rica as a production destination • Film Centre – organises film festivals, rents production equipment, maintains national film archive and media library • Monday Cinematheque – national television programme that promotes national audiovisual artists/technicians and their work
Ecuador	CNCINE: Consejo Nacional de Cinematografía del Ecuador (*National Film Board of Ecuador*)	2006	Law 2006-29	CNCINE is the institution charged with strengthening the Ecuadorian audiovisual industry. It works to promulgate and implement policies for film development in the country.	• Film Development Fund – funds development, production and post-production • National Film Distribution System – promotes distribution across Ecuador • International promotion – establishes partnerships with international film festival funds • Provides education and training for film professionals and private citizens

Mexico	IMCINE: Instituto Mexicano de Cinematografía (*Mexican Film Institute*)	1983	Presidential decree	IMCINE's mission is to encourage the production and promotion of Mexican cinema at home and abroad through industry and artist development.	• Creators Incentive Programme and Production Support Programme – provides funding and training for screenwriting and project development • Coordinates the activities of FOPROCINE and FIDECINE, public funds for the production of artistic and popular cinemas • Facilitates co-production agreements between public and private organisations and audiovisual producers
Panama	DICINE: Dirección General de Cine (*Film Department of the Ministry of Commerce and Industry*)	2012	Law 36	DICINE is in charge of incentivising and promoting domestic production. It also seeks to establish Panama as a hub for the international film industry.	• Film Fund and Film Fund Contest – provides support for the national industry, especially through funding for Panamanian productions • Supports development, promotion and funding for international film events (e.g. IFF Panama, Premios Platino Film Awards) • Ensures distribution for Panamanian productions in national cinemas
Peru	DAFO: Dirección del Audiovisual, la Fonografía, y los Nuevos Medios (*Department of Audiovisual Art, Phonography, and New Media*)	2013	Supreme Decree No. 005-2013-MC	DAFO is responsible for the development, promotion and implementation of policies and strategies that develop and promote of Peru's audiovisual, phonographic and new media industries.	• Film funding – funds film development, production and post-production • Education and training – programmes workshops for audiovisual professionals; provides aid for participation in international training programmes • Promotes international co-production • Promotes citizen access to domestic production • Preserves national audiovisual heritage (e.g. National Film Registry)

Country	Institute	Est	Founding Legislation	Purpose	Selected Services and Programmes
Uruguay	ICAU: Instituto del Cine y Audiovisual del Uruguay (*Cinema and Audiovisual Institute of Uruguay*)	2008	Law 18,284	ICAU is charged with designing national audiovisual policy. Its objectives include support for production, co-production, distribution and exhibition of Uruguayan film and film culture.	• Development Fund – provides funding for national film and television productions • National Audiovisual Training Programme – provides children and teens training in the theory and production of audiovisual products • Conservation of Audiovisual Patrimony – identifies and preserves works of national cinema
Venezuela	CNAC: Centro Nacional Autónomo de Cinematografía (*National Autonomous Film Centre*)	1993	Law 38,281	The CNAC is the governing body of the Venezuelan audiovisual industry. It formulates and implements policies to stimulate, regulate and develop the national audiovisual industry.	• FONPROCINE – provides funds for national productions • Stimulus of the Industrial Base – provides financing for technological improvements and innovations • Film and Audiovisual Lab – provides training in theory and practice for citizens • Venezuelan Film Commission – facilitates international production in Venezuela

Sources: http://www.incaa.gov.ar/; http://www.ancine.gov.br/; http://www.conacinebolivia.com.bo/; http://chileaudiovisual.cultura.gob.cl/; http://www.proimagenescolombia.com/; http://www.centrodecine.go.cr/; www.cubacine.cult.cu; http://www.imcine.gob.mx/; http://dicine.gob.pa/; http://dafo.cultura.pe/; http://www.icau.mec.gub.uy/; http://www.cnac.gob.ve/.

Credit: Courtney Aspen Sanchez.

Notes

CHAPTER 2

1. These are the various workshops that Bojórquez attended and which are listed in the film's credits: Escuela Internacional de Cine y Televisión (EICTV); Diplomado de Producción Cinematográfica Panamá, 2010; Tareula II – Production and scriptwriting course for professional European and Latin American producers, 2010; 4º Encuentro de Nuevas Miradas, EICTV, 2010; III Bolivia Lab, 2011; BrLab, 2011; Encuentros Suchitoto, El Salvador, 2011; Morelia Lab 2011; Foro de Coproducción Tareula II – 58 Festival Internacional de Cine de San Sebastián, 2010; Foro de Coproducción 36 de Cine Iberoamericano de Huelva, 2010; Encuentro Iberoamericano de Coproducción Cinematográfica – 26 Festival Internacional de Cine en Guadalajara, 2011; Cine Qua Non Lab, 2011.

CHAPTER 5

1. My thanks to Isis Sadek for this observation

CHAPTER 6

1. The Programa Ibermedia website lists all of the film institute documents in Spanish and Portuguese: http://www.programaibermedia.com/el-marco-legal/legislacion-por-paises/.
2. Later, in 2011, the sequel *Tropa de elite 2: O inimigo agora é outro* (*Elite Squad 2: The Enemy Within*, dir. José Padilha) became the all-time largest box-office success in Brazil and the highest-grossing film in Brazil with eleven million viewers watching in theatres.

Bibliography and Further Reading

Abascal, Lorena, 'Nicaragua tiene buenas notas en cine', *El nuevo diario* (Nicaragua), 17 January 2015, http://www.elnuevodiario.com.ni/variedades/339503-nicaragua-tiene-buenas-notas-cine/ (accessed 1 July 2015).

Acevedo-Muñoz, Ernesto, *Buñuel in Mexico: The Crisis of National Cinema* (Berkeley: University of California Press, 2003).

Acosta, Delia, 'Microcinemas and Digital Alternatives', *InterPress Service International Association*, 14 May 2005, http://www.ipsnews.org/new_nota.asp?idnews=28616 (accessed 11 January 2009).

Aguiar, José Carlos G., 'La piratería como conflicto. Discursos sobre la propiedad intelectual en México', *Íconos. Revista de Ciencias Sociales* no. 38 (September 2010), pp. 143–56, http://www.redalyc.org/html/509/50918282012/index.html (accessed 16 September 2017).

Aguilera, Laura, and Erik Brannon, 'Telefonica Adds Viacom Channels to Its OTT Movistar Play', IHS Markit, 23 February 2018, https://technology.ihs.com/602072/telefonica-adds-viacom-channels-to-its-ott-movistar-play (accessed 2 December 2018).

Alvaray, Luisela, 'Hybridity and Genre in Transnational Latin American Cinemas', *Transnational Cinemas* vol. 4 no. 1 (2013), pp. 67–87.

Álvarez, Kikí, Personal interview, 9 April 2016.

Álvarez, L. A., 'El cine en la última década del siglo XX: Imágenes colombianas', in Jorge Orlando Melo (ed.), *Colombia hoy* (Bogotá, Colombia: Tercer Mundo Editores, 1995), pp. 359–74.

Ambulante Report, 2015, https://www.dropbox.com/s/6jp5swjyi4ik67h/REPORTE_2015_WEB.pdf?dl=0 (accessed 26 May 2016).

ANCINE, 'ANCINE divulga Informe Anual Preliminar do mercado de exibição em 2013', 2014, https://www.ancine.gov.br/sites/default/files/releases/2014-01-21-informepreliminar.pdf (accessed 28 September 2017).

Anderson, Tre'vell, 'Derbez y "How to Be a Latin Lover" superan expectativas, mientras que "Date" rebasa los mil millones de dólares', *Hoy*, 30 April 2017, http://www.hoylosangeles.com/latimesespanol/hoyla-eugenio-derbez-y-como-ser-un-amante-latino-superan-expectativas-mientras-que-date-rebasa-los-mil-mil-20170430-story.html (accessed 8 September 2017).

Andrade, Daniel Bravo, 'Para que llevar el cine a los barrios?', *El Colombiano*, 6 March
    2016, www.elcolombiano.com/cultura/cine/para-que-llevar-el-cine'a-los-barrios-
    FA3705373 (accessed 26 May 2016).

Anon., 'Argentina Top Producer of Spanish Pictures', *Motion Picture Herald*, 7
    November 1942a.

Anon., 'B.A. vs 42nd Street', *Variety*, 28 July 1942b, p. 15.

Anon., 'Argentine Pic Biz Faces 50 Percent Raw Film Stock Snip', *Variety*, 23 April
    1943a.

Anon., 'U.S. Ups Mex Films, Cuts Argentina for Axis Stand', *Variety*, 17 May 1943b.

Anon., 'Peru Has Tough Anti-Piracy Law, But No One Has Filed Suit Yet', *Variety*, 30
    March 1983, p. 54.

Anon., 'Luis Puenzo habla', *La Maga*, 6 January 1993, p. 20.

Anon., 'Big Push into Latin America by Exhibitor', *Screen Digest*, 1 July 1996.

Anon., 'A Digital Dream of Movies for the Masses', *Financial Times*, 15 September
    2003, www.communicationforsocialchange.org/publications-resources.
    php?=229&printv" (accessed 18 September 2006).

Anon., 'La libertad de Mercado no se da mientras no haya condiciones iguales para
    todo el mundo' (Interview with Pedro Pérez, president of the FAPAE), *Raices* no.
    10, November 2004, www.raicesdelcine.com.ar/Numero%2010/notas10/fapae_10.
    htm (accessed 25 June 2005).

Anon., 'El negocio del cine y del video (pirateria)'. A study sponsored by the MPA,
    INCAA, Union Argentina de Videoeditores, et. al, 2007, n.p.

Anon., 'The Sandman Under Rain Theatres in Brazil', *Yahoo Financial News*, 16 June
    2008a, www.biz.yahoo.com/iw/080616/0407486.html?printer=1 (accessed 20 June
    2008).

Anon., 'Hollywood Moguls See Cinema's Future in 3D', *Phys.org*, 20 November 2008b,
    http://phys.org/news/2008-11-hollywood-moguls-cinema-future-3d.html (accessed
    31 July 2015).

Anon., 'Cinemark Invests $2.5 million in Guatemala', *Central American Data*, 31
    March 2009a, http://en.centralamericadata.com/en/article/home/Cinemark_
    Invests_25_Million_in_Guatemala (accessed 23 December 2011).

Anon., 'Cine mexicano contra el corte del presupuesto', *El Universal*, 1 October 2009b,
    http://www.eluniversal.com.mx/notas/630449.html (accessed 27 July 2015).

Anon., 'Directores de Colombia y Chile seleccionados por la Résidence de
    Cinéfondation', *LatAmCinema.com*, 22 July 2010a, http://www.latamcinema.com/
    noticia.php?id=2791 (accessed 12 October 2011).

Anon., '"Hacer cine en Guatemala no es algo logico" dice Julio Hernández
    Cordón', *Hola Ciudad* (Guatemala), 9 September 2010b, www.holaciudad.com/
    HacercineenGuatemalanoesalgológico-n107333 (accessed 30 July 2015).

Anon., 'Strong Competition from Cinema Chains in Guatemala', *Central American Data*, 28 September 2010c, http://www.centralamericadata.biz/en/article/home/Strong_Competition_from_Cinema_Chains_in_Guatemala (accessed 23 December 2011).

Anon., 'Mexico's First 3D Animated Feature Arrives in El Paso Theaters', *El Paso, Inc*, 7 December 2011, http://www.elpasoinc.com/whatsup/arts_culture/movies/article_c0c8bd9e-20f8-11e1-b070-001a4bcf6878.html (accessed 21 December 2011).

Anon., 'Kramer en la cima', *24horasCL TVN*, 24 October 2012a, http://www.24horas.cl/tendencias/cineytelevision/stefan-vs-kramer-pelicula-mas-vista-de-la-historia-en-chile-361449 (accessed 8 July 2015).

Anon., 'Cuán seria es la lucha antipiratería en América Latina?', *BBC Mundo*, 12 July 2012b, http://www.bbc.com/mundo/noticias/2012/07/120713_tecnologia_lucha_pirateria_aa.shtml (accessed 9 September 2017).

Anon., 'Jorge Luis Serrano: El CNCine aporta con unos 700 mil dólares anuales', *El telégrafo*, 23 October 2012c, https://www.eltelegrafo.com.ec/noticias/espectaculos/1/jorge-luis-serrano-el-cncine-aporta-con-unos-700-mil-dolares-anuales (accessed 2 December 2018).

Anon., '"22 Jump Street" Films in Puerto Rico', *Caribbean Journal*, 2013a, http://caribjournal.com/2013/12/10/22-jump-street-films-in-puerto-rico/ (accessed 22 July 2015).

Anon., 'Animated Film *Metegol* Breaks Opening Day Records in Argentina', *Cinema Tropical*, 20 July 2013b, http://www.cinematropical.com/Cinema-Tropical/animated-film-metegol-breaks-opening-day-records-in-argentina.html (accessed 5 March 2014).

Anon., 'No se aceptan devoluciones', *The Numbers*, 2013c, https://www.the-numbers.com/movie/No-se-Aceptan-Devoluciones#tab=summary (accessed 1 December 2018).

Anon., 'How Government Incentives are Boosting Latin American Films' 1 October 2013d http://knowledge.wharton.upenn.edu/article/lights-camera-action-government-incentives-latin-american-film-industry/ (accessed 30 December 2018).

Anon., 'El Foprocine apoyará 15 proyectos este año', 7 July 2014a, https://www.eleconomista.com.mx/arteseideas/El-Foprocine-apoyara-15-proyectos-este-ano--20140707-0055.html (accessed 7 December 2018).

Anon., 'Netflix Takes Two-Thirds of Over-the-Top Video Subscriptions in Latin America', *Emarketer.com*, 14 September 2014b, http://www.emarketer.com/Article/Netflix-Takes-Two-Thirds-of-Over-the-Top-Video-Subscriptions-Latin-America/1011581 (accessed 30 July 2015).

Anon., 'Latin American Internet Audience Nears 310 Million', *Emarketer.com*, 4 December 2014c, https://www.emarketer.com/Article/Latin-American-Internet-Audience-Nears-310-Million/1011667 (accessed 1 December 2018).

Anon., 'Naked Screen Will Premiere in November', *ViaNica.com*, 26 September 2014d, https://vianica.com/headline/971 (accessed 2 December 2018).

Anon., 'Cinemart Profile', International Film Festival Rotterdam, 2015a, https://www.iffr.com/professionals/cinemine/cinemart-profile/ (accessed 30 July 2015).

Anon., 'Con gran suceso en el exterior, "Relatos Salvajes" se convirtió en el filme más exitoso del país', *Telam*, 24 March 2015b, http://www.telam.com.ar/notas/201503/99113-relatos-salvajes-cine-pelicula-exito-historia.html (accessed 7 June 2017).

Anon., 'Interview with Spanish Producer at the Panama International Film Festival', 2015c.

Anon., 'La Residencia Andina de Guion Documental prepara su primera edición', *LatAmCinema.com*, 23 June 2015d, https://www.latamcinema.com/la-residencia-andina-de-guion-documental-prepara-su-primera-edicion/ (accessed 21 June 2017).

Anon., 'El Centro de Cine anunció los ocho proyectos ganadores del fondo "El Fauno"', *Revista Delelfoco*, 2 December 2015e, https://revista.delefoco.com/7554-el-centro-de-cine-anunci-los-ocho-proyectos-ganadores-del-fondo-el-fauno.aspx (accessed 2 December 2018).

Anon., 'Brazil to Surpass Mexico in OTT Video Revenues', *Emarketer.com*, 24 February 2016a, http://www.emarketer.com/Article/Brazil-Surpass-Mexico-OTT-Video-Revenues/1013623 (accessed 10 August 2016).

Anon., 'Centro de Cine abre convocatoria 2016 del Fondo para el Fomento Audiovisual y Cinematográfico el Fauno', 15 April 2016b, http://www.centrodecine.go.cr/index.php/noticias/1244-centro-de-cine-abre-convocatoria-2016-del-fondo-para-el-fomento-audiovisual-y-cinematografico-el-fauno (accessed 12 May 2016).

Anon., 'Internet Users by Country', 2016c, http://www.internetlivestats.com/internet-users-by-country/ (accessed 30 September 2017).

Anon., 'A Peek into Latin America's Video Streaming Market', *Muvi*, 2017, https://www.muvi.com/blogs/peek-latin-americas-video-streaming-market.html (accessed 8 December 2018).

Appelo, Tim, 'How "Wild Tales" Director Damian Szifron Wrote a Foreign-Language Oscar Contender in His Bathtub', *Hollywood Reporter*, 12 September 2014, http://www.hollywoodreporter.com/news/how-wild-tales-director-damian-755131 (accessed 28 July 2015).

Araújo Castro, 'Introduction', in Fundación Patrimonio Fílmico Colombiano, *Largometrajes colombianos: En cine y video* (Bogotá, Colombia: Ministerio de Cultura, 2005).

Arena, Constanza, Interview on Bio Bio Televisión, 'Chilean Cinema: A Debate Between a Common Good and Private Interest', 2015, http://tv.biobiochile.cl/notas/2015/01/12/constanza-arena-el-cine-chileno-se-debate-entre-el-bien-comun-y-el-interes-privado.shtml (accessed 27 July 2015).

Aronczyk, Melissa, *Branding the Nation: The Global Business of National Identity* (New York: Oxford University Press, 2013).

Australab website, 2018, http://ficvaldivia.cl/australab/ (accessed 4 December 2018).

Avilés Molina, M., 'Análisis de la evolución del cine en el Ecuador desde un punto de vista técnico y cultural', BA thesis, Facultad de Ciencias de la Comunicacion, Universidad de las Americas, Quito, 2013, http://dspace.udla.edu.ec/handle/33000/1609 (accessed 4 December 2018).

Ayala Blanco, Jorge, *La aventura del cine mexicano: En la época de oro y después* (Mexico City: Ediciones era, 1968).

Ayala Blanco, Jorge, *La búsqueda del cine mexicano* (Mexico City: UNAM, 1974).

Báez Sánchez, Eunice, 'Película tica El Regreso recolectó $62 mil dólares en contribuciones', *RedCultura.com*, 25 April 2011, http://www.redcultura.com/php/Articulos691.htm (accessed 2 December 2018).

Banegas Flores, Cecilia and Cecilia Quiroga San Martín, 'Bolivia: Ley de cine y su impacto el mercado cinematografico', *Industria cinematográfica latinoamericana: Políticas públicas y su impacto en un Mercado digital. El caso Bolivia*, 2011, https://www.academia.edu/3517155/Bolivia_Ley_del_cine_y_su_impacto_el_mercado_cinematogr%C3%A1fico (accessed 27 July 2015).

Barnes, Carolina, José A. Borello, and Adrián Pérez Llahí, 'La producción cinematográfica en la Argentina: Datos, formas de organización y tipos de empresas', *H-industria* vol. 8 no. 14 (Spring 2014), pp. 17–49, https://ojs.econ.uba.ar/ojs/index.php/H-ind/article/view/655 (accessed 8 July 2015).

Batlle, Diego et al., 'Los problemas de exhibición en el cine argentino: El caso Las Acacias', *OtrosCines.com*, 18 November 2011, http://micropsia.otroscines.com/2011/11/los-problemas-de-exhibicion-del-cine-argentino-el-caso-las-acacias/ (accessed 25 November 2014).

Batlle, Diego, 'Taquilla: El cine argentino se quedó con el 10,3% del público total entre enero y junio', *OtrosCines.com*, 2015, http://www.otroscines.com/nota?idnota=9869 (accessed 31 July 2015).

Baz, Verónica, Lorena Becerra, Ximena López and Gabriela Esquinca, *Reporte piratería: Entendiendo el mercado 'sombra' en México*, 2015, PIRATERIA_Entendiendo_el_mercado_sombra_en_Mexico__1.pdf (accessed 9 September 2017).

Bellos, Alex, 'Brazil Takes Lead Role in Move to All-Digital Cinema', *The Guardian*, 4 December 2003, www.communicationforsocialchange.org/publications-resources.php?=229&printv" (accessed 18 September 2006).

Benaim, Abner, and Gema Juárez Allen, Personal interviews, 14 April 2015.

Bensinger, Ken, 'Film Companies Fight Piracy by Taking to Mexico's Streets', *Wall Street Journal*, 17 December 2003, http://www.wsj.com/articles/SB107162806666489600 (accessed 18 November 2016).

Bernardes, Horacio, 'Cine: Balance de lo sucedido en la producción argentina 2009', *Página 12*, 29 December 2009, http://recursosculturales.com.ar/blog/?p=852 (accessed 17 July 2011).

Bernades, Horacio, Diego Lerer and Sergio Wolf (eds), *Nuevo cine argentino: Temas, autores, y estilos de una renovación* (Buenos Aires: FIPRESCI/Ediciones Tanaka, 2002).

Bernardo, Fabiano, 'The Hottest Pay TV Markets in Latin America', *Latin Link*, 2014, http://latinlink.usmediaconsulting.com/2014/08/the-hottest-pay-tv-markets-in-latin-america (accessed 29 August 2017).

Berneri, Anahí, 'Roundtable at Panama International Film Festival', 14 April 2015.

Berrendo Pérez, Oscar, Juan Antonio Serrano Fernández and Enrique Encinas Puebla (eds), *Panorama Audiovisual 2014* (Madrid: EGEDA, 2014), http://www.egeda.com/documentos/PANORAMA_AUDIOVISUAL_IBEROAMERICANO_2014_300dpi.pdf (accessed 9 July 2015).

Bettati, Bruno (ed.), *Reflections on Audiovisual Distribution* (Santiago, Chile: Cine Sin Fronteras/Austral Lab, 2012a).

Bettati, Bruno, *Why Not? Política industrial para el audiovisual chileno* (Santiago, Chile: Ebooks Patagonia, 2012b).

Bohan, Merwin L., 'Reasons Why American Industry Should Give Enthusiastic, Strong Support for Plan', OCIAA collection, Motion Picture Division Folder, Rockefeller Archive Center, Sleepy Hollow, New York, 26 May 1942.

Bojórquez, Ana V., Personal interview, 13 April 2015.

Bojórquez, Ana V., Email correspondence, 30 June 2015.

Bollier, David, 'Piracy Creates a Hit Film in Brazil', *On the Commons*, 26 November 2007, http://onthecommons.org/piracy-creates-hit-film-brazil (accessed 3 March 2014).

Bordat, Elodie, 'Cine e identidad: Un análisis de las políticas de fomento al cine en Argentina y en México en el siglo XX'. *Independencias – Dependencias – Interdependencias, VI Congreso CEISAL 2010* conference, Toulouse, France, 30 June 2010, http://halshs.archives-ouvertes.fr/halshs-00496199/en/ (accessed 11 January 2012).

Bourdieu, Pierre, *La distinción. Criterio y bases sociales del gusto* (Mexico City: Taurus, 2002).

Brown, Tomas, 'Indie Films in Brazil Get New Online Channel', *Rio Times Online*, 2014, http://riotimesonline.com/brazil-news/rio-entertainment/indie-films-in-brazil-get-new-online-channel/#sthash.vuqwUEKQ.dpuf (accessed 20 September 2016).

Burton, Julianne, 'Revolutionary Cuban Cinema', *Jump Cut* no. 19 (December 1978), pp. 17–20, http://www.ejumpcut.org/archive/onlinessays/JC19folder/CubanFilmIntro.html (accessed 13 December, 2011).

Burton, Julianne, 'Film and Revolution in Cuba: The First Twenty-Five Years', in Michael T. Martin (ed.), *The New Latin American Cinema, Volume 2* (Detroit, MI: Wayne State University Press, 1997; originally published 1985), pp. 123–42.

Cajueiro, Marcelo, 'Brazil: The 3D Phenom Expands Ticket Sales', *Variety* vol. 420 no. 6 (20–26 September 2010), pp. A15–A16.

Cajueiro, Marcelo, 'South's Good News', *Variety* vol. 424 no. 8 (3–9 October 2011), p. 43.

Calistro, Mariano, 'Aspectos del nuevo cine, 1957–1968', in Jorge Miguel Couselo, Mariano Calistro and Claudio España (eds), *Historia del cine argentino* (Buenos Aires: Centro Editor de América Latina, 1992), pp. 109–38.

Canadian Trade Commissioner Service, 'Film and Television Sector Profile – Argentina', 24 June 2006, http://www.infoexport.gc.ca/ie-en/DisplayDocument. jsp?did=5231531/ (accessed 19 December 2011).

Castells, Manuel and Gustavo Cardoso (eds), *Piracy Cultures: How a Growing Portion of the Global Population Is Building Media Relationships Through Alternate Channels of Obtaining Content*, Kindle edition (Los Angeles: USC Annenberg Press, 2013).

Castro Cobos, Mario, and Fernando Vílchez R., 'El cine peruano no existe' (Interview with Josué Méndez), 20 February 2007, http://lacinefilianoespatriota.blogspot. com/2007/02/dioses-la-segunda-pelcula-de-josu-mndez.html (accessed 12 October 2011).

Catarse, 2017, https://www.catarse.me/ (accessed 28 June 2017).

Cavallo, Ascanio, and Gonzalo Maza (eds), *El novisimo cine chileno* (Santiago, Chile: Uqbar, 2010).

Centro de Cine, 'Centro de Cine crea fondo de producción audiovisual', 12 February 2015, http://www.centrodecine.go.cr/index.php/noticias/1049-centro-de-cine-crea-fondo-de-produccion-audiovisual (accessed 1 July 2015).

Chanan, Michael, 'Sound Cinema 1930–1960', in Geoffrey Nowell-Smith (ed.), *The Oxford History of World Cinema* (Oxford: Oxford University Press, 1996), Section 2, pp. 427–35.

Chanan, Michael, *Cuban Cinema* (Minneapolis: University of Minnesota Press, 2004).

Christofoli, Eduardo Pires, 'A exibição de conteúdos digitais: O caso da Rain Networks', 2010, http://www.pucrs.br/edipucrs/Vmostra/V_MOSTRA_PDF/ Comunicacao_Social/83958-EDUARDO_PIRES_CHRISTOFOLI.pdf (accessed 29 July 2015).

Cine&Tele, 'Italia ya forma parte de Ibermedia', 24 October 2016, http://www. cineytele.com/2016/10/24/italia-ya-forma-parte-de-ibermedia/ (accessed 20 September 2017).

CinemaChile, 2017, www.cinemachile.cl/en/ (accessed 9 September 2017).

Circuito Grande Cine, Venezuela, http://www.circuitograncine.net/cine_movil_popular.php (accessed 7 April 2014).

Cobo, María M., 'Venezuela: La tarea de la Villa del Cine es impulsar el cine venezolano', *Tiwy.com*, http://www.tiwy.com/pais/venezuela/materiales/villa_del_cine.phtml (accessed 10 August 2010).

Cornelio-Marí, Elia Margarita, 'Digital Delivery in Mexico: A Global Newcomer Stirs the Local Giants', in Cory Barker and Myc Wiatrowski (eds), *The Age of Netflix: Critical Essays on Streaming Media, Digital Delivery and Instant Access* (Jefferson, NC: McFarland, 2017), pp. 201–28.

Cortés, María Lourdes, Personal interview, 24 November 2005.

Cortés, María Lourdes, Personal interview, 24 April 2015.

Coscia, Jorge, 'The Screen Quota: A Fundamental Step Forward', *Raíces de cine* no. 9 (September 2004). Reprinted in Coscia, *Del estallido a la esperanza* (Buenos Aires: Corregidor, 2005), pp. 94–122.

Coulter, Susan Weeks, Personal interview, 15 September 2011.

Cubanet, 'Megacompania de comunicaciones quiere llevar su cable de fibra óptica hasta Cuba', *Cubanet*, 21 August 2017, https://www.cubanet.org/noticias/megacompania-de-comunicaciones-quiere-llevar-su-cable-de-fibra-optica-hasta-cuba/ (accessed 8 December 2018).

Curubeto, Diego, *Babilonia gaucha: Hollywood en la Argentina, la Argentina en Hollywood* (Buenos Aires: Editorial Planeta, 1993).

Dager, Nick, 'Despicable Me 2 First Satellite Delivered Movie in Mexico', *Digital Cinema Report*, 8 July 2013, http://www.digitalcinemareport.com/article/despicable-me-2-first-satellite-delivered-movie-mexico#.VblPZkYsCX4 (accessed 29 July 2015).

Davies, Vanessa, 'El cine nacional cerró 2013 con más de 1 millón de espectadores', *Correo del Orinoco*, 30 December 2013, http://www.correodelorinoco.gob.ve/nacionales/cine-nacional-cerro-2013-mas-1-millon-espectadores/ (accessed 17 July 2015).

Dávila, Arlene, *El Mall: The Spatial and Class Politics of Shopping Malls in Latin America* (Oakland: University of California Press, 2016).

Davis, Charles H., and Janice Kaye, 'International Production Outsourcing and the Development of Indigenous Film and Television Capabilities: The Case of Canada', in Greg Elmer, Charles Davis, Janine Marchessault and John McCollough (eds.), *Locating Migrating Media* (Lanham, MD: Lexington Books, 2010), pp. 3–22.

Davis, Robert E., 'The Instantaneous Worldwide Release: Coming Soon to Everyone, Everywhere', in Elizabeth Ezra and Terry Rowden (eds), *Transnational Cinema: The Film Reader* (London and New York: Routledge, 2006), pp. 73–80.

Departamento de Estudio e Investigación del Sindicato de la Industria Cinematográfica Argentina (DEISICA), *Deisica 22. Informe sobre los aspectos económicos y culturales de la industria cinematográfica argentina* (Buenos Aires: DEISICA, 2012).

de la Fuente, Anna Marie, 'Rebate Boosts Production', *Variety*, 22–28 November 2004, p. 18.

de la Fuente, Anna Marie, 'Latin Biz Thrives as Local Pic Funds Mature', *Variety*, 7–13 February 2011a, p. A4.

de la Fuente, Anna Marie, 'Distrib Focuses on Latin American Pics', *Variety*, 19 November 2011b, http://www.variety.com/article/VR1118046327#.Ttaw6PxLFfd. email (accessed 2 August 2012).

de la Fuente, Anna Marie, 'Exhib Moves into Rio's Favelas', *Variety* vol. 421 no. 10 (2011c), p. 3.

de la Fuente, Anna Marie, 'Chile Pics Heat Up Abroad: Local Auds Still Chilly to Homemade Fare, Though Genre Pics Could Turn Tide (SPOTLIGHT: CHILE)', *Variety*, 9 May 2011d, http://www.accessmylibrary.com/article-1G1-258356562/ chile-pics-heat-up.html (accessed 21 December 2011).

de la Fuente, Anna Marie, 'Colombia Lures Productions with Financial Rewards', *Variety*, 19 May 2013, http://variety.com/2013/film/features/scout-about-colombia-1200442277/ (accessed 18 March 2015).

de la Fuente, Anna Marie, 'Prolific Mexican Producer Alex Garcia Is Just Getting Started', 28 March 2014a, https://variety.com/2014/film/global/prolific-mexican-producer-alex-garcia-is-just-getting-started-1201146654/ (accessed 2 December 2018).

de la Fuente, Anna Marie, 'Big Foreign Shoots in Mexico Down but Not Out', *Variety*, 24 March 2014b, https://variety.com/2014/film/global/big-foreign-shoots-in-mexico-down-but-not-out-1201144520/ (accessed 2 December 2018).

de la Fuente, Anna Marie, 'Cannes: Mexico's Film Distribution Business Faces Challenging Future', *Variety*, 16 May 2015, http://variety.com/2015/film/festivals/ mexicos-distribution-business-faces-challenging-future-1201497917/ (accessed 7 July 2015).

de la Fuente, Anna Marie, 'Film, TV Shoots in Mexico on the Rise', *Variety*, 13 March 2017a, http://variety.com/2017/film/festivals/shooting-mexico-film-tv-production-rise-1202007628/ (accessed 12 June 2017).

de la Fuente, Anna María, 'New Distributor–Exhibitor Alliance Aldea Launched', 2 August 2017b, http://variety.com/2017/film/festivals/new-distrib-exhib-alliance-aldea-launches-lima-film-fest-august-1202514067/ (accessed 28 September 2017).

De Naipes, Castillo, 'Why Netflix Is Entering Cuba Even Though the Internet Barely Works There', *Quartz*, 9 February 2015, http://qz.com/341368/why-netflix-is-entering-cuba-even-though-the-internet-barely-works-there/ (accessed 14 July 2015).

De Pablos, Emiliano, 'Cannes: Cannes Market, Los Cabos Team for Pic-in-Post Showcase', *Variety*, 8 May 2015, http://variety.com/2015/film/global/cannes-film-market-paillard-los-cabos-festival-1201490934/ (accessed 26 July 2015).

Dennison, Stephanie, and Lisa Shaw, *Popular Cinema in Brazil* (Manchester: Manchester University Press, 2004).

Desser, David, 'Global Noir: Genre Film in the Age of Transnationalism', in Barry Keith Grant (ed.), *Film Genre Reader III* (Austin: University of Texas Press, 2003), pp. 516–36.

de Usabel, Gaizka S., *The High Noon of American Films in Latin America* (Ann Arbor: UMI Research Press, 1982).

de Valck, Marijke, *Film Festivals: From European Geopolitics to Global Cinephilia* (Amsterdam: Amsterdam University Press, 2007).

de Valck, Marijke, 'Sites of Initiation: Film Training Programs at Film Festivals', in Mette Hjort (ed.), *The Education of the Filmmaker in Europe, Australia, and Asia* (New York: Palgrave Macmillan, 2013), pp. 127–45.

Díaz, José Mariano, 'Porque es tan difícil hacer cine en Guatemala?', *Brújula*, 20 January 2014, http://brujula.com.gt/por-que-es-tan-dificil-hacer-cine-en-guatemala/ (accessed 7 July 2015).

Díaz López, Marina, 'América siempre inédita: esbozo de las politíca cultural de las instituciones públicas cinematográficas españolas de ámbito nacional hacia América Latina', in Oscar Berrendo Pérez, Juan Antonio Serrano Fernández and Enrique Encinas Puebla (eds), *Panorama Audiovisual 2014* (Madrid: EGEDA, 2014), http://www.egeda.com/documentos/PANORAMA_AUDIOVISUAL_IBEROAMERICANO_2014_300dpi.pdf (accessed 9 July 2015).

Diegues, Carlos, 'The Cinema That Brazil Deserves', in Lucia Nagib (ed.), *The New Brazilian Cinema* (London: I.B. Taurus, 2003), pp. 23–35.

DiOrio, Carl, 'D-Cinema Lags in Latin Region', *Hollywood Reporter*, 13 October 2008, p. 2.

Donoghue, Courtney Brannon, 'The Rise of the Brazilian Blockbuster: How Ideas of Exceptionality and Scale Shape a Booming Cinema', *Media Culture Society* vol. 36 no. 4 (2014), pp. 536–50.

Dos Santos, Suzy, 'The Central Role of Broadcast Television in Brazil's Film Industry: The Economic, Political, and Social Implications of Global Markets and National Concentration', *International Journal of Communication* vol. 3 (2009), pp. 695–712.

Downie, Andrew, 'Brazil Takes Lead Role in Move to All Digital Cinema', *Christian Science Monitor*, 5 February 2004, www.csmonitor.com/2004/0205/p07s01-woam. html (accessed 18 September 2006).

Durán, Cecilia, Email correspondence and Skype discussion on 15 August with the director of the Ícaro Film Festival Honduras and member of the 'Magic Lantern' Film Association about the state of the proposed Honduran film law, 2016.

Durán, Rodolfo, 'Los eternos problemas para conseguir salas: el caso de la pelicula Vecinos', *OtrosCines.com* (letter written in 2010), 2013, https://www.otroscines.com/nota-4366-los-eternos-problemas-para-conseguir-salas-el-caso-de-licardo (accessed 8 December 2018).

Durón, Hispano, 'The New Central American Cinema, 2001–2010', PhD dissertation, University of Kansas, Lawrence, 2014, http://kuscholarworks.ku.edu/bitstream/handle/1808/14530/Durn_ku_0099D_13296_DATA_1.pdf?sequence=1 (accessed 25 June 2015).

Eguigure, Rossy, 'Have Docs, Will Travel: Mexico's Moveable Film Fest', *Documentary. org*, Spring 2010, http://www.documentary.org/content/have-docs-will-travel-mexicos-moveable-film-fest (accessed 3 March 2014).

Elmer, Greg, and Mike Gasher (eds), *Contracting Out Hollywood: Runaway Productions and Foreign Locations Shooting* (Lanham, MD: Rowman and Littlefield, 2005).

Erazo, Vanessa, '*Instructions Not Included* a Game Changer for Latinos in Film?', *Latin Heat*, 22 January 2014, http://www.latinheat.com/everything-related-to-film/film/instructions-not-included-a-game-changer-for-latinos-in-film/ (accessed 8 September 2017).

España, Claudio, 'El cine sonoro y su expansion', in Jorge Miguel Couselo (ed.), *Historia del cine argentino* (Buenos Aires: Centro Editor de América Latina, 1992), pp. 47–88.

European Audiovisual Observatory, *World Film Market Trends* (France: Global Rouge, 2009).

Expansión por CNN 'México firma El Acuerdo comercial antifalsificación (ACTA) en Japón', *Expansión por CNN México*, 11 July 2012, http://expansion.mx/nacional/2012/07/11/mexico-firma-el-acuerdo-comercial-contra-la-falsificacion-acta-en-japon?newscnn1=%5B20120712%5D (accessed 2 November 2016).

Falicov, Tamara L., 'Argentina's Blockbuster Movies and the Politics of Culture Under Neoliberalism, 1989–1998', *Media, Culture & Society* vol. 22 (2000), pp. 327–42.

Falicov, Tamara L., 'Television for the Big Screen: How *Comodines* Became Argentina's First Blockbuster Phenomenon', in Julian Stringer (ed.), *Movie Blockbusters* (London: Routledge, 2003), pp. 242–54.

Falicov, Tamara L., 'US–Argentine Co-Productions 1982–1990: Roger Corman, Aries Productions, "Schlockbuster" Movies, and the International Market', *Film and History* vol. 34 no. 1 (2004), pp. 31–9. Special Issue on Latin American Cinema.

Falicov, Tamara L., 'Hollywood's Rogue Neighbor: The Argentine Film Industry During the Good Neighbor Policy, 1939–1945', *The Americas: A Quarterly Review of Inter-American Cultural History* vol. 63 no. 2, Guest edited by Ana M. López (2006), pp. 245–60.

Falicov, Tamara L., *The Cinematic Tango: Contemporary Argentine Film* (London: Wallflower Press, 2007a).

Falicov, Tamara L., 'Programa Ibermedia: Co-Production and the Cultural Politics of Constructing an Ibero-American Audiovisual Space', *Spectator* vol. 27 no. 2 (2007b), pp. 21–30.

Falicov, Tamara L., 'Hollywood in Latin America: How Mexico and Argentina Cope and Cooperate with the Behemoth of the North', in Janet Wasko and Paul McDonald (eds), *The Contemporary Hollywood Film Industry* (Oxford: Blackwell, 2008), pp. 264–76.

Falicov, Tamara L., 'Cine en Construcción (Films in Progress): How Spanish and Latin American Filmmakers Negotiate the Construction of a Globalized Art House Aesthetic', *Transnational Cinemas* vol. 4 no. 2, Special issue guest edited by Sarah Barrow and Tamara L. Falicov (London: Intellect Press, 2013a), pp. 253–72.

Falicov, Tamara L., 'Ibero-Latin American Co-Productions: Transnational Cinema, Spain's Public Relations Venture or Both?', in Stephanie Dennison (ed.), *Contemporary Hispanic Cinema: Interrogating the Transnational in Spanish and Latin American Film* (Woodbridge, Suffolk: Tamesis/Boydell and Brewer, 2013b), pp. 67–88.

Falicov, Tamara L., 'Film Funding Opportunities for Latin American Filmmakers: A Case for Further North–South Collaboration in Training and Film Festival Initiatives', in Maria Delgado, Stephen Hart and Randal Johnson (eds), *Companion to Contemporary Latin American Film* (New York: Blackwell-Wiley, 2017), pp. 85–98.

Feigenbaum, Harvey, 'Is Technology the Enemy of Culture?', *International Journal of Cultural Policy* vol. 10 no. 3 (2004), pp. 251–63.

Fein, Seth, 'Hollywood, US–Mexican Relations, and the Devolution of the "Golden Age" of Mexican Cinema', *Film-Historia* vol. 4 no. 2 (1994), pp. 103–35.

Fein, Seth, 'Transcultured Anticommunism: Cold War Hollywood in Postwar Mexico', in C. Noriega (ed.), *Visible Nations: Latin American Cinema and Video* (Minneapolis: University of Minnesota Press, 2000), pp. 82–114.

Fermin, Zuri, Personal interview, 30 May 2003.

Fernandes, Sujatha, *Cuba Represent!: Cuban Arts, State Power and the Making of New Revolutionary Cultures* (Durham, NC, and London: Duke University Press, 2006).

Festival Scope, Festival Internacional Cine de Morelia (Morelia International Film Festival), 2016, https://www.festivalscope.com/all/festival/morelia-international-film-festival/2016 (accessed 14 November 2016).

Finley, Adam, 'Venezuelan Film Gets International Distribution', *Moviefone.com*, 2005, http://blog.moviefone.com/2005/08/05/venezuelan-film-gets-international-distribution/ (accessed 30 July 2015).

Floángel Gómez and M. Romero, 'En 2011 la Villa del Cine estará al 100% de su capacidad', *Correo del Orinoco*, 15 August 2010, p. 14.

Fondeadora.mx, 2016, https://fondeadora.mx/ (accessed 14 December 2016).

Foreman, Liza, 'How a New Generation of Filmmakers, Tax Incentives Are Buoying the Latin American Film Sector', *Hollywood Reporter*, 12 May 2011, http://www.hollywoodreporter.com/news/how-a-new-generation-filmmakers-187937 (accessed 18 March).

Fosk, Alejandro, '2013 Latin America Digital Future in Focus', *Comscore*, 29 May 2013, https://www.comscore.com/Insights/Presentations-and-Whitepapers/2013/2013-Latin-America-Digital-Future-in-Focus (accessed 1 December 2018).

Frau-Meigs, Divina, '"Cultural Exception", National Policies and Globalisation Imperatives in Democratisation and Promotion of Contemporary Culture',

Quaderns del CAC no. 14 (2003), http://www.audiovisualcat.net/publicationsing/
Q14france.pdf (accessed 11 August 2005).

Friedlander, F., 'Balance 2015: las distribuidoras cinematográficas independientes',
Ultracine, 29 December 2015, http://www.ultracine.com/index.php/balance-2015-
las-companias-distribuidoras-independientes-cinematograficas/ (accessed 1 August
2016).

Fritz, Ben, 'Netflix Sees Mexico Profitability in Two Years as Latin America
Launches', *Los Angeles Times,* 12 September 2011, http://latimesblogs.latimes.com/
entertainmentnewsbuzz/2011/09/netflix-sees-mexico-profitability-in-two-years-as-
latin-america-launches.html (accessed 23 December 2011).

Fuchs, Alejandro, 'Global Family: Cinepolis' Alejandro Ramírez Discusses Outreach
and Opportunity', *Film Journal,* 15 April 2013, http://www.filmjournal.
com/filmjournal/content_display/news-and-features/features/cinemas/
e3i647f3e5c89c4b75ca0c5ce063d0334fc (accessed 2 April 2014).

Fuertes, Marta, and Guillermo Mastrini (eds), *Industria cinematográfica latinoamericana*
(Buenos Aires: La Cruijia Ediciones, 2014).

García, Facundo, 'Un poco de aire para el cine nacional', 8 January 2009, http://www.
pagina12.com.ar/diario/suplementos/espectaculos/5-12508-2009-01-08.html
(accessed 14 November 2012).

García Canclini, Néstor, *Hybrid Cultures: Strategies for Entering and Leaving Modernity*
(Minneapolis: University of Minnesota Press, 1995).

García Canclini, Néstor, 'Comunicación y cultura: Encuentros y desencuentros', in
Enrique Bustamente (ed.), *La cooperación cultura-comunicación en Iberoamérica*
(Madrid: Agencia Española de Cooperación Internacional para el Desarrollo,
2007). http://www.ccemx.org/descargas/files/ccci.pdf (accessed 2 December 2018).

García Reira, Emilio, *Historia documental del cine mexicano* (Mexico: University of
Guadalajara, 1992).

Garnham, Nicholas, 'Media Policy', in A. Briggs and P. Cobey (eds), *The Media: An
Introduction* (Hong Kong: Longman, 1998), pp. 210–33.

Garnham, Nicholas, *Emancipation, the Media, and Modernity. Arguments About the
Media and Social Theory* (New York: Oxford University Press, 2000).

Getino, Octavio, *Cine y televisión en América Latina: Producción y mercados* (Buenos
Aires: CICCUS, 2000).

Getino, Octavio, *Cine Argentino: Entre lo posible y lo deseable,* 2nd edition (Buenos Aires:
CICCUS, 2005).

Getino, Octavio, *Cine Iberoamericano: Los desafíos del nuevo siglo* (San José, Costa Rica:
Veritas, 2006).

Getino, Octavio, 'Los desafíos de la industria del cine en América Latina y el Caribe',
2007, http://www.ehu.eus/zer/hemeroteca/pdfs/zer22-08-getino.pdf (accessed 5
July 2015).

Getino, Octavio, *Cuaderno 7: Estudio de producción y mercados del cine latinoamericano en la primera década del siglo XXI* (Havana: Fundación del Nuevo Cine Latinoamericano, 2012), http://cinelatinoamericano.org/assets/docs/Cuaderno%20 7%20WEB.pdf (accessed 30 November 2018).

Giardina, C., 'MediaMation Grows 4D Footprint in Latin America', *Hollywood Reporter*, 2015, http://www.hollywoodreporter.com/behind-screen/mediamation-grows-4d-cinema-footprint-845009 (accessed 22 May 2016).

Goldsmith, Ben and Tom O'Regan, *The Film Studio: Film Production in the Global Economy* (Lanham, MD: Rowman and Littlefield, 2005).

Gomery, Douglas, 'The Hollywood Studio System, 1930–1949' (1986), reprinted in Thomas Schatz, *Hollywood: Critical Concepts in Media and Cultural Studies*, vol. 1 (New York: Routledge, 2004), pp. 107–28.

Gómez García, Rodrigo, 'Media Industries and Policy in Digital Times: A Latin American Perspective of Notes and Methods', in Ingrid Volkmer (ed.), *The Handbook of Global Media Research*, 1st edition (Hoboken, NJ: Wiley-Blackwell, 2012), pp. 212–26.

González, Erick, 'Instances and Problematic of Distribution', in Bruno Bettati (ed.), *Reflections on Audiovisual Distribution* (Chile: Cine Sin Fronteras/Austral Lab, 2012), pp. 13–22.

González, Leandro, Carolina Barnes and José A. Borello, 'El talón de Aquiles: Exhibición y distribución de cine en la Argentina, *H-industri@* vol. 8 no. 14 (2014), pp. 51–79.

González, Roque, Personal Interview, 22 December 2009.

González, Roque, 'Catching Up with Digital: 3D Drives the Rollout South of the Border', *Film Journal International*, 14 October 2011, http://www.filmjournal.com/filmjournal/content_display/news-and-features/features/cinemas/e3i61f2bfa2d77f2f132878a3c266236ad3 (accessed 21 December 2011).

Gonazalez, Roque, Email correspondence, 3 January 2012.

González, Roque, 'Emerging Markets and the Digitalization of the Film Industry', produced with the UNESCO Office of Statistics (UIS), UIS Information Paper no. 14, Quebec, Canada, 2013.

González, Velda, Sub-director of Programming, Puerto Rico Film Commission, email correspondence, 30 October 2006.

Gross, Steven R., and Katherine Ashton (Partners), Jasmine Powers and Lisa Gan (Associates), Debevoise & Plimpton LLP, 'The Globopar Financial Restructuring: A New Model for International Workouts', *International Corporate Rescue* vol. 3 no. 2 (2006), http://www.chasecambria.com/site/journal/article.php?id=21 (accessed 14 June 2012).

Gruenwedel, Erik, 'Getting a Kick in Latin America', *Home Media Magazine*, 9 June 2014, http://www.homemediamagazine.com/news/getting-kick-latin-america-33372 (accessed 2 September 2016).

Grupo Chaski, 'Red de microcines', 2015, http://grupochaski.org/red-de-microcines/ (accessed 31 July 2015).

Gubern, Roman, *Historia de cine*, vol. II (Barcelona: Lumen, 1971).

Guerra, Gerardo, 'Una mirada al cine boliviano', *Revista Trendy* vol. 5 no. 77 (April 2011), http://www.sbb.com.bo/articulo.php?edicion=66&id=10368 (accessed 22 April 2014).

Guerschuny, Hernán, 'Diseccionando el aura', *Haciendo cine* vol. 9 no. 52 (October 2005), pp. 22–3.

Guerschuny, Hernán, 'No se puede seguir creciendo sin salir al mundo' (Interview with Octavio Nadal), *Raices* vol. 4 no. 16 (May 2006), pp. 12–13.

Gurza, Agustín, 'Milestone Mexican Film to Screen in LA', *Los Angeles Times*, 10 July 2001, http://articles.latimes.com/2001/jul/10/entertainment/ca-20420 (accessed 9 October 2013).

Gutiérrez, Vicente, 'El cine mexicano rompe récord en taquilla', *El Economista*, 8 January 2010, http://eleconomista.com.mx/entretenimiento/2012/01/10/cine-mexico-rompe-record (accessed 7 March 2014).

Gutiérrez, Vicente, 'Cancela México apoyo a películas extranjeras', *El Economista*, 11 June 2017, http://eleconomista.com.mx/entretenimiento/2017/06/11/cancela-mexico-apoyo-peliculas-extranjeras (accessed 13 June 2017).

Guzmán, Laura Amelia, and Israel Cárdenas, Personal interview, 12 April 2015.

Harrison, Haskell, and John Gnuschke, 'An Overview of Film Production Incentives', *Business Perspectives*, 22 September 2005, https://www.questia.com/magazine/1G1-141803475/an-overview-of-film-production-incentives (accessed 2 December 2018).

Harvey, Edwin, *Film Policy and Public Finance. Iberoamerican Countries in an International Context: Antecedents, Institutions, and Experiences* (Madrid: Iberautor Promociones Culturales, 2005).

Hawley, Chris, 'Hollywood Casts Mexico in Starring Role', *The Arizona Republic*, 4 October 2004, www.chateaumanzanillo.com/movies_mexico.html (accessed 16 December 2005).

Hecht, John, 'Von Damm Exits Videocine', *Hollywood Reporter*, 1 November 2006, https://www.hollywoodreporter.com/news/von-damm-exits-videocine-141444 (accessed 8 December 2018).

Hecht, John, 'Cinemark Selling Mexico Theatre Chain', *Hollywood Reporter*, 19 February 2013a, http://www.hollywoodreporter.com/news/cinemark-selling-mexico-theater-chain-422326 (accessed 10 May 2016).

Hecht, John, 'Mexico's "Instructions Not Included" Has Record Box Office Opening', *Hollywood Reporter*, 23 September 2013b, http://www.hollywoodreporter.com/news/mexicos-instructions-not-included-has-634751 (accessed 1 August 2016).

Hernández Castillo, Juan Manuel, *Claves del cine móvil? Tecnologías vivenciales* (Caracas, Venezuela: CNAC, 2016), https://issuu.com/juanjoseespinozaaguilar/docs/libro___claves_del_cine_mo__vil-_im (accessed 30 November 2018).

Hernández Cordón, Julio, Personal interview, 13 April 2015.

Hesmondhalgh, David, *Cultural Industries* (London: Sage, 2007).

Higson, Andrew, 'The Limiting Imagination of National Cinema', in Elizabeth Ezra and Terry Rowden (eds), *Transnational Cinema: The Film Reader* (London: Routledge, 2006), pp. 15–25.

Hill, John, 'The Issue of National Cinema and British Film Production', in Duncan Petrie (ed.), *New Questions of British Cinema* (London: British Film Institute, 1992).

Hill, John, 'British Film Policy', in Albert Moran (ed.), *Film Policy: International, National, and Regional Perspectives* (London: Routledge, 1996), pp. 101–13.

Himpele, Jeffrey D., *Circuits of Culture: Media, Politics and Indigenous Identity in the Andes* (Minneapolis: University of Minnesota Press, 2008).

Hinojosa Córdova, Lucila, 'Economía política del cine mexicano: Dos décadas de transformaciones', *Revista Rae-IC* (*Revista de la Asociación Española de Investigación de la Comunicación*) vol. 1 no. 2 (2014), http://www.novosmedios.org/revista/index.php/AEICp/article/view/49/51 (accessed 12 July 2015).

Hjort, Mette, 'On the Plurality of Cinematic Transnationalism', in Nataša Ďurovičová and Kathleen Newman (eds), *World Cinemas, Transnational Perspectives* (New York: Routledge, 2010), pp. 12–33.

Hoad, Phil, 'Is Hollywood Backing a Blessing for Local-Language Films – Or a Curse?', *The Guardian*, 13 August 2013, http://www.theguardian.com/film/filmblog/2013/aug/13/hollywood-backing-local-language-films (accessed 16 October 2013).

Hopewell, John, 'Brazil Boosts Indie Film', *The Rio Times*, 7 March 2009, http://riotimesonline.com/brazil-news/rio-entertainment/brazil-boosts-indie-film/# (accessed 22 December 2011).

Hopewell, John, 'VOD Grows Fast in Latin America', *Variety*, 30 December 2011, http://www.variety.com/article/VR1118047990?refcadid=19 (accessed 3 January 2012).

Hopewell, John, 'Big Players Take Control of Brazil's Market', *Variety*, 26 January 2013a, http://variety.com/2013/film/news/big-players-take-control-of-brazil-s-market-1118064912/ (accessed 23 June 2015).

Hopewell, John, 'RioFilme Fuels Brazilian Biz', *Variety*, 26 January 2013b, http://variety.com/2013/film/news/riofilme-fuels-brazilian-biz-1118064911/ (accessed 3 March 2014).

Hopewell, John, 'Mundial Moves into Brazil', *Variety*, 21 August 2013c, http://variety.com/2013/film/global/mundial-moves-into-brazil-exclusive-1200583912/ (accessed 23 June 2015).

Hopewell, John, 'Latin American Horror Booming at Blood Window Market', *Variety*, 20 November 2013d, http://variety.com/2013/biz/global/scarefare-surges-in-latin-america-1200857018/ (accessed 26 July 2015).

Hopewell, John, 'Telefe Drives into New Productions, Telefónica Commits to Projects in Spain', *Variety*, 5 December 2013e, http://variety.com/2013/film/global/telefonica-studios-pushes-production-investment-in-argentina-and-spain-exclusive-1200923203/ (accessed 18 March 2015).

Hopewell, John, 'Brazil New Year Bonanza', *Variety*, 31 December 2013f, http://variety.com/2013/film/global/brazil-new-year-bonanza-1201014875/ (accessed 23 June 2015).

Hopewell, John, 'Garcia Powers Up LatAm Distribution', *Variety*, 5 March 2013g, http://variety.com/2013/film/global/garcia-powers-up-latam-distribution-1200003403/ (accessed 28 September 2017).

Hopewell, John, 'Aggressive Brazil Exhib Build to Continue', *Variety*, 4 October 2014, http://variety.com/2014/film/festivals/cinepolis-aggressive-brazil-exhib-build-to-continue-exclusive-1201320867/ (accessed 10 May 2016).

Hopewell, John, 'Brazil Films Get Boost from State Aid', *Variety*, 12 May 2016, http://variety.com/2016/film/festivals/brazil-films-get-boost-from-state-aid-1201772955/ (accessed 10 October 2016).

Hopewell, John, and Jonathan Holland, 'Pix in Progress Find Funders', *Variety*, 20–26 September 2004, p. 14.

Hopewell, John, and Emiliano de Pablos, 'Telefónica Studios Ups Production Slate', *Variety*, 2013, http://variety.com/2013/film/news/telefonica-studios-ups-production-slate-1200662004/ (accessed 18 March 2015).

Hopewell, John, and Jonathan Holland, 'Pix in Progress Find Funders', *Variety*, 20–26 September 2004, p. 14.

Huddleston, Jr Tom, 'Your Netflix Experience Is About to Look a Lot Different', 15 June 2015, *Fortune*, http://fortune.com/2015/06/15/netflix-new-website-design/ (accessed 7 July 2015).

Hughan, Ilse, 'Mientras tanto en la ciudad … La experiencia del mercado de coproducción cinematográfica para proyectos de América Latina', in Eduardo Russo (ed.), *Hacer cine: Producción audiovisual en América Latina* (Buenos Aires: Editorial Paidos, 2008), pp. 431–9.

Humphreys, Keith, 'How a Landmark Antitrust Case Changed the Movies', *The Washington Monthly*, 1 May 2013, http://washingtonmonthly.com/2013/05/01/how-a-landmark-antitrust-case-changed-the-movies/ (accessed 8 July 2016).

Ibermedia, Summit of the Americas (Chile: 10–11 November, 1996), p. x.

Ibermedia, 'Ibermedia en cifras', 2015, http://www.programaibermedia.com/el-programa/ibermedia-en-cifras/ (accessed 2 December 2018).

IIPA, 'About IIPA', 2017, http://www.iipawebsite.com/aboutiipa.html (accessed 25 September 2017).

IMCINE, Statistical Yearbook of Mexican Cinema, 2013, http://
www.imcine.gob.mx/sites/536bfc0fa137610966000002/content_
entry537f86d593e05abc55000247/53ce9ce49d727985f20002be/files/anuario_2013.
pdf (accessed 21 July 2015).

IMCINE, Statistical Yearbook of Mexican Cinema, 2014, http://
www.imcine.gob.mx/sites/536bfc0fa137610966000002/content_
entry537f86d593e05abc55000247/53ce9ce49d727985f20002be/files/ANUARIO_
ESTAD_STICO_DE_CINE_MEXICANO_2014_ON_LINE.pdf (accessed 8
July 2015).

IMCINE, 'Presenta IMCINE nueva plataforma digital para el cine mexicano', 19 June
2015, http://www.imcine.gob.mx/comunicacion-social/comunicados-y-noticias/
presenta-imcine-nueva-plataforma-digital-para-el-cine-mexicano (accessed 7 July 2015).

IMCINE, Mission statement on website, 2016, http://www.imcine.gob.mx/imcine/el-
instituto (accessed 25 October 2016).

INCAA, Mission statement on website, 2016, http://www.incaa.gob.ar/incaa (accessed
25 October 2016).

Irmer, Marc, Personal interview, February 2011.

Ituralde, María Eugenia, and Diego Gabriel Lingeri, 'Qué miramos en Olavarría?
Cuota de pantalla, cine nacional e industria de cine', *Aura, revista de historia y teoria
de arte* no. 1 (2013), pp. 46–60.

Jaafar, Ali, 'Alex Garcia Launches AG Capital, Will Finance High-End English-
Language Film and TV', *Deadline Hollywood*, 18 May 2015, http://deadline.
com/2015/05/alex-garcia-launches-ag-capital-will-finance-high-end-english-
language-film-and-tv-cannes-1201428918/ (accessed 30 July 2015).

Jäckel, Anne, *European Film Industries* (London: British Film Institute/Palgrave
Macmillan, 2008).

Jarvinen, Lisa, *The Rise of Spanish-Language Filmmaking: Out from Hollywood's Shadow,
1929–1939* (New Brunswick, NJ, and London: Rutgers University Press, 2012).

Jaugey, Florence, Personal interview, 16 April 2015.

Jeancolas, Jean-Pierre, 'The Inexportable: The Case of French Cinema and Radio in the
1950s', in Richard Dyer and Ginette Vincendeau (eds), *Popular European Cinema*
(London and New York: Routledge, 1992), pp. 141–8.

Jiménez, Hernán, Kickstarter video campaign, 2011, https://www.kickstarter.com/
projects/1052685152/costa-rican-feature-film-the-return (accessed 2 December
2018).

Jiménez Hinestrosa, C. P., 'Cineplex: Una empresa colombiana que exporta cine
nacional a Centroamérica', *D.H.P* (Colombia), 2005, http://base.d-p-h.info/es/
fiches/dph/fiche-dph-6742.html (accessed 14 July 2015).

Johnson, Randal, *The Film Industry in Brazil: Culture and the State* (Pittsburgh, PA:
University of Pittsburgh, 1987).

Johnson, Randal, 'The Rise and Fall of Brazilian Cinema, 1960–1990', in Randal Johnson and Robert Stam (eds), *Brazilian Cinema*, expanded edition (New York: Columbia University Press, 1995), pp. 362–86.

Johnson, Randal, 'Film Policy in Latin America', in Albert Moran (ed.), *Film Policy: International, National and Regional Perspectives* (London: Routledge, 1996), pp. 128–47.

Johnson, Randal, 'TV Globo, the MPA, and Contemporary Brazilian Cinema', in Stephanie Dennison and Lisa Shaw (eds), *Latin American Cinema: Essays on Modernity, Gender, and National Identity* (Jefferson, NC: McFarland, 2005), pp. 11–38.

Johnson, Randal, 'The Brazilian Retomada and Global Hollywood', in Gastón Lillo and Walter Moser (eds), *History and Society: Argentinian and Brazilian Cinema Since the 1980s* (Ottawa: Legas Publishing, 2007), pp. 87–100.

Johnson, Reed, 'Gael Garcia Bernal, Diego Luna's Ambulante Film Fest Plays LA', *Los Angeles Times*, 21 October 2013, http://articles.latimes.com/2013/oct/21/ entertainment/la-et-mn-garcia-bernal-luna-ambulante-20131021 (accessed 3 March 2014).

Johnson-Yale, Camille, '"So-Called Runaway Film Production": Countering Hollywood's Outsourcing Narrative in the Canadian Press', *Critical Studies in Media Communication* vol. 25 no. 2 (June 2008), pp. 113–34.

Jordan, Wilfredo, 'El negocio de CDs "piratas" se yergue entre la informalidad y el contraband, 15 December 2008, http://wilfredojordan.blogspot.com/2008/12/el- negocio-de-cd-piratas-se-yergue.html (accessed 29 May 2014).

Juárez Allen, Gema J., Personal interview, 2015.

Karaganis, Joe (ed.), *Media Piracy in Emerging Economies* (New York: Social Sciences Research Council, 2011).

Kay, Jeremy, 'Viacom Buys Argentina's Telefe Network for $345m', *Screen Daily. com*, 15 November 2016, http://www.screendaily.com/5111356.article?utm_ source=newsletter&utm_medium=email&utm_campaign=Newsletter79 (accessed 15 November 2016).

King, John, 'Cinema', in Leslie Bethell (ed.), *A Cultural History of Latin America: Literature, Music and the Visual Arts in the 19th and 20th Centuries* (Cambridge: Cambridge University Press, 1998), pp. 455–518.

King, John, *Magical Reels: A History of Cinema in Latin America* London: Verso, 2000).

Koehne, M. A., 'Iguana Set Resurrected as a Restaurant', *The Milwaukee Journal Sentinel*, 28 February 1999, http://www.findarticles.com/p/articles/mi_qn4196/ is_19990228/ai_n10487779 (accessed 28 January 2006).

Kozloff, Nikolas, 'Danny Glover, Haiti, and the Politics of Revolutionary Cinema in Venezuela', *NACLA*, 14 August 2008, http://venezuelanalysis.com/analysis/3719 (accessed 17 July 2015).

Laborde, Antonia, 'Así se logró romper el récord de estrenos chilenos en cines locales', *El Definido*, 21 July 2014, http://www.eldefinido.cl/actualidad/pais/2633/Asi_se_logro_romper_el_record_de_estrenos_chilenos_en_cines_locales/ (accessed 27 July 2015).

Lara, Hugo, 'Los inicios del cine mexicano (1895–1910)', 2002, http://www.correcamara.com.mx/inicio/int.php?mod=historia_detalle&id_historia=43#sthash.OetHyuDB.dpuf (accessed 31 March 2014).

Lenti, Paul, 'Central American Traveler's Diary', *Variety*, 23 March 1987, pp. 70–1.

LatAm Cinema, 'La Residencia Andina de Guion Documental prepara su primera edición', 23 June 2015, http://www.latamcinema.com/la-residencia-andina-de-guion-documental-prepara-su-primera-edicion/ (accessed 1 July 2015).

Levine, Sydney, 'Why the Fenix Awards Matter and Los Cabos International Film Festival', *Indiewire*, 2014a, http://www.indiewire.com/2014/11/why-the-fenix-awards-matter-and-los-cabos-international-film-festival-171791/ (accessed 3 August 2016).

Levine, Sydney, 'Case Study: "Wakolda" or "The German Doctor" (Argentina's Submission for the Oscar Nomination as Best Foreign Language Film)', *Indiewire*, 25 April 2014b, http://www.indiewire.com/2014/04/case-studywakolda-or-the-german-doctor-argentinas-submission-for-the-oscar-nomination-as-best-foreign-language-film-168719/ (accessed 3 August 2016).

Lima, Fernando E. Juan, 'Distribuidoras independientes: Especie en extinción?', Guest column, *OtrosCines.com*, 4 February 2015, http://www.otroscines.com/nota?idnota=9413 (accessed 1 August 2016).

Loayza, Marcos, 'Mirrors on the Periphery', in Eduardo Russo (ed.), *The Film Edge: Contemporary Filmmaking in Latin America* (Buenos Aires: Editorial Teseo/Fundación TyPa, 2010), pp. 159–72.

López, Ana M., 'Argentina, 1955–1976', in John King and Nissa Torrents (eds), *The Garden of the Forking Paths: Argentine Cinema* (London: British Film Institute, 1987).

Lowe, Florence S., 'Washington Hullabaloo', *Variety*, 8 February 1944.

Luca, Luiz Gonzalez Assis de, *A hora do cinema digital: A democratização e globalização do audiovisual* (São Paulo: Imprensa Oficial do Estado de São Paulo/Fundação Padre Anchieta, 2009).

Maciel, David R., 'Cinema and the State in Contemporary Mexico, 1970–1999', in Joanne Hershfield and David R. Maciel (eds), *Mexico's Cinema: A Century of Film and Filmmakers* (Wilmington, DE: Scholarly Resources, 1999), pp. 197–232.

MacLaird, Misha, *Aesthetics and Politics in the Mexican Film Industry* (New York: Palgrave Macmillan, 2013).

Mango, Agustín, 'Cinemark Argentina Buys Out Hoyts Multiplexes', *Hollywood Reporter*, 25 August 2011, http://www.hollywoodreporter.com/news/cinemark-argentina-buys-hoyts-multiplexes-227974 (accessed 31 March 2014).

Mango, Agustín, 'Argentine Gov't Boosts Film Sector to Industry Standards', *Hollywood Reporter*, 30 August 2012, http://www.hollywoodreporter.com/news/argentine-cinema-gets-industry-treatment-366847 (accessed 21 November 2012).

Mango, Augustín, 'Dominican Republic Strengthens Tax Credit Film Incentive', *The Hollywood Reporter*, 7 March 2013, https://www.hollywoodreporter.com/news/dominican-republic-strengthens-tax-credit-579899 (accessed 2 December 2018).

Mango, Agustín, and John Hecht, 'Latin America's Film Industry Paradox: 5 Countries with Loud Fest Titles (and Quiet Box Office Payoffs)', *Hollywood Reporter*, 13 February 2016, http://www.hollywoodreporter.com/lists/latin-americas-film-industry-paradox-864913 (accessed 16 May 2016).

Manrique, Elena, Personal interview, 12 April 2015.

Márquez, Humberto, 'Film-Venezuela: Bringing Non-Hollywood Fare to City Squares', *Inter Press Service News Agency*, 7 November 2006, www.ipsnews.net (accessed 19 November 2013).

Márquez, Humberto, 'Venezuela: Petrodollars for Local Film Industry', *Inter Press News Agency*, 12 January 2007, www.ipsnews.net (accessed 19 November 2013).

Martin, Michael T. (ed.), *The New Latin American Cinema*, vols. 1–2 (Detroit, MI: Wayne State University Press, 1997).

Martínez, Gabriela, 'Cinema Law in Latin America: Brazil, Peru and Colombia', *Jump Cut* no. 50 (Spring 2008), https://www.ejumpcut.org/archive/jc50.2008/LAfilmLaw/text.html (accessed 25 July 2017).

Mastrini, Guillermo, 'Preambulo', in Marta Fuertes and Guillermo Mastrini (eds), *Industria cinematográfica latinoamericana* (Buenos Aires: La Cruijia Ediciones, 2014).

Mata, Aquilino José, 'La casa del fin de los tiempos, la película venezolana más taquillera', *El Diario de Caracas*, 6 December 2013, http://diariodecaracas.com/gente/la-casa-del-fin-los-tiempos-la-pelicula-venezolana-mas-taquillera (accessed 17 July 2015).

Mata, Natalia Rodriguez, 'Por qué la pausa en el fondo para el audiovisual Cinergia?', 17 June 2015, http://www.redcultura.com/front/noticias2.php?ref=1%2Fid%3D60 (accessed 7 July 2015).

Mattelhart, Tristan, 'Audiovisual Piracy, Informal Economy, and Cultural Globalization', *International Journal of Communication* vol. 6 (2012), pp. 735–50.

Mayorga, Emilio, 'Ibermedia Boosts Animation Support', *Variety*, 1 May 2018, https://variety.com/2018/film/global/ibermedia-boosts-animation-support-1202793416/ (accessed 10 August 2018).

McAllister, Elba, Personal interview, 14 April 2015.

McDonald, Paul, *Video and DVD Industries* (London: British Film Institute, 2007).

McDonald, Paul, 'Hollywood, the MPAA, and the Formation of Anti-Piracy Policy', *International Journal of Cultural Policy* vol. 22 no. 5 (2016), pp. 686–705.

Middents, Jeffrey, *Writing National Cinema: Film Journals and Film Culture in Peru* (Hanover, NH: Dartmouth College Press. Published by University Press of New England, 2009).

Miller, Toby, Nitin Govil, John McMurria, Ting Wang and Richard Maxwell, *Global Hollywood 2*, 2nd edition (London: British Film Institute, 2004).

Mingant, Nolwenn, Cecilia Tirtaine and Joel Augros (eds), *Film Marketing into the Twenty-First Century* (London: British Film Institute/Palgrave Macmillan, 2015).

Minghetti, Claudio, 'Un golpe de realidad', *La Nacion*, 9 May 2005, http://www.lanacion.com.ar/702595-un-golpe-de-realidad (accessed 31 July 2015).

Mitchell, Wendy, 'Colombia Unveils Cash Rebate Details', *Screen Daily*, 1 March 2013, http://www.screendaily.com/news/production/colombia-unveils-cash-rebate-details/5052522.article (accessed 18 March 2015).

Mohr, Ian, and John Hopewell, '"A New Latin Quarter": Argentine Launches Fund with Weinsteins', *Daily Variety* vol. 291 no. 36 (22 May 2006), p. 10.

Moisés, José Álvaro, 'Cultural Diversity and Development in the Americas', *Cultural Studies Series No. 9*. Unit for Social Development, Education and Culture, Organisation of American States, 2002, http://www.oas.org/udse/espanol/documentos/1hub4.doc (accessed 11 August 2005).

Monteagudo, Luciano, 'Last News from the Battlefront', *El Amante.com*, 7 August 2003, http://www.elamante.com/ar/nota/2/2080.shtml (accessed 8 October 2003).

Monteagudo, Luciano, 'El adios a un talento de alto vuelo', 30 June 2006, *Página 12*, www.pagina12.com.ar/diario.suplementos.espectaculos.5-2983-2006-06 (accessed 13 December 2006).

Mora, Carl J., *Mexican Cinema: Reflections of a Society, 1896–2004*, 3rd edition (Jefferson, NC: McFarland, 2005).

Moreno Domínguez, José Manuel, 'Diversidad audiovisual e integración cultural: Analizando el programa Ibermedia', *Comunicación y sociedad* no. 9 (January–June 2008), pp. 95–118.

Mosco, Vincent, *Political Economy of Communication* (London: Sage, 1996).

Mount, Ian, 'Can an Argentine Animated Film Rival Hollywood Blockbusters?', *The New Yorker*, 25 October 2013, http://www.newyorker.com/business/currency/can-an-argentine-animated-film-rival-hollywood-blockbusters (accessed 24 June 2015).

MPA, 'Motion Picture Association: Submission to the Services Workshop', VIII Americas Business Forum, 17–21 November 2003, www.sice.oas.org/FTAA/miami/ABF/papers/pMtPicAs_e.asp (accessed 12 January 2006).

MPAA, 'Opinion: Reflexiones sobre el público', *Página 12*, 29 December 2009, http://www.pagina12.com.ar/diario/suplementos/espectaculos/subnotas/16506-4646-2009-12-29.html (accessed 31 July 2015).

MPAA, 'Theatrical Market Statistics Report', 2012, http://www.2012-Theatrical-Market-Statistics-Report.pdf (accessed 7 April 2014).

MPAA, 'Theatrical Market Statistics 2014', 2014, http://www.mpaa.org/wp-content/uploads/2015/03/MPAA-Theatrical-Market-Statistics-2014.pdf (accessed 24 June 2015).

MPAA, 'Theatrical Market Statistics Report', 2015b, http://www.mpaa.org/wp-content/uploads/2015/03/MPAA-Theatrical-Market-Statistics-2014.pdf (accessed 22 May 2016).

Muello, Peter, 'Brazil's Movie Industry Eyes Comeback', *SF Gate*, 6 October 2006, http://www.sfgate.com/cgibin/article.cgi?f=/n/a/2006/10/06/entertainment/e111821D34.DTL (accessed 9 June 2008).

Murdock, Graham, 'Comentarios de base: Las condiciones de la práctica cultural', in Y. H. Ferguson and P. Golding (eds), *Economía Política y Estudios Culturales* (Barcelona: Bosch, 2016), pp. 161–84.

Murga, Celina, Roundtable discussion at Panama International Film Festival, 14 April 2015a.

Nagib, Lúcia, 'Going Global: The Brazilian Scripted Film', in Sylvia Harvey (ed.), *Trading Culture: Global Traffic and Local Cultures in Film and Television* (Eastleigh, Hants.: John Libbey Publishing, 2006), pp. 95–104.

Nevarez, Griselda, 'Latinos Are the Biggest Moviegoers', *La Opinión*, 5 April 2014, https://laopinion.com/2014/04/05/latinos-are-the-biggest-moviegoers/ (accessed 30 November 2018).

Newbery, Charles, 'Quotas Give Screen Time to Local Pix', *Variety*, 12 July 2004, p. 12.

Newbery, Charles, 'No sos vos, soy yo sigue batiendo records', *Cómo hacer cine*, 13 July 2005, http://www.comohacercine.com/actualidad_detalle.php?ide+3695&c+Taquillas (accessed 7 August 2005).

Newbery, Charles, 'Digital Cinema Grows in Latin America', Variety, 9 October 2008, http://variety.com/2008/film/markets-festivals/digital-cinema-grows-in-latin-america-1117993755/ (accessed 30 July 2015).

Newbery, Charles, 'Argentina, Venezuela Prep Film Fund', *Variety*, 5 May 2011, http://variety.com/2011/film/news/argentina-venezuela-prep-film-fund-1118036470/ (accessed 13 July 2015).

Nex TV Latam, 'Televisa Launches Its OTT Veo', *Nex TV Latam.com*, 5 June 2013, http://nextvlatam.com/televisa-launches-its-ott-veo/?lang=en (accessed 30 July 2015).

Noble, Andrea, *Mexican National Cinema* (London and New York: Routledge, 2004).

Nornes, Abé Markus, *Cinema Babel: Translating Global Cinema* (Minneapolis: University of Minnesota Press, 2007).

Noticine, 'Cineastas uruguayos en huelga de hambre contra la morosidad hacia Ibermedia', 11 November 2003, http://noticine.com/industria/2015-cineastas-uruguayos-en-huelga-de-hambre-contra-la-morosidad-hacia-ibermedia.html (accessed 24 September 2016).

Novaes, Tereza, '"Tropa de Elite" ja foi visto por 19% dos paulistanos', *Folha de São Paulo*, 6 October 2007, http://www1.folha.uol.com.br/ilustrada/2007/10/334403-tropa-de-elite-ja-foi-visto-por-19-dos-paulistanos.shtml (accessed 3 March 2014).

O'Brien, María, and Maya Ibars, 'Fame, Glamour, Cash', *Latin Finance* no. 156 (April/May 2004), pp. 42–4.

Olivera, Héctor, 'La Nouvelle vague en danger', *Cahiérs du cinema* vol. 578 (27 April 2003), p. 27.

Oliveres, J. J., 'No cambió el guión *Spectre* a pedido de México: James Wilson', *La Jornada*, 19 March 2015, http://www.jornada.unam.mx/2015/03/19/espectaculos/a08n1esp (accessed 22 July 2015).

O'Neill, J., 'Telefónica's $100M Spend on Peru Tech Center Key to Its OTT Growth in LatAm', 10 May 2016a, http://www.ooyala.com/videomind/blog/telef-nica-s-100m-spend-peru-tech-center-key-its-ott (accessed 1 August 2016).

O'Neill, J., 'Report Forecasts Declining Latam Market Share for Netflix', *Ooyala.com*, 26 May 2016b, http://www.ooyala.com/videomind/blog/report-forecasts-declining-latam-market-share-netflix (accessed 1 August 2016).

Ozores, Pedro, 'LatAm's first OTT Association Comes to Life in Brazil', 2 March 2018, http://www.bnamericas.com/en/news/ict/latams-first-ott-association-comes-to-life-in-brazil/ (accessed 10 August 2018).

Pacheco, Joel, 'Netflix Sees Another Competitor Rise in Mexico: Axtel Play (+Analysis)', *MDC Blog*, 2017, https://www.linkedin.com/pulse/netflix-sees-another-competitor-rise-mexico-axtel-play-joel-pacheco/ (accessed 10 August 2018).

Page, Joanna, *Crisis and Capitalism in the New Argentine Cinema* (Durham, NC: Duke University Press, 2009).

Pantelion Films, 2017, http://www.pantelionfilms.com/ (accessed 28 June 2017).

Pardo, José Manuel, '30 meses de cine-movil por los campos de Cuba', *Cine cubano*, 1971.

Patino, Carolina, 'Analysing the Formal and Informal Documentary Film Distribution Markets in Colombia', *Journal of Media Practice* vol. 15 no. 1 (2014), http://www.tandfonline.com/doi/abs/10.1080/14682753.2014.892696 (accessed 27 July 2017).

Peña, William, '50% usuarios Internet en Latinoamérica, ven contenido audiovisual pirata vía online', *PC World*, 22 January 2016, http://www.pcworldenespanol.com/2016/01/22/50-de-usuarios-de-internet-en-latinoamerica-disfrutan-contenidos-audiovisuales-piratas-via-online/ (accessed 26 October 2016).

Perelman, Pablo, and Paulina Seivach, *La industria cinematográfica en la Argentina: Entre los límites del mercado y el fomento estatal* (Buenos Aires: CEDEM/GCBA, 2003).

Pérez, Oscar Berrendo, Juan Antonio Serrano Fernández and Enrique Encinas Puebla, *Panorama audiovisual Iberoamericano 2014* (Madrid: EGEDA, 2014), https://www.google.com/search?q=Panorama+Audiovisual+Iberoamericano+egeda¡utf-8œutf-8 (accessed 16 May 2016).

Pérez, Pedro, Interview in *Raices*, no. 10, 2004.

Picciau, Kevin, 'Cinemark Strengthens Its Position in Latin America', *INA Global*, 11 July 2011, http://www.inaglobal.fr/en/cinema/article/cinemark-strengthens-its-position-south-america (accessed 31 March 2014).

Picciau, Kevin, 'Venezuelan Film Industry: Ten Years Getting Strong, Growing Up', *INA Global*, 23 April 2014, http://www.inaglobal.fr/en/cinema/article/venezuelan-film-industry-ten-years-getting-strong-growing-7550 (accessed 11 July 2016).

Pick, Zuzana, *The New Latin American Cinema: A Continental Project* (Austin: University of Texas Press, 1993).

Picó, María Bird, 'Center Growth Fuels Big Latin American Cinema', International Council of Shopping Centers (ICSC), December, www.icsc.org.srch/sct/sct1205/Latin_cinemas.php (accessed 19 September 2006).

Pinazza, Nátalia, 'The Re-Emergence of Brazilian Cinema: A Brief History', in Natalia Pinazza and Louis Beyman (eds), *Directory of World Cinema: Brazil* (London: Intellect Books, 2013), pp. 32–3.

Pires, Lucas Rodrigues, 'Cinema brasileiro agora é notícia: Por quê?', *Digestivo Cultural*, 2003, http://www.digestivocultural.com/colunistas/coluna.asp?codigo=1097&titulo=Cinema_brasileiro_agora_e_noticia._Por_que? (accessed 23 June 2017).

Piva, Jorge Mario Martínez, Ramón Padilla Pérez, Claudia Schatan Pérez and Verónica Vega Montoya, 'The Mexican Film Industry and Its Participation in the Global Value Chain', *ECLAC*, Sub-regional Headquarters in Mexico, 2011, pp. 1–47, http://repositorio.cepal.org/bitstream/handle/11362/4916/S20111039_en.pdf?sequence=1 (accessed 5 June 2015).

Pragda, *The Return (El regreso)*, 2017, https://pragda.com/film/the-return/ (accessed 28 June 2017).

Prescott, Roberta, 'Netflix to Distribute Televisa Programs', *RCR Wireless Americas*, 27 July 2011, http://www.rcrwireless.com/americas/20110727/enterprise/netflix-to-distribute-televisa-programs/ (accessed 21 December 2011).

ProChile, 2017, www.prochile.gob.cl (accessed 9 September 2017).

Proimágenes, Promotional testimonial video of actor Mickey Rourke, 2015, https://www.youtube.com/watch?v=30RF_FKBQ7M (accessed 5 November 2016).

Puente, Henry, *The Promotion and Distribution of US Latino Films* (New York: Peter Lang, 2011).

Quartesan, Alessandra, Monica Romis and Francisco Lanzafame, *Cultural Industries in Latin America and the Caribbean* (Washington DC: Inter-American Development Bank, 2007), http://publications.iadb.org/bitstream/handle/11319/1143/Cultural%20Industries%20in%20Latin%20America%20and%20the%20Caribbean%3a%20Challenges%20and%20Opportunities.pdf?sequence=1 (accessed 4 February 2015).

Quintín, 'A Provisory Balance', *El Amante.com*, 1 August 2003, www.elamante.com.ar/nota/2/2079.shtml (accessed 5 September 2005).

Ramírez, Diego, Personal interview, 2015.

Ramírez Berg, Charles, *Cinema of Solitude: A Critical Study of Mexican Film, 1967–1983* (Austin: University of Texas Press, 1992).

Ramírez Berg, Charles, *The Classical Mexican Cinema: The Poetics of the Exceptional Golden Age Films* (Austin: University of Texas Press, 2015).

Ramos, Diana, 'Qué tan seria es la lucha antipiratería en América Latina?', 2012, http://www.animalpolitico.com/2012/07/cuan-seria-es-la-lucha-antipirateria-en-america-latina/ (accessed 1 September 2017).

Recktenwald, Nick, 'Latin American Cinema Is the Unexpected Remedy for Hollywood', *Blockbuster Boredom Mic.com*, 19 August 2013, http://mic.com/articles/59613/latin-american-cinema-is-the-unexpected-remedy-for-hollywood-blockbuster-boredom (accessed 21 August 2017).

RECon (The Global Retail Real Estate Convention), 'RECon Summary', 2012, http://www.inmobiliare.com/english-edition/shopping-center/recon-latin-america-summarizing.html (accessed 23 December 2011).

Rêgo, Cacilda M., 'Brazilian Cinema: Its Fall, Rise, and Renewal (1990–2003)', *New Cinemas: Journal of Contemporary Film* vol. 3 no. 2 (2005), pp. 85–100.

Reina, Mauricio, 'Análisis sobre el significado de esta ley', in '10 años de la ley de cine 814', *Cine Colombiano* (article originally published 21 July 2013 in *El Tiempo* newspaper), 30 July 2014, http://cinecolombiano.com/10-anos-de-la-ley-de-cine-814/ (accessed 30 September 2016).

Residence Programme at Cannes Film Festival, http://www.festival-cannes.fr/en/theResidence/generalinformation.html (accessed 25 June 2017).

Rodríguez, Jaime, Personal interview, 2016.

Rodríguez, Juan, and Carlos Adrianzen, 'Festival de Lima-El Cine-Encuentro Latin Americano de cine de Lima', MA thesis, Universidad Complutense de Madrid, 2007.

Rodríguez Sánchez, Raquel, 'El mercado del cine en Argentina', Oficina Económica y Comercial de la Embajada de España en Buenos Aires, *ICEX* (Exportacion España e Inversiones), 2015, https://www.icex.es/icex/es/navegacion-principal/todos-nuestros-servicios/informacion-de-mercados/paises/navegacion-principal/el-mercado/estudios-informes/DOC2015595462.html?idPais=AR&null (accessed 30 November 2018).

Roettgers, Janko, 'Muy Bien: Netflix More Than Doubles Traffic Share in Latin America', *Gigaom.com*, 20 November 2014, https://gigaom.com/2014/11/20/muy-bien-netflix-more-than-doubles-traffic-share-in-latam/ (accessed 14 July 2015).

Rolfe, Pamela, 'Film Future Bright for Venezuela; Spotlight: Venezuela', *Hollywood Reporter*, 24 May 2006, http://www.lacla.org/history.2007.html (accessed 12 December 2011).

Rolfe, Pamela, '15 Latin American Projects Go to Co-Production Forum in San Sebastian', *Hollywood Reporter*, 6 August 2012, http://www.hollywoodreporter.com/news/15-latin-american-projects-go-723713 (accessed 30 July 2015).

Ross, Miriam, 'Grupo Chaski's Microcines: Engaging the Spectator', *eSharp* vol. 11 (2008), pp. 1–21. http://www.gla.ac.uk/media/media_81277_en.pdf (accessed 31 July 2015).

Rossbach, Alma, and Leticia Canel, 'Política cinematográfica del sexenio de Luis Echeverría, 1970–1976', *Hojas de cine* (Mexico) vol. 2 (1988), pp. 93–6.

Rubenstein, Anne, 'Bodies, Cities, Cinema: Pedro Infante's Death as a Political Spectacle', in Gilbert M. Joseph, Anne Rubenstein and Eric Zolov (eds), *Fragments of a Golden Age: The Politics of Culture in Mexico Since 1940* (Durham, NC: Duke University Press, 2000), pp. 199–233.

Russo, Eduardo (ed.), *The Film Edge: Contemporary Filmmaking in Latin America* (Buenos Aires: Editorial Teseo/Fundación TyPA, 2010).

Salcedo, Gerardo, 'Los primeros 25 años', in *Múltiples rostros, múltiples miradas, un imaginario fílmico: 25 años del Instituto Mexicano de Cine* (Mexico: CONACULTA/IMCINE, 2009), pp. 10–14.

Sánchez-Ruiz, Enrique E., 'Las co-producciones en el cine mexicano', in Eduardo de la Vega Alfaro and Enrique E. Sánchez-Ruiz (eds), *Bye Bye Lumiere ... Investigación sobre cine en México* (Guadalajara: University of Guadalajara, 1994), pp. 75–100.

Sawada, Thiago, 'Avanço do streaming sinaliza fim da pirataria', *Estadao*, 15 August 2016, http://link.estadao.com.br/noticias/cultura-digital,avanco-do-streaming-sinaliza-fim-da-pirataria,10000069428 (accessed 10 September 2017).

Schiller, Herbert, *Mass Communications and American Empire*, 2nd edition (Boulder, CO: Westview Press, 1992).

Schnitman, Jorge, *Film Industries in Latin America: Dependency and Development* (Norwood, NJ: Ablex, 1984).

Schoon, Robert, 'Online Piracy in Latin America: Half of South American Internet Users Steal Media: Report', *Latin Trade*, 27 January 2016, http://www.latinpost.com/articles/111879/20160127/online-piracy-in-latin-america-half-of-south-american-internet-users-steal-media-report.htm (accessed 19 October 2016).

Schroeder Rodriguez, Paul A., 'After New Latin American Cinema', *Cinema Journal* vol. 51 no. 2 (Winter 2012), pp. 87–112.

Sedeño Valdellós, Ana, 'Globalización y transnacionalidad en el cine: Coproducciones internationales y festivales para un cine de arte emergente', *Fonseca: Journal of Communication* no. 6 (2013), pp. 296–315.

Segoviano, Rogelio, 'Nosotros los nobles: Un éxito inesperado', *Forbes Mexico*, 24 December 2013, https://www.forbes.com.mx/nosotros-los-nobles-un-exito-cinematografico-inesperado/ (accessed 25 September 2017).

Shaw, Deborah, *The Three Amigos: The Transnational Films of Guillermo del Toro, Alejandro González Iñárritu, and Alfonso Cuarón* (Manchester: Manchester University Press, 2013).

Shaw, Lisa, and Stephanie Dennison, *Brazilian National Cinema* (London and New York: Routledge, 2007).

Shurlock, Geoffrey, 'Versions: The Problem of Making Foreign Language Pictures', *American Cinematographer* vol. 11 no. 9 (January 1931), p. 22, quoted in Nornes, *Cinema Babel*, fn 58, p. 262.

Silva Neto, A. L., *Dicionário de filmes brasileiros* (São Paulo: A. L. Silva Neto, 2002).

Soles, Diane, 'The Cuban Film Industry: Between a Rock and a Hard Place', in Eloise Langer and John Cotman (eds), *Cuban Transitions at the Millennium* (Largo, MD: International Development Options, 2000), pp. 123–35.

Sousa Crespo, Mauricio, 'Crash Course on Bolivian Cinema', *ReVista: Harvard Review of Latin America* (Fall 2011), http://revista.drclas.harvard.edu/book/crash-course-bolivian-cinema (accessed 27 July 2015).

Statista, 'Number of Cinema Screens in Brazil', 2014a, http://www.statista.com/statistics/316838/number-cinema-screens-brazil/ (accessed 16 May 2016).

Statista, 'Number of Cinema Screens in Latin America', 2014b, http://www.statista.com/statistics/316868/number-cinema-screen-country-type-latin-america/ (accessed 27 April 2016).

Statista, 'Number of Internet Users in Latin America from 2014 to 2018 (in Millions)', 2018, https://www.statista.com/statistics/274860/number-of-internet-users-in-latin-america/ (accessed 1 December 2018).

Stewart, Andrew, 'Hollywood Gets Instructions from Latino Audiences', *Variety*, 24 September 2013, http://variety.com/2013/film/box-office/hollywood-gets-instructions-from-latino-audiences-1200665085/ (accessed 8 September 2017).

Stock, Anne Marie, 'Migrancy and the Latin American Cinemascape: Towards a Post-National Critical Praxis', in Elizabeth Ezra and Terry Rowden (eds), *Transnational Cinema: The Film Reader* (New York: Routledge, 2006), pp. 157–66.

Stock, Anne Marie, *On Location in Cuba: Street Filmmaking During Times of Transition* (Chapel Hill: University of North Carolina Press, 2009).

Straubhaar, Joseph, 'Beyond Media Imperialism: Asymmetrical Interdependence and Cultural Proximity', *Critical Studies in Mass Communication*, 8 March 1991, pp. 39–59.

Suárez, Juana, *Critical Essays on Colombian Cinema and Culture: Cinembargo Colombia*, trans. Laura Chesak (New York: Palgrave Macmillan, 2012).

Sutherland, Elizabeth, 'Cinema of Revolution: 90 Miles from Home', *Film Quarterly* vol. 15 no. 2 (Winter 1961), pp. 42–9.

Swartzel, Erick, and Ben Fritz, 'Fewer Americans Go to the Movies', *Wall Street Journal*, 25 March 2014, http://online.wsj.com/news/

article_email/SB10001424052702303949704579461813982237426-
lMyQjAxMTA0MDMwMTEzNDEyWj (accessed 31 March 2014).

Tegel, Simeon, 'Cue the Governor's Helicopter: Mexico's Film Hungry States
Compete for Tinsel Town Bucks', *Latin Trade*, www.latintrade.com (accessed 16
December 2005).

Thompson, Anne, 'Why Hollywood Is Discovering Colombia: From Medellín
and Bogotá to Cartagena', *Indiewire*, 22 March 2015, http://www.indiewire.
com/2015/03/why-hollywood-is-discovering-colombia-from-medellin-and-bogota-
to-cartagena-188390/ (accessed 27 July 2017).

Tierney, Dolores, *Emilio Fernández: Pictures in the Margins* (Manchester: University of
Manchester Press, 2007).

Tierney, Dolores, 'Alejandro González Iñárritu: Director Without Borders', *New
Cinemas: Journal of Contemporary Film* vol. 7 no. 2 (2009), pp. 101–17.

Treviño, Jesús, 'New Mexican Cinema', *Film Quarterly* vol. 32 no. 3 (Spring 1979), pp.
26–37.

Triana-Toribio, Núria, 'Building Latin American Cinema in Europe: Cine en
Construcción/Cinéma en Construction', in Stephanie Dennison (ed.), *Interrogating
the Transnational in Hispanic Film* (London: Tamesis, 2013).

Tucker, Duncan, 'Cinépolis Offers Online Rentals & "4D" Cinema', *The Tequila Files*,
6 November 2013, http://thetequilafiles.com/2013/11/06/cinepolis-offers-online-
rentals-4d-cinema/ (accessed 2 April 2014).

Turdiman, Daniel, '3D Cinema Tech Taking on a Starring Role', 16 May 2007, CNET
News on *CNet.com* (accessed 8 January 2009).

UNESCO, World Anti-Piracy Observatory, 'Causes of Piracy', 2010, http://
webarchive.unesco.org/20161022102714/http://portal.unesco.org/culture/en/
ev.php-URL_ID=39405&URL_DO=DO_TOPIC&URL_SECTION=201.html
(accessed 9 September 2017).

Unidad Especializada en Investigación de Delitos contra los Derechos de Autor y
la Propiedad Industrial (Specialised Unit for the Investigation of Crimes against
Copyright and Intellectual Property), 2016, https://www.gob.mx/pgr/acciones-y-
programas/unidad-especializada-en-investigacion-de-delitos-contra-los-derechos-
de-autor-y-la-propiedad-industrial (accessed 20 September 2017).

United States Trade Representative (USTR), 'Mission of the USTR', n.d., https://ustr.
gov/about-us/ (accessed 16 September 2017).

United States Trade Representative (USTR), 'Out of Cycle Review of Notorious
Markets', 2016a, https://ustr.gov/sites/default/files/2016-Out-of-Cycle-Review-
Notorious-Markets.pdf (accessed 16 September 2017).

United States Trade Representative (USTR), '2016 Notorious Markets List
Spotlights Fight against Global Piracy and Counterfeiting of American Products',
Press release, December 2016b, https://ustr.gov/about-us/policy-offices/press-

office/press-releases/2016/december/2016-notorious-markets-list (accessed 20 September 2017).

United States Trade Representative (USTR), '2017 Special 301 Report', 2017, https://ustr.gov/sites/default/files/301/2017%20Special%20301%20Report%20FINAL.PDF (accessed 16 November 2017).

van der Zalm, J., 'Villa de Cine: Venezuelan Government as Film Producer', *The Power of Culture*, December 2007, http://www.krachtvancultuur.nl/en/current/2007/december/villadelcine (accessed 20 December 2011).

Venegas, Cristina, 'Filmmaking with Foreigners', in Ariana Hernandez-Reguant (ed.), *Cuba in the Special Period: Culture and Ideology in the 1990s* (New York: Palgrave, 2009a), pp. 37–52.

Venegas, Cristina, 'Thinking Regionally: Singular in Diversity and Diverse in Unity', in Jennifer Holt and Alisa Perren (eds), *Media Industries: History, Theory, Method* (Malden, MA: Blackwell, 2009b), pp. 120–31.

Venegas, Cristina, *Digital Dilemmas: The State, the Individual and Digital Media in Cuba* (New Brunswick, NJ: Rutgers University Press, 2010).

Vertiz de la Fuente, Columba, 'Fondeadora.mx: Para conseguir fondos a proyectos creativos', *Proceso* (Mexico), 3 March 2013, p. 70.

Villaça, Mariana Martins, 'O Instituto Cubano del Arte e Industria Cinematográficos (ICAIC) e a política cultural em Cuba (1959–1991)', PhD dissertation, Universidade de São Paulo, 2006.

Villazana, Libia, 'De una política cultural a una cultura politizada: La República Bolivariana de Venezuela y su revolución cultural en el sector audiovisual', in Josef Raab and Sebastian Thies (eds), *E Pluribus Unum? National and Transnational Identities in the Americas* (Inter-American Perspectives/Perspectivas Interamericanas) (Münster: LIT/Tempe, AZ: Bilingual Press, 2008), pp. 161–73.

Villazana, Libia, *Transnational Financial Structures in the Cinema of Latin America: Programa Ibermedia in Study* (Berlin: VWM Verlag, 2009).

Villegas, Juan, Roundtable discussion, Panama International Film Festival, 14 April 2015.

Von Sychowski, Patrick, 'Cinépolis Acquisition of Chile's Cine Hoyts Signals Global Ambition', *Celluloid Junkie*, 8 January 2015, https://celluloidjunkie.com/2015/01/08/cinepolis-acquisition-chiles-cine-hoyts-signals-global-ambition/ (accessed 30 November 2018).

Werner, Michael (ed.), *A Concise Encyclopedia of Mexico*, 2nd edition (London: Routledge, 2015).

Whitney, John Hay, and Francis Alstock, Memo dated 15 June, signed by John Hay Whitney and Francis Alstock declaring support for the Mexican moving-picture industry, OCIAA collection, Motion Picture Division folder, box 7, Rockefeller Archive Center, 1942.

Woo, Kristina, 'Brazil Launches New Film Biz Effort in Cannes', *Indiewire*, 19 May 2006, http://www.indiewire.com/ots/2006/05/cannes_06_marke_2.html (accessed 20 March 2007).

Young, James, 'Mexico Tries to Lure Shoots to Troubled Country', *Variety*, 19 March 2010, https://variety.com/2010/film/features/mexico-tries-to-lure-shoots-to-troubled-country-1118016700/ (accessed 2 December 2018).

Young, James, 'Mexico's Canana Pacts with Netflix', *Variety*, 19 December 2011, http://www.variety.com/article/VR1118047741?refCatId=19 (accessed 22 December 2011).

Young, James, 'Cinépolis Theater Chain Expands to the US', *Variety*, 27 June 2013, http://variety.com/2013/biz/news/cinepolis-1200502669/ (accessed 3 April 2014).

Young, James, 'Mexico Reportedly Paid Millions to Hollywood for Better Portrayal in Upcoming 007 Film', 23 March 2015, *Vice News*, https://news.vice.com/article/mexico-reportedly-paid-millions-to-hollywood-for-better-portrayal-in-upcoming-007-film (accessed 22 July 2015).

Zhang, Xin, 'Cinema Exhibition in Central and Latin America', *IHS Technology*, 14 January 2014, https://technology.ihs.com/520103/cinema-exhibition-in-central-and-latin-america (accessed 10 May 2016).

Zullo-Ruiz, Fernanda, 'The "Cine Argentino" Brand: The Politics of a Geographical-Cultural Trademark'. Paper presented at the Geographical Imaginaries and Hispanic Film conference, 4–6 November 2009, Tulane University, New Orleans.

Zupnik, Bernardo, Roundtable discussion at BAFICI, 2004.

Zweig, Noah, 'Villa del Cine (Cinema City): Constructing Bolivarian Citizens for the Twenty-First Century', *Situations: Project of the Radical Imagination* vol. 4 no. 1 (2011), pp. 139–49, https://radicalimagination.institute/wp-content/uploads/2017/02/zweig-2011.pdf (accessed 7 December 2018).

Index